15.95

The Emergence of American
Literary Narrative,
1820–1860

The Emergence of American Literary Narrative, 1820–1860

JONATHAN ARAC

Harvard University Press

Cambridge, Massachusetts

London, England

2005

Acknowledgments

I am grateful for the support of the institutions I served while working on this project: the University of Illinois at Chicago, Duke University, Columbia University, and the University of Pittsburgh. A Fellowship from the National Endowment for the Humanities in 1986–87 allowed necessary time for reading and starting to write. My initial work was greatly aided by the Library of America, which generously provided copies of the relevant volumes then available. Sacvan Bercovitch, Andrew Brown, and Cyrus Patell did exemplary editorial work in founding, fostering, and carrying through this project, and in making occasions that allowed me to benefit from the responses of my fellow contributors Michael Bell, Barbara Packer, and Eric Sundquist. Friends and colleagues were generous in critical dialogue over my work, especially those who read all or most of the manuscript: Lauren Berlant, Paul Bove, Nancy Glazener, Carol Kay, Daniel O'Hara, Donald Pease, and Bruce Robbins. I appreciate the assistance of Columbia University students Laura Coradetti and Vanessa Schneider in re-examining the text for this republication. For his commitment to making this book available to a wider group of readers, I thank Lindsay Waters, and for critical encouragement in the final preparation of this edition, my thanks to Susan Andrade.

Contents

The Emergence of American
Literary Narrative,
1820–1860

1

Establishing National Narrative

Of the American writers from the mid-nineteenth century whose names are still recognized today, the majority are writers of prose narrative, such as Cooper, Poe, Hawthorne, Melville, and Stowe. Beyond these better-known writers, others will also appear in these pages, for the canon changes, and some writers who have never before, or not recently, played a significant part in American literary histories now seem important, such as the historians George Bancroft and Francis Parkman and the abolitionist Frederick Douglass. From the 1820s through the 1860s American prose narrative was produced and distributed within an increasingly established, yet conflict-ridden, publishing business. Narratives arose from, responded to, and contributed to continental and overseas expansion, racial struggles, and political debates, and elsewhere. But the production of narratives in a culture may be seen not only as a function of other institutions and structures but also as an institution that has a history and structure of its own, relatively independent of these others. Such a relatively internal history, in which the fundamental organizing terms are drawn from literary analysis rather than from economic or social analysis, is the work of this section. For in this period writers of prose narratives helped to form a definition of literature that still exerts power now.

The central event in the literary history of mid-nineteenth-century American prose narrative is the emergence, around 1850, of works, preeminently *The Scarlet Letter* and *Moby-Dick,* that still count as "literature" for many readers of the late twentieth century. Yet other valuable prose narratives of the time often trouble today's readers because there is no clear conceptual category into which the works fit. To understand this emergence requires acknowledging the problem of "genre," that is, the problem of defining different kinds of writing. In the discussion of narrative forms that follows, Chapter 4 addresses the newly emerging genre of literary narrative; Chapters 1 through 3 define the competing, earlier generic types in relation to which the specificity of literary narrative may be understood; and Chapter 5 sketches the fate of literary narrative in the period of its first emergence. Although literary narrative dominates late-twentieth-century views of this period, the works that are now valued did not immediately establish themselves, and the very genre of literary narrative itself almost disappeared in the intense national crisis of the Civil War.

In the late eighteenth century, "literature" meant all culturally valued writing, including what would now be distinguished as "nonfiction," such as history, travel, philosophy, and science. By the late twentieth century, however, the most widely accepted meaning of "literature" is fiction that does not fit any defined marketing genre (science fiction, western, crime, romance, and so on). In the United States, mid-nineteenth-century prose narrative was a crucial place for this change in meaning. As a result of this change, it is now expected that literary culture and national culture will stand at a tense distance from each other. This historically limited conception often makes it difficult to understand the value of works that are based on a different relation to the national.

The dominant narrative type that preceded literary narrative, and that continued to flourish even after literary narrative had appeared, I call "national narrative." From the standpoint of America's present existence as an independent union, national narrative told the story of the nation's colonial beginnings and looked forward to its future as a model for the world. This story, which still has much force in the United States, began to take on its fully articulated form around the presidency of Andrew Jackson (1829–1837). It could be told with equal power through fiction, especially in the work of James Fenimore Cooper, beginning in the 1820s, and through history, especially in the work of George Bancroft, beginning in the 1830s. When it first took shape, there was no fully operative national culture. National narrative was part of the process by which the nation was forming itself and not merely a reflection of an accomplished fact, yet it defined the ground against which the other major narrative types would stand out.

Within the imaginative space opened by the articulation of national narrative, two important smaller types of narrative flourished and competed with the national. First, in the 1830s, came what I call "local narratives." These were more restricted than was national narrative, either in the geographical area they encompassed or in the scale of the human experience with which they dealt. Following the example of Washington Irving's New York sketches, local narratives include stories by the "southwestern humorists" of Georgia, Alabama, Mississippi, and Tennessee; the northeastern tales of Nathaniel Hawthorne; and the works in which Edgar Allan Poe began to define the city as a new American locale. In the 1840s what I call "personal narratives" became prominent. Rather than express the collectivity of the nation, these works place in the foreground a single first-person narrator. Yet, contrary to both Puritan tradition and twentieth-century expectation, this "I" is a rather extroverted reporter, bringing news from the margins of the dominant culture rather than exploring spiritual or psychological inwardness. This narrative form includes works by travelers, such as Herman Melville, Richard Henry Dana *(Two Years before the Mast),* and Francis Parkman *(The Oregon Trail),* and also narratives by escaped slaves, such as Frederick Douglass.

Literary narrative emerged in 1850 together with a political crisis over slavery, which threatened the nation's existence and produced a compromise intended to subdue the controversy. At this moment, Melville and Hawthorne emphasized certain elements present in their own earlier writings and in those of Poe and set their work apart from national narrative. The "Custom-House" introduction to Hawthorne's *Scarlet Letter* illustrates this distancing from national concerns. In contrast not only to national narrative but also to local and personal narratives, which both addressed and reflected the concerns of everyday public life, the literary narrative of *The Scarlet Letter* turns away to develop a freely imaginative space. Whether through the hyperbole of Poe, the allegory of Melville, or the irony of Hawthorne, works of literary narrative not only differed from but seemed also to transcend and, implicitly, to criticize the world of common life. Yet their critical authority depended on their being limited to elite audiences, esoteric subjects, and indirect means. The possible glory of forming a "world elsewhere" through writing often was experienced by the authors themselves as deadeningly repetitive, solitary labor. This moment in which the "literary" writer was redefined as an "artist" marks a crisis in the relation of narrative to its public, for the work of the artist was understood to draw its primary value from its private relation to the writer's self.

This turn of American literary narrative was not unique. Since the later eighteenth century, Romantic writers in England and Germany had elaborated a new understanding of the place occupied by highly skilled writing within a culture. Conceptions such as "originality," "genius," and "imagination" defined literature as independent from the public world rather than interrelated with it, and notions of "psychology" and "development" defined new areas of attention and new techniques. Therefore, in analyzing American prose narrative in the mid-nineteenth century it is necessary also to discuss the transatlantic writers who were important as examples and resources. Especially significant were the English poets and critics William Wordsworth and Samuel Taylor Coleridge, for, paradoxically, they provided in theory and in practice models of writing newly democratic in spirit yet also newly difficult for readers to grasp and to enjoy.

James Fenimore Cooper

The power of national narrative codified by George Bancroft and James Fenimore Cooper continues to be felt in the United States. It circulates through media that are not understood as literary. Bancroft's conceptions of America are still common in the civic discourse of political education and debate. Cooper's images of America still prevail in the mass-cultural forms of movies and television. Bancroft's story tells of an America where freedom is established through the self-government of ever-larger communal groups, from Puritan congregations to revolutionary town meetings to the joining of states in a union. Cooper's story depends upon a version of Bancroft's. From the first, however, Cooper's readers have found his power to be less compelling in treating groups than solitary individuals; less in treating settlements than wilderness; less in treating government than the margins of the law. His most powerful figure is the solitary woodsman Natty Bumppo. Both Bancroft and Cooper enjoyed wide sales and acclaim, and both explicitly identified themselves with the side of "the people" in politics. The twentieth-century genre that has most fully integrated the modes of Bancroft and Cooper into a single narrative frame is the Hollywood western, which typically focuses on a solitary male figure who furthers the causes of civilization and the people, even if he cannot live in the town he has saved.

Cooper's work troubles modern readers because it is not realistic in its technique, but it is emphatically referential in its substance. More familiar and honored now are those works that are scrupulously precise in registering a world that stands at a fictional distance from specific national issues. Yet Cooper was the first author of what was accepted without question in the United States and abroad as truly "American" writing. Moreover, his importance is not merely historical, for his work, both in its ideas and in its technique, instances many problems that continue to cause concern in the culture of the United States.

Although Cooper wrote national narrative, to understand him requires an international context. American literary history thus resembles American economic history, which also, in a seeming paradox, requires international context. In Cooper's time, Americans liked to believe that the economy of the United States depended on self-sufficient farming. In reality, American involvement in export production and merchant shipping was so great that the international system was the primary generator of the nation's internal economic growth. Cooper's international dimension was recognized from his first successful novel onward. With the publication of *The Spy* in 1821, Cooper forever after was either praised or condemned as the "American Scott" (referring to the Scottish novelist Sir Walter Scott). A difference between history and literary history here emerges. Although it may be possible to place America within world history only to show, like George Bancroft, how America has transcended that history, no one has claimed that Cooper actually manifested the high point of the history of world literature, only that he was significantly different from, say, Scott.

The very process of establishing Cooper's American difference from Scott relies upon similarities that give the comparison its point. Starting with *Waverley* (1814), Scott wrote a series of historical romances set in periods ranging from the not-so-distant past ("'tis sixty years since" is the subtitle of *Waverley)* all the way back to the Middle Ages. Writing as a Scot, whose nation had been united for more than a century with England, Scott especially focused on the border country between Scotland and England, historically a zone of conflict. This terrain clearly prefigures the "neutral ground" between revolutionary and Loyalist forces on which Cooper set *The Spy*. Moreover, although the recurrent pattern of captivity among the Indians in Cooper's Leatherstocking novels looks back to colonial American captivity narratives, it also echoes the misadventures of Scott's passive heroes, whom the author typically placed in the power of those threatening, but ultimately defeated, forces that opposed the course of history.

Cooper and Scott shared a broad cultural–historical understanding of the course of civilization, derived from the theorists of the Scottish Enlightenment. In Scott, the Romantic energies of the Highland clan system (*Rob Roy*, 1817) or the passionate enthusiasm of radical religious dissent seeking to remake the polity (*Old Mortality*, 1816) must yield to a more humdrum yet more progressive and beneficent way of life, which is associated with the lowland Scots, the union of Scotland with England, and the triumph of the Established church. So in Cooper the qualities of his most noble Indians, and of Natty Bumppo himself, must yield to the common day of civilization. In the works of both writers, glamorized, yet firmly derogated, "primitive" figures are the center of attention for most of the book, and banal, yet positively presented, figures are the ones given the future, as those who will carry on life through marriage.

Both Cooper and Scott thought about and were involved with the issues of their time and nations. Nevertheless, in the works by which they are still known, they meditate only obliquely on the concerns of their own time, projecting the issues into the past and subjecting them to plot devices that insure their safe containment. For example, social divisions troubling to 1820s Americans could be negotiated through the plot in *The Spy*. The title figure first appears disguised as a peddler, haggling and seductively oriented toward consumption. Yet this character proves to be fundamental to the national well-being. He is the trusted secret agent of Harper (General Washington in disguise), a figure who passes through the novel as its iconic promise that all will turn out well. The birth of the new nation as depicted here is not only martial but also marital: witness the respective fates of the two daughters of the British-leaning Wharton family. Sarah, the elder, is betrayed by her false, aristocratic beau from the British forces, while her sister Frances is united with the less socially elevated American revolutionary officer.

Similarly, in Cooper's *The Pioneers* (1823) the marriage of Judge Temple's daughter Elizabeth to Oliver Edwards, companion of Natty Bumppo and Indian John, provides a way to reconcile social differences. Not only does the marriage link an apparently contrasting couple—high social status to low, settled life to still-woodsy—but, through revelations of the mystery plot, it also links the now-American Temple family with the Loyalist Effingham family, spiritual adoptees of the Indians and the first white possessors of the lands that Temple now holds. Loyalist and revolutionary, white and red, high and low are symbolically integrated in the novel.

Not all of the parties are so integrated, however. Drunken Indian John—whose people bestowed the land—is burned to death, and Natty Bumppo—whose woodcraft made Effingham's success possible—sets out for the wilderness. *The Pioneers,* then, as opposed to *The Spy,* diverges importantly from Scott. In *Ivanhoe* (1819) Scott went back to the Middle Ages to tell his story of the making of the English through joining the Norman king Richard with the Saxon Ivanhoe; meanwhile, the evil Norman leader dies. Both Scott's fable and *The Spy* proceed by incorporation of the oppositional element (Norman or Loyalist) into the united, progressive, national whole (although the opposition leaders must die). The plot of *The Pioneers,* in contrast, operates by exclusion. Cooper does not depict the Indians and woodsmen as part of the future in *The Pioneers,* even though they are central to the Leatherstocking novels that follow. In *The Last of the Mohicans* (1826) the exclusion of the Indians is fully elaborated and rationalized. Thus the "good" Indians, the Mohicans, are already dying out. Their "last" hope, Uncas, dies

tragically, and the good chief Tanemund is grotesquely superannu-
ated. Only the "bad" Indians survive as a group, and they must be
exterminated, as is their heroic, passionate, but villainous leader,
Magua.

The Pioneers imaginatively works through the confrontation of
two ways of life, the residual forest life of Natty Bumppo and the
recently emergent and now dominant settlement life of Judge Temple. In *The Last of the Mohicans* the confrontation is more abstract.
"Nature," represented by the heroic and unspoiled good Indians, is
set against "civilization," represented by the British. Civilization
triumphs as Major Duncan Heyward marries Alice, the daughter
of Colonel Munro. Nature is defeated as Uncas dies, along with
Munro's other daughter, Cora, with whom he might have been
united (Cora's West Indian, racially mixed origins having made her
an inappropriate wife for a white man). This battle between the
white British and the red Indians for possession of North America is
not, however, the explicit conflict of the book. Instead, the natural
Indians and the civilized British are shown united against their negative counterparts. The unnatural French are corrupted into weakness by the failure of their civilization (their great leader Montcalm
cannot prevent the slaughter of British prisoners by Indians). Allied
with the French are the savage Mingoes, the bad Indians of the
story. The villain of the book is the Mingo leader Magua, who has
lived among whites. He combines the worst of the uncivil and the
unnatural, the savage and the corrupt. The hero of the book is
Natty Bumppo. A white man "without a cross" of Indian ancestry,
Natty nonetheless combines "natural" Indian skills with a mastery
of the weapon of civilization, the long rifle.

The Last of the Mohicans also offers a phantom possibility of another ideal figure. Cora Munro is a woman with the spirit of a man,
as opposed to her weak, blond sister. Cora combines the natural energies attributed to her parent of African ancestry with the civilization attributed to her father's people, and therefore her union with

Uncas would unite the three most prominent racial groups of North America in the strongest couple that the book imagines. But that imagination is contained as purely optative, contrary to fact. America is defined in this founding national narrative as the land of pureblooded whites and male domination, not a land of interracial, multicultural equality of the sexes. Moreover, as shown in *The Pioneers,* Natty himself is not in the long run the victor. By the irony of history, none of the participants in *The Last of the Mohicans* is the hero so much as are Cooper's chosen readers, the Americans who are the actual possessors of the continent for which the British, French, and Indians believed themselves to be struggling.

The Prairie (1827) again sets "good" Indian against "bad" Indian. The machinery of plot resembles that in *The Last of the Mohicans,* but Cooper's concerns are quite different. *The Last of the Mohicans* went back in time to treat the forest life seen as vanishing in *The Pioneers. The Prairie* moves forward in time to treat the problem of law posed in *The Pioneers* by the confrontation of Natty with the hunting regulations established by Judge Temple. In *The Prairie* the conflict that in *The Last of the Mohicans* set civilization against nature here sets civilization against freedom. The lack of freedom in *The Prairie* is imagined as settlement—entirely absent from the represented world of the novel, though implicit in its frame of reference and that of its readers. The lack of civilization is imagined as a condition of lawlessness, an anarchy that may be either the exercise of arbitrary power or the absence of power.

This conflict is elaborated through the relations among the white characters; the Indians do no more than provide occasions for the various contrasting and conflicted relations among the whites. Ishmael Bush, the squatter patriarch, by combining the negative terms of anarchy and settlement, functions as the book's villain. Although Natty Bumppo is idealized in this work, his values nonetheless are set in a carefully qualified context, and if he embodies most fully the positive good of freedom, he also partakes like Bush of the dangers of anarchy. At the other extreme from Natty is the bee hunter Paul Hover. From the beginning, Paul is associated with civilization because the honeybee, as an import from Europe, was widely understood to live only within a certain proximity to settlements and thus to prefigure the frontier, where settlement encroaches on wilderness. By the book's end, Paul is ready to give up bee hunting and settle down. The closest the book comes to offering an ideal combination of the two conflicting positive values, freedom and civilization, is in the figure of the young soldier Duncan Middleton, whose middle name is Uncas because he is a descendant of Major Duncan Heyward from *The Last of the Mohicans*. Yet this genealogy, and Middleton's cross-cultural love for Doña Inez de Certevallos, give Middleton only an abstract association with the value of freedom, and readers have not experienced his as an ideal combination. Middleton is Cooper's unsuccessful attempt to place his imaginative emphasis where he placed his intellectual and political commitment.

This partial failure illustrates a crucial historical feature. Cooper's fictions operate as strategies of containment, that is, as imaginary techniques for negotiating the complexities of the life that both he and his readers were living. Yet the containments do not hold perfectly; the myth does not stand wholly free from the reality. Cooper never developed formal techniques wholly adequate to what he was trying to accomplish. Reviewers observed, or complained, that his works did not really have plots in the sense of an Aristotelian close meshing in which each element leads seamlessly to the next. He certainly did, however, have plots in the sense that by the end of the works a change in affairs has occurred from the initial state. But to achieve these changes, he called upon devices that seemed arbitrary and thus drew attention to the role of wish rather than necessity in what he was representing.

Moreover, while it is perfectly clear what kind, or genre, of work Cooper was producing—historical romance—the ground rules for that genre were not well established. Was it more like comedy or tragedy? *The Last of the Mohicans* sounds an elegiac note of loss beginning with its title, yet thirteen of its thirty-three chapters bear epigraphs from Shakespearean comedies, including five from *A Midsummer Night's Dream*. One reviewer protested passionately that readers were not prepared for the deaths of Cora and Uncas, that the book had been giving quite contrary signals heralding a happy union of the two. Echoing closely a famous essay by Charles Lamb, this reviewer complained that readers had been as badly served by Cooper as they had been by the Nahum Tate version of *King Lear,* which transforms the tragedy by allowing Lear and Cordelia to survive. In other words, to this reader the aesthetic satisfactions of generic coherence were much more important than the national issues. National narrative did not permit an alternative history of America in which the most heroic of Indians and the most passionate of mulattoes founded a new line. Yet this reviewer found that the logic of romance demanded such a deviation from national narrative. At issue here, then, are the concerns that led the "literary" to emerge as an independent realm, answerable only to the requirements of its own coherent fantasy rather than engaged in concerned dialogue with the life of the times.

If Cooper's large-scale management of his materials was open to criticism and question even from admiring readers (the comparison to *King Lear* is hardly unflattering), objections were also raised to his management of the local details of language. Mark Twain's 1895 essay on Cooper's literary offenses codifies these objections most tellingly, but it is worth trying to understand what Cooper has done, even if it is less the result of mastery than of struggle. In presenting characters whose language marks them as a radically incoherent set of attributes rather than as a psychologically plausible whole, Cooper is struggling with complex social issues.

Natty Bumppo is uneducated and culturally limited, and he often speaks a language that marks these social limitations. On the other hand, he embodies a way of life that is extremely different from that lived by anyone who reads about him. This way of life Cooper found immensely attractive, and he wished his readers to feel its value. At times, therefore, Cooper gave Natty a much grander syntax and diction than he otherwise possessed. The problem this causes is familiar from British Romanticism. Some twenty years before Cooper wrote, Wordsworth had argued, in his preface to *Lyrical Ballads,* that uneducated people leading a life close to nature are capable of intensely vivid figurative language when they are moved by passion. Cooper clearly shares Wordsworth's view. And just as Cooper was criticized, Wordsworth had been accused of inconsistencies in the relation of character to language.

Twain's criticism of Cooper resumed this line of attack. Cooper, however, took his Indians and Natty more seriously than Twain would take his own historically marginalized characters. For all of Twain's boasting about the accurate dialect in *Huckleberry Finn* (1884), none of the characters whose language he so precisely registered has anything to say that effectively challenges the values of Huck and Jim. Readers never waver in their allegiance to the two historically progressive forces in Twain's book, the boy breaking through to an intuitive recognition of racial equality, and the slave winning his freedom. In other words, Twain devised a technique to bring to life his "positive" characters, the structural equivalents to Cooper's Major Heyward and Middleton.

This accomplishment of Twain's is aesthetically powerful, and it has also been held to promote democratic values, but in placing readers' sympathies so entirely with the progressive characters, Twain excludes the losers of history from serious attention. Even though Twain, like Bancroft and unlike Cooper, found the cutting edge of progress in "plebeian" characters, his work, like Cooper's, expresses a hierarchy of social values.

This difference between Cooper and Twain resembles also the difference between Cooper and Parkman. Parkman testified that several of Cooper's novels had so deeply influenced his life that "I sometimes find it difficult to separate them distinctly from the recollections of my own past experiences," and his massive history of the French, English, and Indians in the American wilderness aims to substantiate the reality that *The Last of the Mohicans* had only suggested. Yet the overwhelming coherence of Parkman's vision and prose produces much greater restriction than is found in Cooper. In his overview of Cooper's career, Parkman wholly rejects Uncas, instead finding in Magua the essential truth of all Indians, and he underwrites this judgment in his history. New standards of realistic technique in fiction and in history did not ensure writing that would embrace more of humanity than was embraced by the world roughly shared between Cooper's fictions and the reality of his times.

Cooper's challenge to the attempt to isolate "literature" as a separate sphere can be marked in Poe's review of *Wyandotté*. According to Poe, Cooper won readers by relying on the appeal of things of the world: of life in the forest, or of life on the ocean. In contrast, Poe argues, a "man of genius" would have eschewed such "hackneyed" themes. Poe distinguishes "two great classes of fictions." One is "popular and widely circulated." It is read with "pleasure" but without "admiration" and, above all, without thinking of "the author." The other class, less popular, provides, "at every paragraph," pleasure "springing from our perception and appreciation of the skill employed, of the genius evinced in the composition." Here, readers think of "the author," not merely of "the book." The popularity of the first class is in contrast to the "fame" open to the second: if popular books "sometimes live," nonetheless, their "authors usually die"; but, in the case of genius, "even when the works perish, the man survives." Poe places in the class of genius Charles Brockden Brown and Hawthorne and in the popular class, Cooper. History, however, suggests that Cooper too was a genius, for his books now hardly survive. Yet his work made possible the dime novels and movies by which the American frontier has fixed itself in the world's shared cultural imagination; his sea novels were acknowledged as examples by writers such as Herman Melville and Joseph Conrad. Thus, the "man survives," and the problems he poses for meditation are immensely challenging.

Cooper succeeded, moreover, in surprising ways. His younger French contemporary Honoré de Balzac (1799–1850) found in Cooper's wilderness the inspiration for a certain mode of sensitivity to the city. Balzac had responded to Cooper from the beginning. In 1829 Balzac published the first of the novels that formed his massive *Human Comedy*, a historical novel about the French Revolution in Brittany called, after the Mohicans, *The Last Chouan*. A few years later, in his first great novel of Paris, *Old Goriot* (1834), Balzac's most powerful figure Vautrin asserts that Paris "is like a forest in the New World, where a score of savage tribes . . . struggle for existence." And in the next decade, *Splendors and Miseries of Courtesans* presents a character harassed by "invisible enemies" and searching for an abducted woman. The narrator observes,

> Thus, that poetry of terror which the strategems of enemy tribes at war spread in the heart of the forests of America, and of which Cooper has made such good use, was attached to the smallest details of Parisian life. The passers-by, the shops, the hackney carriages, a person standing at a window . . . everything presented the ominous interest that in Cooper's novels resides in a tree-trunk, a beaver-lodge, a rock, a buffalo skin, a motionless canoe, a branch even with the water.

The "poetry of terror" in Cooper's wilderness enriched the resources of urban realism. This intensity of attention had been fostered by the historical romance, for the form asserted that in the past even apparently commonplace individuals had been involved in a process of great significance, the making of world history. Natty Bumppo's "hawk-eye" functioned in the wilderness of New

York during the Seven Years' War, and it helped to make possible, through the British defeat of the French, the eventual American defeat of the British. The same "hawk-eye" functioned also to validate for Balzac a history of the present in fiction, in which even the most trivial and socially discredited elements of life played a role and thus demanded attention. In politics Balzac was a royalist, but as a novelist he learned from Cooper to be a democrat.

Alexis de Tocqueville

Not Balzac, but Alexis de Tocqueville (1805–59) was the French writer who had the most famous encounter with American democracy. Tocqueville came to the United States in 1831 with Gustave de Beaumont (1802–66). These two youthful, liberal noblemen had been commissioned by the French Ministry of Justice to study the country's penal system, which had attracted international attention for its innovative techniques for moral reform. For nearly a year after their arrival in New York, the two traveled all over the nation, as far north as Boston (and even into Canada), as far west as the still scarcely settled Wisconsin territory, and as far south as New Orleans. Their report, *On the Penitentiary System in the United States and Its Application in France,* was immediately translated and published in the United States (1833).

The report contains a remarkable thumbnail analysis of a characteristically American type of reformer, which looks forward to Hollingsworth in Hawthorne's *Blithedale Romance* (1852). For this type, prisons become "the subject to which all the labours of their life bear reference. Philanthropy has become for them a kind of profession; and they have caught the *monomanie* of the penitentiary system, which to them seems the remedy for all the evils of society." *"Monomanie"* remains in French because "monomania" had not yet fully entered the English language. This concept, which is so crucial for understanding many characters in Poe and Hawthorne and, above all, for thinking about Captain Ahab in Melville's *Moby-Dick,* began to circulate widely in the United States only with Isaac Ray's *Treatise on the Medical Jurisprudence of Insanity* (1838). Even in their government report, Tocqueville and Beaumont showed that they were in touch with the emerging crucial concerns for Americans of their time, and Beaumont wrote a novel on the effects of slavery, *Marie,* published in France in 1835. Tocqueville wrote on his own the far more ambitious work *Democracy in America* (Volume I, 1835; Volume 2, 1840), which from its first American translation by Henry Reeve in 1838 to the present has remained an essential resource for Americans in thinking about themselves. Although written by a Frenchman, Tocqueville's work has become part of the American national narrative.

The second volume of *Democracy in America* contains a chapter on "the Sources of Poetry among the Americans" in which Tocqueville has grasped a duality that helps to define also the particular perspective of Cooper's work discussed earlier. According to Tocqueville, the fundamental equality of all citizens in the United States means that there is no poetic inspiration to be received from great single individuals. Instead, "the nation itself" awakens imagination. Although Europeans "talk a great deal of the wilds of America," Tocqueville has learned that "the Americans themselves never think about them." Americans do not "perceive the mighty forests that surround them till they fall beneath the hatchet."

Tocqueville's analysis helps to make clear that Cooper's Natty Bumppo is the retrospective construction of an age in which the "hatchet" of settlement has already leveled enough American forest so that the historical loss of all wilderness begins to become conceivable. Natty prophetically mourns this loss in *The Pioneers;* nevertheless, the last sentence of the book places Natty not as a solitary mourner, but amidst what Tocqueville called "the nation itself." Natty has left for the frontier, and so, "He had gone far towards the setting sun,—the foremost in that band of Pioneers, who are opening the way for the march of the nation across the continent." Tocqueville finds that precisely "this magnificent image of themselves" is always present "before the mind" of Americans, so as to "haunt every one of them in his least as well as in his most important actions." Tocqueville registers this image in language much like Cooper's: "the American people views its own march across these wilds, draining swamps, turning the course of rivers, peopling solitudes, and subduing nature."

Tocqueville's primary goal is to understand a worldwide process that he calls the "democratic revolution." This revolution first occurs in the United States, and the United States therefore holds lessons for the future of Europe and the rest of the world. In using the notion of "equality" as the key concept for his analysis, Tocqueville is self-consciously participating in the democratic spirit, which, he argues, prefers abstractions and generalizations to the concrete, often personalized, specificity that marked aristocratic societies. Tocqueville's abstract conception of the democratic destiny of the United States echoes closely, as will be seen, the abstractions with which George Bancroft organizes his history of the United States.

Much of what Tocqueville shares with Bancroft has become common American self-understanding, even though it will not hold up to rigorous historiographic analysis. Tocqueville states in the introduction to his first volume *of Democracy in America* that "the gradual development of the principle of equality . . . is a providential fact," because "it is universal, it is lasting, it constantly eludes all human interference; and all events as well as all men contribute to its progress." Consequently, in studying democracy and equality in the United States, Tocqueville has been impressed with a "religious awe" from the force of "that irresistible revolution." The United States has a special historical role because America from its beginning has most fully embodied the principle that is providentially transforming the world: "the emigrants who colonized the shores of America in the seventeenth century somehow separated the democratic principle from all the principles that it had to contend with in the old communities of Europe, and transplanted it alone to the New World."

Tocqueville's national narrative begins in New England and spreads throughout the rest of America: "The principles of New England spread at first to the neighboring states; they then passed successively to the more distant ones; and at last, if I may so speak, they *interpenetrated* the whole confederation. They now extend their influence beyond its limits, over the whole American world." In a biblical figure that links American political discourse from John Winthrop's "Model of Christian Charity" (1630) to Ronald Reagan, Tocqueville sees this civilization as "a beacon lit on a hill." Tocqueville emphasizes the organic principle by which the democratic-egalitarian structure of America has developed. It has not, he argues, worked on the aristocratic principle of organization from the top down by central authority. Instead, "in America . . . the township was organized before the county, the county before the state, and the state before the union." In principle, therefore, no tension can arise between the nation as a whole and any of its local components, because they are what have made it.

Tocqueville's democratic abstractions take on the power of myth. His work gains credibility from its empirical detail, yet these details vanish into a national narrative. Indians are erased by the argument that they "occupied" the land without "possessing" it. Despite his knowledge that Virginia was colonized before New England, Tocqueville's definition of American "national character" does not take into account that there were numerous initial settlements, and so he does not recognize any contradiction between his claim for the priority of New England and his theory of harmonious national development. He writes as if there were only one single "origin of the Americans," which assures the continued favorable development of the nation: "their forefathers imported that equality of condition and of intellect into the country whence the democratic republic has very naturally taken its rise." Therefore, Tocqueville claims to see "the destiny of America embodied in the first Puritan who landed on these shores, just as the whole human race was represented by the first man."

Yet Tocqueville also at moments acknowledged that the United States could not wholly be explained by the national narrative of equality and the myth of New England. America was a land not only of freedom but also of slavery. Slavery depended on a principle of brutal inequality, which threatened the United States: "If ever America undergoes great revolutions, they will be brought about by the presence of the black race on the soil of the United States; that is to say, they will owe their origin, not to the equality, but to the inequality of condition." Tocqueville saw another potential for destabilizing inequality in the urbanization of America. An extraordinary footnote in Tocqueville's first volume warned that the growing size and heterogeneous population of "certain American cities" made them a "real danger" for the "future security of the democratic republics of the New World." He imagined that it would require a national armed force, "independent of the town population," in order to "repress its excesses." Tocqueville's critical capacity to conceive the problems, and not only the power and success, of American democracy has made his work the version of American national narrative from this period that is now still read.

George Bancroft

Like Tocqueville, who came to the United States on a mission for the French government and who returned home to play a significant political role, George Bancroft compels interest as an example of the relations between writing and political power. He shaped the story of America both through his national narrative and through his service to the state. Born in 1800, the son of a clergyman in Worcester, Massachusetts, he graduated from Harvard in 1817, where his diligence and capacity won him special favor. Like the scholar George Ticknor before him and the poet Henry Wadsworth Longfellow after him, Bancroft was sent to Germany with the idea that his studies there would fit him for leadership on the Harvard faculty. But his studies at Göttingen and Berlin, and his further travels in France and Spain, apparently unfitted him for Harvard and Harvard for him. Within a year after his return, he had left Cambridge to collaborate in an experimental, progressive school at Northampton, Massachusetts, which he conducted with considerable success from 1823 to 1831. During these years Bancroft published verse, translations from the German, and essays on recent German literature and thought, much as his older contemporary the Scot Thomas Carlyle was doing before Carlyle found his vocation as historian and social critic.

Bancroft's personal connections marked him as a conservative New Englander and a likely Federalist. He married into the Dwight family of Springfield, Massachusetts, who were prominent in banking and in midwestern land speculation; his brother-in-law, "Honest John" Davis, became Whig governor of the state. Bancroft himself, however, developed in quite different directions. His German education opened to him the body of ideas in philosophy, theology, and history that also inspired the transcendentalist movement in New England at this time; and his first public appearances on political matters pointed in a popular, Jeffersonian direction. By the early 1830s, as he was leaving schoolteaching, Bancroft moved into his major activities in both scholarship and politics. He formed the plan for his *History of the United States* that was finally fulfilled in 1874, after ten volumes, with the settlement of the revolutionary war. He also formed a lifelong allegiance to the Jacksonian, Democratic party. His commitments to "the Democracy," as the Democratic party was known, and to his history seemed to arise together and to sustain each other.

Published to great acclaim and large sales, the first volume of

Bancroft's *History* appeared in 1834, carrying the story of America from Columbus through the English Civil War and Restoration (1660). The second volume (1837) progressed through the English Glorious Revolution and its immediate colonial consequences (1689). In 1838, when the Democrats, almost always the opposition party in those days in Massachusetts, won a state election, Bancroft moved to Boston to become collector of the Port of Boston, the major patronage position in the state. As Democratic boss of Massachusetts, he appointed Nathaniel Hawthorne the weigher and gauger at Boston Custom House, the first of the three patronage positions that Hawthorne held. Bancroft's political activity did not prevent his completing the third volume of the *History* (1840), bringing the story up to the mid-eighteenth century.

For the next decade, politics, on an increasingly larger scale, took the main share of Bancroft's time. In 1844, the same year in which he ran unsuccessfully for the governorship of Massachusetts, his support at the national convention was decisive for James K. Polk's presidential nomination, and he was rewarded with a cabinet position when Polk was elected president. As secretary of the navy, Bancroft was instrumental in establishing the U.S. Naval Academy, and during the Mexican War he was also in de facto charge of the Army Department. This was a difficult position for him, because New England opinion from the Whig right to the transcendental left solidly opposed the war. He was rewarded with the greatest prize in the federal government's patronage system, the position of ambassador to the Court of St. James. In London from 1846 until 1849, he used his position to gain access to a wealth of English and French documentation on the revolutionary period that had never been studied before. When he returned to writing his history, he held incomparable authority, through both his public position and his research. From 1852 through 1860, on the verge of the Civil War, volumes 4 through 8 appeared, at last bringing the story to July 4, 1776, the first actual moment in the history of those United

States upon which he had already lavished some four thousand pages.

In the crisis of the Civil War, Bancroft stood with the Union, offering advice to Lincoln and even drafting the first message to Congress by Andrew Johnson after Lincoln's death. Although he still identified himself as a Democrat, he was invited to present the official Lincoln memorial oration to Congress in 1866, the same year in which volume 9 appeared. He was appointed ambassador to Berlin, where he served from 1867 through 1874. During these years, which encompassed the Franco-Prussian War, Bancroft associated closely not only with Otto von Bismarck and other leaders of the German military and political establishment but also with the great senior historians of what was then considered the world's leading center for the study of history. When he returned from Berlin to the United States in 1874, he published the last volume of the *History.* Bancroft lived until 1891, an honored figure in the political, diplomatic, and cultural life of Washington D.C., and he put the *History* through two sets of revisions. First he reduced the ten volumes to six for the 1876 Centennial; next he produced, in 1882, the *History of the Formation of the Federal Constitution;* and finally he integrated the two sets into the "author's Final" six volumes in 1886.

It is one indication of Bancroft's accomplishment in writing his *History* that over the forty years in which it was produced, years that saw so much change in the history of the United States, it was not necessary for him to alter his tone or standpoint. The revisions of the 1870s and 1880s trimmed what had come to seem antiquated rhetorical flourishes, but for all this, in the originally published ten volumes, no more than one single word at the end of the last sentence of the preface to the ninth volume (1866) was required to register awareness of the Civil War: "This contribution to the history of the country I lay reverently on the altar of freedom and union." As early as the end of the second volume Bancroft had declared that the two volumes thus far completed "show why we are a free people" and that the volumes to come would show "why we are a united people." In other words, the key terms of value around which the Civil War was fought by the North were already firmly in place in Bancroft's discourse.

Bancroft did not think of himself as an inventor. He conceived his task to resemble that of a primitive bard. He wanted to articulate what his people already knew and believed and had been telling each other, but to give it a shape and scope that would include as much of the story as possible, more than could be directly known by any single person or local tradition, and that would thus make possible the continuation of the people, their knowledge, and their story. Yet this nation-building narrative was something new. In giving formal expression to the inchoate ideas of the American people, Bancroft was performing what is etymologically the basic act of "ideo-logy," and by making this expression not in the form of analysis, but as a coherent narrative shape, he was providing an American "myth" in the sense that Aristotle uses the term in the *Poetics*. Twentieth-century readers are likely to notice the optimism and nationalism that make Bancroft's national myth seem untrue and dangerous and the racial categories that make the ideology seem a false consciousness.

Bancroft's position, however, has a centrality that will not allow it simply to be dismissed. It is instructive to compare Bancroft with another important political voice of his time, Nathaniel Hawthorne's friend John L. O'Sullivan (1813–95). In 1837 O'Sullivan founded and edited the *United States Magazine and Democratic Review* and was closely allied with Bancroft. In the *Democratic Review* the notion of America's "manifest destiny" to expand across and to rule the North American continent began to figure as early as 1845, in close conjunction with the Mexican War in which Bancroft played so prominent a role. Within a few years, though, O'Sullivan had discredited himself with adventurist schemes to conquer Cuba for the United States. He long lived abroad, during the Civil War trying to mobilize British support for recognizing the Confederacy.

As early as in the lead editorial of the first issue of the *Democratic Review*, the limitations of O'Sullivan's position were clear. In the editorial O'Sullivan analyzed the recent nullification controversy involving South Carolina, arguing that its crux was "the relative rights of majorities and minorities." The substance of O'Sullivan's argument shows that in American political discourse at this time "minorities" was a code word for the South and not, as it is now, a term for racial or ethnic groups that are vulnerable to discrimination. O'Sullivan was deeply involved in social reform of the sort that had brought Tocqueville to the United States. In 1841 he wrote a notable report urging the state of New York to abolish capital punishment. Yet in an exemplary 1840 article, "Democracy," O'Sullivan wrote about "human rights" in political theory and American practice, without any attention to the fact of slavery in the nation.

Bancroft, on the other hand, was unequivocal in his notion of human rights, and he took political heat for his position. In 1845 his record had to be vetted by a southern senator before he could be nominated to the Cabinet, and, after the Civil War, Wendell Phillips could express the judgment that Bancroft had "remodelled his chapters" in order to negotiate the issue of slavery. Nonetheless, Bancroft opposed the racism of his time. Unlike those who welcomed theories of the multiple origins of humanity, theories that claimed to demonstrate scientifically that races other than the white were not fully human, Bancroft insisted, "All are men. When we know the Hottentot better, we shall despise him less." Unlike O'Sullivan, Bancroft saw the southern arguments in the nullification controversy as "recklessly insulting the free labor of the North." The southern arguments did not, for Bancroft, represent the fundamental concerns of American democracy. Rather, they were "subversive of liberty" and tended toward "treason and disunion."

Yet if Bancroft could differ so significantly from his closest political associates, it was also the case that those on the other side of party lines could find almost nothing to object to in his works. William Hickling Prescott, best known today for his account of Cortés's triumph over the Aztecs in his *History of the Conquest of Mexico* (1843), was a largely apolitical, deeply conservative member of the prosperous Boston Whig establishment—the group to which Bancroft "should" have aspired. Prescott opposed the annexation of Texas and the Mexican War, which Bancroft supported. Nonetheless, appearing in the solidly traditional *North American Review,* Prescott's 1841 review of Bancroft's third volume demonstrates how much actually was shared across the party spectrum. This in turn explains why Bancroft and most other northern Democrats could later join the Republicans on the Union side in the Civil War.

In his review, Prescott uses as his own the progressive, democratic language that modern readers might wrongly assume to be the polemical, "Jacksonian," portion of Bancroft. Like Bancroft, Prescott sees in the history of America the "progress of freedom" based on concern for "the natural rights of humanity." Prescott connects this progress to the "contest between light and darkness" that is at issue in the democratic strivings of Europe in the 1840s. Like Bancroft and Tocqueville, Prescott sees American freedom as divinely planned. America was discovered and settled only after the "glorious Reformation" had assured that the right, Protestant principles would predominate among the settlers. For Prescott, this fact was no accident: it was not merely "fortunate," it was "providential."

The United States were not ready for a full-scale history immediately after independence, Prescott argues, but only for "local narratives, personal biographies, political discussions," and the like. But now that the country has acquired some history of its own, the time has come for national narrative. It can be seen that a "tendency" to self-government "connects" colonial history to the history of the modern union and gives a "true point of view" from which colonial history might be narrated. The great task that Prescott envisions for the historian of colonial America is to find some principle of "unity." Prescott's own work found unity in its biographical focus, as in his *History of the Reign of Ferdinand and Isabella* (1838) and in his concentration on Cortes in the *Conquest of Mexico*. But Bancroft's scope is too vast both geographically and chronologically for a single figure, or even for a string of biographies, to organize it fully. To achieve a "central point of interest among so many petty states," to find "an animating principle of his narrative," Bancroft needs to tell the story of freedom. His work is a history of ideas and of institutions, of principles more than of persons, even though it is always conducted in the name of the "people." This is the abstraction that Tocqueville connected with democracy.

In its narrative organization, Bancroft's history depends on two principles that are in considerable tension with each other: the figure of prolepsis and the trope of development. Prolepsis is not mere anachronistic error. It is the figure of anticipation, of placing something earlier than it would usually be expected. So, by prolepsis, Bancroft begins the history of the United States in the seventeenth century, thereby identifying the later political entity with the already existing, quasi-eternal, land itself. In the first volume, after the initial chapter, "Early Voyages. French Settlements," and a second chapter on the Spaniards, the third chapter is entitled "England Takes Possession of the United States." Centuries before the Declaration of Independence, the "United States" is made to live in Bancroft's pages. But if the United States are there already, what is the point of the history? Bancroft is always in the position of having to tell how something that is already present would nonetheless fully accomplish, realize, and manifest itself over time. Often his figure for this process is organic, modeled on the life of an individual. He asserts, like Tocqueville, that the first period of American history "contains the germ of our institutions" and that "the maturity of a nation is but a continuation of its youth."

Equally fundamental to Bancroft is the metaphor of light. Seventeenth-century Virginia witnessed "the happy dawn of legislative liberty in America." Before Darwin, the problem of change obscured the perspicuity of developmental metaphors. Light was clearer. No one can doubt that at dawn light is present and yet that a day will follow in which this light undergoes variations over time that may aptly figure history. So the light of freedom is present from the beginning: "As the Pilgrims landed, their institutions were already perfected. Democratic liberty and independent Christian worship at once existed in America." And yet noon is more glorious than dawn; a climax remains. Just as the first three chapters in the first volume of Bancroft's *History* move climactically from France to Spain to England so in this volume as a whole the story of New England occupies the last three chapters (of ten) but almost half the total pages; and in the overall construction of the *History,* three volumes get the story to the mid-eighteenth century, but seven more are required for the next thirty years.

It is also possible, moreover, that noon has not yet been reached. The conservative Tory looks to the past, and the Whig grasps the present, but democracy rules the future. Democracy is "the party of progress and reform"—the best is yet to be. Bancroft, in the middle of the first volume, summarizes his theme:

The enfranchisement of the mind from religious despotism led directly to inquiries into the nature of civil government; and the doctrines of popular liberty, which sheltered their infancy in the wildernesses of the newly-discovered continent, within the short space of two centuries, have infused themselves into the life-blood of every rising state from Labrador to Chili, have erected outposts on the Or-

egon and in Liberia, and . . . have distributed all the ancient govern-
ments of Europe . . . from the shores of Portugal to the palaces of the
Czars.

Bancroft's narrative structure and his historical analysis both depend on dialectical procedures. His story moves by a principle of
supersession. Institutions that at one historical moment are progressive, at a later moment cease to be so. This tension between
immutable principles and transitory institutions produces considerable complexity. For example, in the later seventeenth century
(Volume 3),

> A revolution in opinion was impending. The reformation had rested
> truth on the Bible, as the Catholic church had rested it on tradition;
> and a slavish interpretation of the Bible had led to a blind idolatry of
> the book. But true religion has no alliance with bondage; and, as the
> spirit of the reformation, which was but a less perfect form of free-
> dom of mind, was advancing, reason was summoned to interpret the
> records of the past, and to separate time-hallowed errors from truths
> of the deepest moment.

This increase in the scientific spirit was to change religion, making
Calvinist forms outmoded, and Bancroft saw the Salem witchcraft
trials as arising out of a politically retrograde attempt by ministers
to reclaim their eroding power.

If even the Calvinists, dear to Bancroft for their gifts to freedom
in Massachusetts, were to be transcended, so might the larger religious movement to which they belonged: "Protestantism is not humanity; its name implies a parry struggling to throw off some burdens of the past and ceasing to be a renovating principle when its
protest shall have succeeded. It was now [in the Seven Years' War]
for the last time, as a political element, summoned to appear upon
the theatre of the nations" (Volume 4). In turn, the "last war" of
Protestantism proved to be "first in a new series of the great wars of

revolution that founded for the world of mankind the power of the people." The American Revolution marked the moment when "the idea of freedom . . . for the first time . . . found a region and a race, where it could be professed with the earnestness of an indwelling conviction and be defended with the enthusiasm that had hitherto marked no wars but those for religion" (Volume 7). In the sphere of power politics, similar reversals and transformations may occur. By the eighteenth century, the "great European colonial system had united the world" (Volume 3). This united world formed a theater in which the American struggle for liberty could achieve the greatest resonance and be insured of a future as universal on earth as it was in spirit. By the time of Volume 5 (1852), Bancroft himself, now living in New York City, could find that the American principle of free trade had so effectually united the world in freedom that the multitude of races, cultures, and languages of New York made it "the representative city of all Europe."

This vision of an America that contained the world, by containing the principle that was reshaping and bettering the world, was an American ideology that was most fully articulated in Bancroft's national narrative and that was played out, in the years he was writing, by the national expansion that brought the United States all the way to the Pacific coast and that threatened to go further into Central America and the Caribbean. This national narrative emerged in the 1820s and 1830s, together with the strong presidency of Andrew Jackson, but it was not yet dominant. Space remained for local narratives that offered alternative emphases. The actual differences among the regions of the United States meant that the story of America was not the only story.

2

Local Narratives

Washington Irving

In *The Sketch Book of Geoffrey Crayon, Gent.* (1819) Washington Irving established for decades the norms defining American local narratives, that is, small-scale pieces with regional subject matter. The basic modes of writing in Irving's work, as in the English periodicals of his time and in American periodicals for decades, were the sketch and the tale. The sketch, as its name suggests, is like a picture. Nothing happens in the sketch, except for the verbal action of displaying to the reader something that the narrating voice considers of interest. In the tale something does happen, often something rather remarkable. The sketch highlights the first-person narrative, as of the "Crayon" figure; the tale, in contrast, presents a third-person narration or else gives the narrative to another voice than that of the sponsoring narrator. Irving's voice echoed British tradition in periodical writing, and much of his subject matter resembled the colorful regionalism in Walter Scott's full-length romances. A sketch was, in effect, a descriptive chapter torn from its narrative context. By the same process, during the 1830s and 1840s, while George Bancroft and James Fenimore Cooper continued their writing, national narrative was being fragmented into local scenes by periodical writers following Irving.

Irving's most famous tales from *The Sketch Book* display a problematic relation between local and national. "Rip Van Winkle" notoriously passes over the founding American national events during Rip's protracted slumber, and the tale itself is attributed to Diedrich Knickerbocker, Irving's fictional antiquarian historian of Dutch New York. It is said to derive, moreover, from "legendary lore," which is available not from books and records—the materials of such a national history as Bancroft's—but only from men and women long at home in their locale. "The Legend of Sleepy Hollow" shows the resentment of the local community in the early days of the nation (like Cooper's *The Pioneers,* the story is set in the 1790s) against a Yankee intruder. The ghost, whose legend is mobilized to terrorize Ichabod Crane, comes from a dead Hessian officer, so that, in the overall structure of the tale, the conflict between two regions, Dutch New York and Yankee Connecticut, also comes to represent an old, quiet, and even colonial way of life set against a graceless, grasping yet inept, new national life. Schoolmaster, psalm singer, and would-be go-getter, Crane immortalized one American type, as did his rival Brom Bones, a horse racer, cock fighter, humorist, and village Hercules "always ready for either a fight or a frolick." These two regional varieties would appear in many other places and guises long after Irving himself had turned his attention to work on a national scale, from his life of Columbus, to his history of John Jacob Astor's fur-trading empire, to his life of Washington.

Southwestern Humor

Starting in the 1830s, a group of writers followed Irving in writing regionally based sketches and tales. They did not deal with the long-settled regions of New York, as he had, or with New England, as Hawthorne did. Instead, they took on the newly settled areas of the frontier in the South reaching from Georgia into Tennessee,

Alabama, Mississippi, and Arkansas, known at the time as the "South-West." Their work typically first appeared in the local newspapers where the writers might happen to live, but it soon was being published in regional newspapers, such as the St. Louis *Reveille* and the New Orleans *Picayune,* and in the journal, based in New York, that became the flagship for southwestern-humor writing, the *Spirit of the Times.* This intricate hierarchy of journals exemplifies the complex participation of southwestern humor in levels of cultural activity including the local, the regional, and the national.

Founded in 1831, the *Spirit of the Times* aimed at a national readership interested in horse racing, and the single greatest readership with that interest was southern planters. William Porter, the Vermont-born editor, defined his journal as "designed to promote the views and interests of but an infinitesimal division of those classes of society composing the great mass. . . . We are addressing ourselves to gentlemen of standing, wealth, and intelligence—the very corinthian pillars of the community." "Corinthian" pillars suggest the luxurious efflorescence of ornament that wealth allows and also echo the British slang term "Corinthian" used for wealthy amateur sportsmen or genteel profligates, as in Pierce Egan's *Life in London* (1824) about the adventures of young Jerry and his friend "Corinthian Tom." (Transformed into cat and mouse, "Tom and Jerry" would remain a comic pair in twentieth-century American cartoon art.) Porter's journal, which would become identified with a distinctively American subject matter, began from (and maintained) imaginative relations with British culture, and a metropolitan model stood behind its appeal to the far-flung corners of American leisure activity. After the Panic of 1837 damaged the financial base for horse racing, the journal shifted its emphasis away from news of the turf. Porter filled his pages from two main sources: he combed newspapers from all over the South and Southwest looking for items to reprint, and he invited readers of the journal to submit material of their own. Such writers' gentlemanly standing was emphasized by the fact that Porter did not pay contributors, although he boasted in 1856 a circulation of forty thousand.

The typical writer of the sketches and tales in the *Spirit of the Times* was a person of considerable cultural authority: white, male, a practitioner of a highly literate profession such as journalism or the law, and politically active. For example, Porter's contributor who called himself "Turkey Runner" was James McNutt, two-term governor of Mississippi (1838–42). McNutt was in favor of hard money and temperance, but his tales focused on backwoods hunters like "Chunkey," who liked easy credit and hard liquor.

In their social and political conservatism, these writers were typically associated with the Whig party. The rise of the southwestern "school" of writing coincided remarkably closely with the emergence of the Whigs as a focus of multiregional resistance to the presidency of Andrew Jackson. Although himself a slaveholder from Tennessee, Jackson as president proved to be more radically, autocratically, national than seemed right to many southerners who had been Democrats. When South Carolina declared its right as a state to "nullify" the federal tariffs of 1828 and 1832, Jackson threatened to use federal troops to enforce central political authority. Yet Jackson also held back from using federal economic power to further the "internal improvements" of roads and canals that appealed to many westerners. Finally, Jackson was repugnant to many northerners, both for his popular, democratic style and for his attack on the central Bank of the United States.

Thus, in the years from 1832 to 1834, the Whig party came into existence, uniting Daniel Webster of the North, Henry Clay of the West, and John Calhoun of the South. This was the moment not only of the nullification crisis but also of other distinct developments that changed the nation by changing the status of slavery in the South. A boom in cotton prices fueled the settlement of new lands on the southwestern frontier and dramatically enhanced the value of the slaves owned in the Old South. Meanwhile, in 1831 Nat Turner led the nation's most important slave rebellion in Southampton, Virginia, and opposition to slavery entered a new, passionate phase, as William Lloyd Garrison began publishing the *Liberator.*

The Whig opposition to Jackson immediately produced local narratives that attempted to seize the imaginative initiative on Jackson's own terrain. *The Narrative of the Life of David Crockett* (1834), along with associated works written about and often purporting to be written by Davy Crockett, marks the attempt by the Whigs to exploit the backwoods prowess and jokes of an ambitious Tennessee politician who had broken with Jackson and who still lives in American popular memory. Almanacs continued to spin yarns about him even after his 1836 death. In their long afterlife, the Crockett narratives ceased to count as local. By the time Walt Disney took them up into massively circulated television, film, and song materials in the 1950s, they had become integrated into national narrative, standing no longer for a part or a party but for the whole of America.

The kind of writing these southwestern figures produced was known as "humor," but the term covered a wide variety of stances and practices. Along the frontier, for instance, there flourished a well-established oral practice of exaggerated self-display, which was reported back to civilization by travelers along the Ohio and Mississippi rivers. As early as 1808, two rivermen were heard arguing at Natchez, Mississippi: "One said, 'I am a man; I am a horse; I am a team. I can whip any man *in all Kentucky,* by G-d.' The other replied, 'I am an alligator, half man, half horse; can whip any man on the *Mississippi,* by G-d,'" and after several more verbal exchanges, a great fight followed. The primary sense, however, in which this whole body of work is "humor" is because it displays the eccentricities of people of lower social standing than that of its

writers and presumed readers. As far back as Aristotle, the difference between tragedy and comedy had been defined not as pertain-
ing to happy or sad endings, but rather in relation to the standing—
in principle moral, but in practice social—of the characters por-
trayed.

Even though cultural developments as old as Christianity and as
recent as the Romantic movement and democratic politics offered
alternatives to this view, and, by the twentieth century, had largely
changed it, it was still an established perspective, especially among
the cultural conservatives who practiced southwestern writing. Although in their attention to life among the lower social strata and
in their detail and frequent grotesquerie, the southwestern writers
prefigure what is called realism and regionalist writing, in general
they do not grant their characters the moral seriousness usual in
these later movements. Nonetheless, this body of writing has taken
on increasing importance over the last fifty years because modern
readers recognize that southwestern "humor" was a major resource
for writers now valued highly, such as Herman Melville, Mark
Twain, and William Faulkner. These writers do grant their characters moral seriousness, but like the humorists they often provoke
laughter and exceed the decorum of realistic verisimilitude.

The inaugural figure in the literature of southwestern humor is
Augustus Baldwin Longstreet (1790–1870). Born in Augusta,
Georgia, and educated in South Carolina and at Yale, Longstreet
returned to his native state to practice law. His career encapsulates
almost every form of professional standing that his society offered:
Longstreet won elections to the Georgia General Assembly and as
judge of the state superior court (1822); in 1829 he was licensed as
a Methodist minister; from 1834 to 1836, he edited the Augusta
State Rights' Sentinel; and he went on to a career as a college and
university president and a polemicist on behalf of the South (for example, he wrote *The Connections of Apostolical Christianity with
Slavery* [1845]). In 1833 Longstreet started publishing his sketches

and tales in the Milledgeville *Southern Recorder,* and he continued their publication in his own paper. Finally, he collected and published them himself (anonymously) in Augusta as *Georgia Scenes, Characters, Incidents, &c. in the first Half Century of the Republic: By a Native Georgian* (1835). The success *of Georgia Scenes* was great and enduring. Poe hailed it in the *Southern Literary Messenger,* and Longstreet boasted of selling thousands of copies without going north of the Mason-Dixon line. By 1840 Longstreet's collection was taken up nationally by Harper and Brothers in New York, and by 1897 it had gone through eleven editions.

Longstreet's collection includes such pieces as "A Sage Conversation," in which the narrator overhears several old women chatting desultorily through the night, trying to piece together a sexual scandal; "The Shooting-Match," where the narrator falls in among the "boys" of Upper Hogthief and by luck wins a prize; "The Turf," with "men, women, children, whites and blacks, all betting" at a horse race, but where the five-hundred-dollar prize proves to be no more than forty-eight dollars plus promissory notes; "The Gander-Pulling"; "The Turn-Out," a rebellion of students against their schoolmaster; "The Fight," where the clay-eating dwarf Ransy Sniffle tricks two handsome friends into mutilating each other, no holds barred; and "The Horse-Swap." In each of these pieces, the scene is set among dirty, uneducated people, and the polite, gentlemanly narrator's voice is contrasted to or at moments supplanted by, a character's racy, colloquial vernacular speech. Yet this speech, so welcome to modern readers, signals a social level and way of life that Longstreet keeps in close check. His own morality is not only decent, but "improving." He aims to record odd features of a way of life that he is happy to announce is passing. Here, as in many other ways, he resembles Twain rather than Cooper.

The opening sketch of the collection, "Georgia Theatrics," begins by warning readers that its account is not now "characteristic of the county in which it occurred." But, back in 1809, "The Dark

Corner" of Lincoln County was known for its "moral darkness."
Longstreet continues, "Since that time, however (all humor aside)
. . . could I venture to mingle the solemn with the ludicrous, even
for the purpose of honorable contrast, I could adduce from this
county instances of the most numerous and wonderful transitions
from vice and folly to virtue and holiness."

Longstreet is sincere in the sanctimony of this moral and cultural-
historical stance, but he must shift away from it to energize his narrative. For after denying that he would "mingle the solemn with the
ludicrous," Longstreet immediately sets against his solemn narrative voice the voices that he hears, "loud, profane, and boisterous,"
over the way and out of sight: "You kin, kin you?" "Yes, I kin, and
am able to do it! Boo-oo-oo! Oh, wake snakes, and walk your
chalks!" Further boasting prepares the way for a big fight, which
the narrator continues to overhear, right up to the climax, as he
comes upon the scene: "I saw the uppermost one (for I could not see
the other) make a heavy plunge with both his thumbs, and at the
same instant I heard a cry in the accent of keenest torture, 'Enough!
My eye's out!' "Horror-struck," the narrator "stood transfixed."
But he discovers that the whole thing had been a "rehearsal," in
which a single teenager "had played all the parts of all the characters in a court-house fight."

This case offers humor in a usual and welcome sense. The trick is
on the narrator who recounts it and on the reader who has been ex-
pecting terrible, sensational events. The vernacular character has
the chance of retort, "You needn't kick before you're spurr'd. There
a'n't nobody there, nor ha'n't been nother. I was jist seein' how I
could 'a' fout." The comedy arises from the mingling of the voices
and from readers' relief that the mutilation was only play. Nonetheless, the boy has not been granted any moral authority to match the
narrator's. He remains part of a culture so savage that children play
at eye gouging. The sketch closes with images that testify to fierce
energies uncontrolled in the terrifying absence of civilization: "I

went to the ground from which he had risen, and there were the prints of his two thumbs, plunged up to the balls in the mellow earth, about the distance of a man's eyes apart; and the ground around was broken up as if two stags had been engaged upon it."

In the process that made southwestern-humor writing a nationally circulated form, probably no author was more important than Thomas Bangs Thorpe (1815–75). Born in Massachusetts and raised in New York, Thorpe went to Louisiana in 1837, where he remained, for the most part, until 1854. In 1839 he published his first sketch, "Tom Owen, the Bee Hunter," "By a New Yorker in Louisiana." Rejected by a local paper, it was printed in the *Spirit of the Times,* where it proved immensely popular. A short piece with an Irvingesque narrator, the sketch has little appeal today, but it was reprinted in Rufus Griswold's *The Prose Writers of America* (1847) and along with "Georgia Theatrics" was the only piece of southwestern humor in the Duyckinck brothers' massive *Cyclopaedia of American Literature* (1855). In 1841 the *Spirit* published Thorpe's other important piece, "The Big Bear of Arkansas," which gave its title to the first anthology of southwestern humor. Published by Carey and Lea of Philadelphia in 1845 (under the editorship of Porter from the *Spirit), The Big Bear of Arkansas and Other Sketches, Illustrative of Characters and Incidents in the South and South-West* sparked a considerable publishing boom of southwestern humor. After this success, Thorpe went off to the Mexican War, accompanying Zachary Taylor, and his reports back from the war were among the major sources not only of news but also for early histories of the war. Thorpe's long involvement with Whig politics in Louisiana ended in frustration, and he returned to New York in 1854, serving with the Union in the Civil War, one of the few southwestern humorists not to side with the Confederacy.

Thorpe's "Big Bear" narrates an encounter between hunter and bear that rests on persuasive local detail but moves into the mysterious and the mythical, while featuring an unconventional narrative voice. This model obviously influenced William Faulkner's "The Bear" (1942), and it has resonance from *Moby-Dick* through much of Ernest Hemingway and on to Norman Mailer's *Why Are We in Vietnam?* (1967). As in Longstreet, a sketch narrator sets a frame within which vernacular voices appear, but in this case the vernacular voice is allowed to take over the bulk of the piece, and unlike in Longstreet, there is no moral dimension to the framing. The vernacular speaker, himself the "Big Bar of Arkansaw" after whom the story is named, appears not on his home ground, but on a Mississippi steamboat. He personally represents his locale, but the scene represents "every State in the Union":

> Here may be seen jostling together the wealthy Southern planter, and the pedlar of tin-ware from New England—the Northern merchant and the Southern jockey—a venerable bishop and a desperate gambler—the land speculator, and the honest farmer . . . Wolvereens, Suckers, Hoosiers, Buckeyes, and Corncrackers, beside a "plentiful sprinkling" of the half-horse and half-alligator species of men, who are peculiar to "old Mississippi."

The narrator, aboard such a boat, behaves like a gentleman. He sits, "critically" reading, amidst the "heterogeneous" crowd, when all are interrupted by the arrival of the "Big Bar," who quickly charms them despite his rough manner. The "Bar" explains to the genteel hunters that animals are not "game" in Arkansas. In Arkansas, the main "game" is poker, but if you are hunting, "that's *meat.*" When "twenty voices" cry out in astonishment at his mention of a wild turkey weighing forty pounds, he answers, "Yes, strangers, and wasn't it a whopper?" Thorpe shows the "Bar" playing humorously with his interlocutors, asserting the whopping size of his native fauna, while at the same time acknowledging that his narrative is itself somewhat a whopper. His Arkansas is "the creation State," and its bears, "feeding as they do upon the *spontenacious* productions of the sile," are fat all year round. After his protracted boast of the qualities of Arkansas, the "Bar" then tells at length the story of one particular hunt, quite unlike the usual hunt that may be "told in two sentences—a bar is started, and he is killed." (One short chapter of Crockett's *Autobiography* describes a season in which he killed one hundred and five bears.)

The hunter discovers traces of the largest bear he has ever seen or heard of; the bear mocks him by repeatedly marauding his pigs; and the hunter is consumed with anger, while feeling that the bear has reversed roles and is hunting him. Glimpsing the bear on a hunt, the "Bar" is awed by his beauty and "loved him like a brother"; nonetheless, he pursues the hunt, to an extended, frustrating, and unsuccessful conclusion. Finally, his pride at stake, he tries once more, and to his amazement, before he has even set out in the morning, the bear appears: "he loomed up like a *black mist,* he seemed so large, and he . . . *walked through the fence* like a falling tree would through a cobweb." Before the hunter has any chance to kill him, the bear has died, for he *"was an unhuntable bar, and died when his time come."* Thorpe's "creation bar" proved one of the great creations of this body of writing, the primary icon that the southwestern humorists fixed in national tradition.

The publishing opportunities opened by the success of *The Big Bear of Arkansas* were quickly exploited by Johnson Jones Hooper (1815–62). Born in North Carolina, Hooper by 1835 was learning law in his brother's office in Alabama. In 1842 he became editor of the *East Alabamian,* where he published his first sketch, "Taking the Census in Alabama." Hooper's subject too is a focus for the tension between local and national. Only as an employee of the federal government, performing a task so resented and feared by the local population that it was considered dangerous, did Hooper come into contact with the common people whose oddities became the stuff of his humor. His piece was a hit, taken up by Porter for the *Spirit of the Times.* Encouraged by Porter, Hooper produced a book that made him famous.

Published by Carey in 1845, Hooper's *Some Adventures of Captain Simon Suggs, Late of the Tallapoosa Volunteers; Together with "Taking the Census" and Other Alabama Sketches* enjoyed eleven editions in the next decade. Although occupying only part of the book, the story of Suggs was Hooper's great contribution. To the end of his days he had to endure being himself called by the name of his creation, much to his dismay and embarrassment. *Some Adventures of Simon Suggs,* dedicated to Porter, is a mock campaign biography, with a supposedly infatuated narrator recounting the qualities of his hero in a way that allows readers to laugh at the objects of the hero's roguery while feeling superior to hero and narrator alike. The mode looks back to Henry Fielding's satire on Sir Robert Walpole's political "greatness" in *Jonathan Wild* (1743), and its tone often resembles that of William Makepeace Thackeray in *Catherine* (1839) and *Barry Lyndon* (1844), which ironically represent the vogue for crime literature. Following his slogan "It is good to be shifty in a new country," Suggs moves from playing tricks on his father into land speculation, card playing, and his corrupt, incompetent leadership of the militia, the "Tallapoosa Volunteers."

Probably the most memorable of the chapters in *Some Adventures of Simon Suggs* is "The Captain Attends a Camp-Meeting," which is echoed in Mark Twain's *Huckleberry Finn,* when "The King Turns Parson." Low on cash, Suggs attends a revival meeting, where he is recognized as a notorious sinner, preached at, and apparently undergoes a remarkable conversion, allowing him to raise money from the assembled group and make off with it. As Suggs relates his supposed "experience" of grace, in edifying "discourse" for all to hear, Hooper looks over the crowd to note their reactions and lights upon a Mrs. Dobbs:

"Dear soul alive! *don't* he talk sweet!" cried an old lady in black silk—"Whar's John Dobbs? You Sukey!" screaming at a negro woman on the other side of the square—"ef you don't hunt up your mass John in a minute and have him here to listen to this 'sperience, I'll tuck you up when I git home and give you a hundred and fifty lashes, madam!—see ef I don't! Blessed Lord!"—referring again to the Captain's relation—"ain't it a *precious* 'scource!"

Full pleasure in the narrative requires readers to share Hooper's assumptions that revival meetings are a bad business in themselves and that enthusiastic religion is not only degrading but even dangerous: morally dangerous because it fosters hypocrisy, socially dangerous because it mixes whites and blacks under the heat of passion, and politically dangerous because it is itself a form of demagogy and conducive to that vice in the polity at large. To this day in the United States, religious revival remains an important part of the national life, and almost the same suspicions remain, except now it is generally the political left that holds the views that Hooper held from the right.

Even the southwestern humor that might seem most purely high-spirited local color has a distinct relation to the politics of the decades from the 1830s through the 1850s. In *The Flush Times of Alabama and Mississippi: A Series of Sketches* (1853), Joseph G. Baldwin makes the connection unmistakable. Baldwin (1815–64) was born in the Shenandoah Valley of Virginia, of an old Connecticut family that had come south to run textile mills; in his teens, he left for Mississippi, to practice law where there was less competition. In 1837 he moved to Alabama, where he was active among the Whigs, serving in the state legislature and running unsuccessfully for Congress. He left Alabama for California after the publication of his book. Baldwin began publishing sketches in the *Southern Literary Messenger*—a much more conventionally polite periodical than usual for southwestern humor—and collected them with new pieces in *Flush Times,* which was published in New York and reprinted six times within six months.

"The Flush Times" of the title were "that halcyon period, ranging from the year of Grace 1835, to 1837; that golden era, when shinplasters were the sole currency; when bank-bills were 'as thick as Autumn leaves in Vallambrosa.'" The quoted phrase from Milton's *Paradise Lost* and the mythological reference mark Baldwin as the most belletristic of the southwest-humor writers. At the same time, fidelity to his subject required him to use "shinplasters," the Americanism for a small-denomination bill issued by a wildcat bank—the easy-credit fruits sought by those who supported Jackson's campaign against the Bank of the United States. As a Whig, Baldwin writes a mock-encomium to Democratic easy credit, although a modest nostalgia for the days when he was young ensures a greater equability of tone than in Hooper. The play of inflections within Baldwin's own narrative rather than extensive quotation from vernacular characters on display provides the great majority of the book's humor, but there is one remarkable exception, where a character is given extensive voice.

Baldwin's Alabama lawyer, "Samuel Hele, esq.," speaks with such satirical "directness" that "he tore the feathers off a subject, as a wholesale cook at a restaurant does the plumage off a fowl, when the crowds are clamorously bawling for meat." But Sam is displayed only in one shocking and anachronistic scene. A "strong-minded" Yankee schoolmistress has come to town, and people persuade Sam to help encourage her to leave town. What he does is give voice in grotesque hyperbole to all the worst fantasies that anyone might ever have entertained about the system of slavery and the degradation of life and character in the South. The teacher flees, accidentally leaving behind a letter to "Mrs. Harriet S——" on slavery in the South, "which I should never have thought of again had I not seen something like [its details] in a very popular fiction, or rather book of fictions, in which the slaveholders are handled with something less than feminine delicacy and something more than masculine unfairness." Baldwin has inserted into his reminiscences of the middle 1830s a response to Harriet Beecher Stowe's *Uncle Tom's Cabin*.

Baldwin's use of Hele suggests that the South of gothic fantasy was just big talk to scare Yankees, but the greatest of the southwestern humorists, George Washington Harris, made grotesque violence the essence of his South, embodied in a character named "Sut," to echo his region. Born near Pittsburgh, Harris (1815–69) lived primarily in East Tennessee, where he worked in a variety of trades and enterprises mostly connected to the world of current technology: he was for several years a steamboat pilot; he worked in, and owned, a metal working shop; he managed a sawmill and a copper mine; and he was involved with railroads. From the 1840s he occasionally contributed to the *Spirit of the Times,* but his major work appeared in the later 1850s, almost exclusively in Tennessee papers, including the fire-eating Democratic Nashville *Union.* As the Civil War approached, Harris contributed some remarkably savage political satires, such as a series mocking Abraham Lincoln en route to his inaugural in Washington, or another so antinorthern as to wish the *Mayflower* settlers had been massacred by the Indians. Nonetheless, after the war it was in New York that Harris's one book was published, *Sut Lovingood: Yarns Spun by a "Nat'ral Born Durn'd Fool"* (1867)—testimony to how thoroughly the North had won the conflict and to how harmless it therefore must have considered even something so fiercely unreconstructed as Sut's South.

Sut's yarns are almost always introduced by a gentlemanly narrator known only as George. Sut's powerfully eccentric and idiomatic backcountry language enters only through this initial mediation, but once entered, his is overwhelmingly the prevalent voice. Moreover, Harris goes farther to emphasize the linguistic eccentricity of his character than had any of the other southwestern writers. Sut's speech is rendered in elaborate phonetic reproduction, both to convey the character of his sounds and to emphasize that this is an illiterate we are reading. Himself a strict Presbyterian, Harris nonetheless gave Sut Lovingood the capacity to stand free of his author morally as he stands free from his narrator linguistically. Hooper's

narrator would break into Suggs's discourse frequently to summarize or to point out metaphors, but Sut's language is almost uninterrupted, and, when Sut is interrupted, it is often only so that he can
retort sharply upon his interlocutor. At one point, Sut digresses to
inquire,

> "How is it that bricks fits so clost enyhow? Rocks won't ni du
> hit."
> "Becaze they'se all ove a size," ventured a man with a wen over his
> eye.
> "The devil yu say, ho'ney-head! Haint reapin-mersheens ove a
> size? I'd like tu see two ove em fit clost. Yu wait ontil yu sprouts
> tuther ho'n, afore yu venters to 'splain mix'd questions."

The appeal to the reaping machine, a product of heavy industry, is
perfectly characteristic of Sut's world. It may be the backwoods or a
backwater, but the reach of modern technology extended even that
far—just as American frontier tales involved prowess with rifles,
and the steamboat framed "The Big Bear of Arkansas."

At times Sut appears in surroundings of more precisely rendered
physical detail than even the low-life conventions of southwestern
humor had seen before. A Sunday morning idyll sets the young Sut
"ontu the fence a-shavin seed-ticks ofen my laigs wif a barlow
knife." Even more striking is the intimacy of social detail. Sut's
powerful emotions include fear and shame, and the stories reveal
the social inequalities, the structures of hierarchy, that produce
such feelings among the lower orders. The characters in this hierarchy include the financially gouging squire, who is deeply involved
in the church and so seems to Sut to be "Secon enjineer ove a
mersheen . . . fur the mindin giner'lly ove everybody else's bisness."
The second such character, the sheriff, provoked Sut's first big scare
when he was a child and has ever since figured as the object of
his planned revenges: "'*The sheriff!*' his'd mam in a keen trimblin
whisper; hit sounded to me like the skreech ove a hen when she sez

'hawk,' tu her little roun-sturn'd, fuzzy, bead-eyed, stripid-backs."
The preacher is the third hierarchical character. Parson John Bullen
tells her parents that their daughter has kissed Sut, and, in revenge,
Sut plays him a painful and humiliating prank.

Sut's realistic environment and feelings sprout into fantastic high-
jinks that typically involve considerable preparation and then, as if
of their own volition, explode into frantic, destructive noise and
movement. At one moment Sut himself speaks of his "skeer makin
mersheen." In general, he seeks devices that need only the smallest
incitement to go, while he can "stan clar ove danger, an watch
things happen"; or again, "Jis' pullin a string wer my hole sheer in
all that ar cumbustifikashun, hurtin, an' trubbil." The mechanical
ingenuity of some of Sut's devices, and the machine metaphors in
which the results are often described, make Harris's work seem as if
they could be scripts for the animated cartoons of the 1930s and
1940s: "I sot these yere laigs a-gwine onder three hunder' pound
preshure ove pure skeer. Long es they is, they went apast each uther
as fas' as the spokes ove two spinnin wheels a runnin contrary
ways."

As also in the cartoons, in Sut's yarns the rapidity, complexity,
and intensity of motion produce heroic messes: "Pickil crocks, per-
serves jars, vinegar jugs, seed bags, yarb bunches, paragorick bot-
tles, aig baskits, an' delft war—all mix'd dam permiskusly, an' not
worth the sortin, by a duller an' a 'alf." The subject matter is not
worth sorting out, but the prose sets it in rhythmic order. The sentence is hinged around the dash, with almost an equal number of
words before and after, subdivided into eight shorter units in the
first half, three almost equal longer units in the second half. Despite
its everyday vocabulary and energetic stresses, Harris organizes his
material with the elaborate syntactical constructions of formal rhetoric: "taters, cabbige, meat, soup, beans, sop, dumplins, an' the
truck what yu wallers 'em in; milk, plates, pies, puddins, an' every
durn fixin yu cud think ove in a week, wer thar, mix'd an' mashed,

like it had been thru a thrashin-meesheen." From the beginning of the grammatical subject ("taters") to the beginning of the predicate ("wer thar") almost two lines intervene, a dozen single-word items punctuated by two echoing relative clauses ("what yu wallers" and "yu cud think ove"). Harris is equally effective with more straight-forwardly repetitive structures: "The street wer white wif milk an' aigshells; hit wer red wif cherrys; hit wer black wif blackberrys, an' hit were green wif gardin truck."

Unlike Hooper, who resisted identification with his shifty rogue Suggs, Harris was widely called after his plebeian troublemaker, even though his naming the polite narrator "George" might seem to suggest a different leaning. Taking his own stand with the Democrats, Harris followed through the logic of the Whig political mythology that linked the Democrats with the people and the people with trouble. Bancroft's national theme was the self-governing powers of the people, the capacity of Americans to achieve order without either government or hierarchy. Harris's smaller scale displayed, apparently without regret, a poetry of destruction—what the people's energies might cost someone like himself, a skilled technical craftsman who required a significant degree of inviolate space and calm. In a ruckus that Sut witnesses, a drunken, tall-talking white man kicks a young Negro. At once the young boy is dehumanized into a projectile: "Away hit flew, spread like ontu a flyin squirrel, smash thru a watch-tinker's winder, totin in broken sash, an' glass, an' bull's-eye watches, an' sasser watches, an' spoons, an' doll heads, an' clay pipes, an' fishin reels, an' sum noise." As the watchmaker sat "a-peepin intu an ole watch, arter spiders, wif a thing like a big black wart kiverin one eye," the next thing he knew, "he wer flat ove his back, wif a small, pow'fully skeer'd ash-culler'd nigger, a-straddil his naik, littil brass wheels spinnin on the floor, an' watches singin like rattil-snakes all roun." East Tennessee was not slaveholding country, and there is little place for African Americans in Sut's world, but this scene suggests the animus some southerners felt toward a social system that they believed doomed the region to technological and economic backwardness. Harris's image of the "nigger," surrounded by the chaos he has proximately caused and astraddle the craftsman's neck, constructs a scene that blames the victim. The initiating kick is out of the picture, which makes the slave appear responsible for the destruction that seems to foreshadow what finally came with the Civil War.

Nathaniel Hawthorne

In 1830, just a few years before Augustus Longstreet began publishing his anonymous scenes from the early days of Georgia in the Milledgeville *Southern Recorder*, Nathaniel Hawthorne (1804–64) published anonymously in the Salem *Gazette* five biographical sketches and tales from the early days of Massachusetts. The subjects included "Mrs. Hutchinson," the antinomian leader of the 1630s to whom he would later compare Hester Prynne, and "The Hollow of the Three Hills," a tale of shame and of the violation of privacy—a theme that Hawthorne would make obsessively his own. Perhaps already by the time he left Bowdoin College in 1825 Hawthorne had planned and written much of a projected book of "Seven Tales of My Native Land." No less than that of the southwestern writers, Hawthorne's initial identity as a writer was intensely local. But despite his location in a more culturally developed part of the nation, Hawthorne experienced much greater difficulties in his path to publication than did the southwestern writers. The response to his projected "Tales of My Native Land" was so discouraging that it is not certain whether Hawthorne actually preserved anything from that undertaking, although it seems likely that the fictional pieces in the *Gazette* derived from it.

Returning after college to live with his widowed mother and two sisters in his native city of Salem, Hawthorne began an intensive program of reading in the library of the Salem Athenaeum. For some dozen years he wrote in isolation. By 1829 he had a new book project, "Provincial Tales," and had presented it to a Boston publisher, who would not risk the book but offered to publish pieces in *The Token,* an annual gift book. In *The Token* for 1831, Hawthorne published an anonymous sketch, "Sights from a Steeple." For the next half-dozen years, some of his sketches and tales were published as "By the Author of 'Sights from a Steeple.'" That sketch remains memorable for its fantasy that "The most desirable mode of existence might be that of a spiritualized Paul Pry, hovering invisible around man and woman, witnessing their deeds, searching into their hearts." Such unseen observation was a crucial feature of nineteenth-century culture. It figured fundamentally in defining the stance of the narrator in realistic fiction; it was no less important as the stance of the emerging social sciences; and it comprised an actual practice both in social welfare reform (prisons, poorhouses) and in industrial organization. In this figure of the sensitive spectator, who is also an inquisitor, Hawthorne shows the marks of his age, even in works that have no evident social content.

In *The Token* of 1832, Hawthorne published several pieces from "Provincial Tales." Still only in his late twenties, he had already produced some of the works on which his reputation would rest. "The Gentle Boy," like "Sights from a Steeple," became a signature piece for his subsequent anonymous works; "Roger Malvin's Burial" and "My Kinsman, Major Molineux" ("By the Author of 'Sights from a Steeple'") are two of the works that since the end of the second world war have figured most frequently in anthology selections and critical discussions of Hawthorne. In the years up to 1838, Hawthorne published some score more of tales and sketches in *The Token,* including "The May-Pole of Merry Mount" ("By the Author of 'The Gentle Boy'") and "The Minister's Black Veil" ("By the Author of 'Sights from a Steeple'"), both in 1836.

While parceling out his "Provincial Tales" to *The Token,* Hawthorne conceived yet another project for a book of local character. "The Story-Teller" would be a frame narrative that dramatized its teller and set the pieces in relation to the history and geography of the places encountered on a trip through New England up to Niagara. Once again, Hawthorne's project came to nothing, except for fragments that appeared in periodicals. In 1834 *New England Magazine* published two portions from "The Story-Teller," and over the next year some fifteen further pieces by Hawthorne followed in that journal, including "Wakefield" and "Young Goodman Brown." By 1837 he had published nearly fifty pieces; yet, when he was looking back in the 1851 preface to the third edition of *Twice-told Tales,* Hawthorne judged that at this point he had been "the obscurest man of letters in America."

For the gentlemen who wrote the southwestern tales and sketches, obscurity was not troubling as it was for Hawthorne. They might even seek obscurity in order to stand clear of the lower-class associations of their subject matter. Hawthorne's case was quite different. Although his paternal ancestors, as Hawthorne learned through his intensive reading of local history in the later 1820s, had included several distinguished figures in earlier colonial times, his own family, especially after his father's premature death, was financially dependent. Hawthorne went to college with considerable reluctance, not wanting to be "living upon Uncle Robert for four years longer." In a letter to his mother from college, he rejected the professions of law, medicine, and divinity, and then exclaimed, "Oh that I was rich enough to live without a profession." He then immediately went on to ask his mother, "What do you think of my becoming an Author, and relying for support upon my pen?" The emotional logic of this sequence suggests that Hawthorne considered writing a profession that was not quite a profession. It offered him greater freedom, but, economically, the pen was a weak "support."

Hawthorne left Salem for Boston in 1836 to become editor of

the *American Magazine of Useful and Entertaining Knowledge,* but the promised five-hundred-dollar salary yielded him no more than twenty dollars in the six months that he stuck out the work before the publisher went bankrupt. He and his sister Maria Louisa then worked together as hacks for *Peter Parley's Universal History, on the Basis of Geography.* For one hundred dollars they put together a work that is said to have sold over a million copies. By 1837, Hawthorne's financial situation was worsening, for the family stagecoach business, linking Boston and Salem, was about to be ruined by the construction of the first railroad between the cities. It became necessary for Hawthorne to "scribble for a living," to become a "scribbler by profession." This exigency drove him to produce four more history books for children: *Grandfather's Chair, Famous Old People,* and *Liberty Tree* (all 1841) and *Biographical Stories for Children* (1842).

To earn a decent living by writing, Hawthorne needed to earn a name for himself. Achieving an identity as a known writer of quality was all that stood between Hawthorne and endless drudging hack work; it made the difference between the "author" Hawthorne had dreamed of becoming and the "scribbler" that he had become. Yet not only was Hawthorne's work appearing without his name, it was even appearing under different rubrics. Such a strategy served the publisher of *The Token,* who did not want it known that a single writer was responsible for eight pieces in the 1837 annual, but it was not in Hawthorne's interest. Hawthorne's friend Horatio Bridge argued, "You scatter your strength by fighting under various banners." Hawthorne's writings were admired by a readership to whom his name was unknown. Bridge therefore urged Hawthorne, "Put your name upon the title-page" of a book. With Bridge's secret financial guarantee, *Twice-told Tales* appeared in 1837, collecting nineteen of the pieces Hawthorne had published up to that point. Although sales began well, with six to seven hundred copies sold in the first months, the Panic of 1837 and the ensuing depression chilled sales and bankrupted the publisher. Yet as Hawthorne reflected in the preface to the reissued edition in 1851, it had served to "open up an intercourse with the world."

From this point, Hawthorne's career was strikingly worldly; like the amateur writers of the southwest, he did not make writing his primary concern. In the twenty years from the publication of *Twice-told Tales*, Hawthorne devoted himself primarily to writing for less than half the time: 1838, when he wrote some dozen pieces that would help make up a second volume *of Twice-told Tales* (1842); the three-and-a half years at the "Old Manse" in Concord, where he lived with his wife Sophia immediately after their marriage and wrote most of the materials for *Mosses from an Old Manse* (1846); and the years from mid-1849 through 1852, in which he wrote full-length romances (*The Scarlet Letter* [1850], *The House of the Seven Gables* [1851], *The Blithedale Romance* [1852]), more stories, collected in *The Snow-Image* (1851), along with more children's books (*True Stories from History and Biography* [1851], *A Wonder-Book* [1852], and *Tanglewood Tales* [1853]), and finally the campaign biography of Franklin Pierce, his old college friend who became president of the United States in 1853.

The intervals between writing were spent primarily in political office. From the mid-1830s through the mid-1850s, each time a Democratic president came into office, Hawthorne received a patronage appointment: in the Boston Custom House, 1839–41; in the Salem Custom House, 1846–9; and as consul in Liverpool and Manchester, England 1853–7. The one other interval was spent in an experiment in a different kind of politics, at the Brook Farm Utopian community in 1841. When Hawthorne completed his service as consul in 1857, he published only one more romance, *The Marble Faun* (1860), and a collection of essays reflecting on England, *Our Old Home* (1863). Along with his journals, the bulk of his writing in the years before his death in 1864 remained unpublished until his family found in them a continuing financial resource. As a famous author, Hawthorne could continue to earn from beyond the grave.

Once Hawthorne had set his name to the title page of a book, an extraordinary process of construction became possible. His college friend Henry Wadsworth Longfellow reviewed *Twice-told Tales* in the weightiest American cultural organ, the *North American Review*. Longfellow undertook to define the "point of view" from which the tales and sketches were produced—that is, he began to make a rich, complex, and integral figure out of what had been a fragmented assortment of writings. Meanwhile, Elizabeth Peabody, the sister of Hawthorne's future wife, Sophia Peabody, used her connections to bring him to the attention of George Bancroft. Bancroft not only came through with patronage employment, he also connected Hawthorne with an important journal. From its very first issue, Hawthorne appeared in John O'Sullivan's *Democratic Review,* and from 1837 through 1845, he published some two-dozen pieces there, about half of his total output for the period.

Now that he was appearing in a national journal, Hawthorne could be taken up in yet further reaches of cultural politics. The strongest advocate for an American national literature, understood as significantly different from British or any other foreign literature, was Evert Duyckinck of New York, and in 1841 he published in the first volume of his new journal *Arcturus* a powerful appreciation of Hawthorne's work. Duyckinck had admired Hawthorne for as long as there had been an identity to be known. In 1838 he and a friend called on Hawthorne in Salem; Hawthorne later recollected this as the first attention ever paid him in his character as "literary man." In the *Arcturus* essay, Duyckinck figured Hawthorne's literary character in the terms that Romanticism had made exemplary for literature itself. Hawthorne was a "Hamlet," whose "consciousness" and "imagination" were immense, but whose "will" lagged behind. He was conceived as a figure whose inwardness was the chief locus of value, and for whom action would be quite secondary, if not impossible.

A few years later, Duyckinck again wrote about Hawthorne, this time in the *Democratic Review*, with which he too had associated himself. James K. Polk had already been elected, and Hawthorne was looking forward to a patronage position. O'Sullivan was playing the angles. He wrote to Hawthorne, "For the purpose of presenting you more advantageously, I have got Duyckinck to write an article about you in the April Democratic, . . . and I want you to consent to sit for a daguerrotype. By manufacturing you thus into a personage, I want to raise your mark higher in Polk's appreciation." In this essay, Duyckinck compared Hawthorne's moral passion to that of King Lear—a comparison that would stick in the mind of Duyckinck's protégé Herman Melville when in 1850 he wrote "Hawthorne and His Mosses" for the *Literary World*, edited by Duyckinck and his brother George. Duyckinck himself in fact was responsible for the publication of *Mosses* in the Library of American Books series he was editing for Wiley and Putnam.

The southwestern writers were Whigs; Hawthorne was a Democrat, like Cooper and Bancroft. Yet Hawthorne was not a popular writer like his fellow Democrats, nor did he follow the Whig humorists in vernacular writing. From the beginning, those who most memorably supported Hawthorne were those most associated with the development in America of the separate, high aesthetic sphere of "literature": Longfellow, Duyckinck, Poe. In 1842, just the year before his critique of Cooper's popularity, Poe had hailed Hawthorne for the "creation," "originality," and "genius"—all key terms of the new Romantic aesthetic—that placed his work in "the highest region of Art." Throughout his career, Hawthorne was praised as a cultivated stylist, who like Irving avoided the Romantic eccentricities of Charles Lamb and followed the eighteenth-century norm of Joseph Addison. Nonetheless, his work was considered difficult.

Hawthorne was a Massachusetts local writer not by virtue of his employing Yankee vernacular diction, but by his historical resurrection of the colonial past. This was not merely a choice of subject matter. It involved his use of a larger strategy that had had greater influence in New England than in any other part of the United States. Hawthorne was notorious for his use of allegory, a mode that looked back to the practices of the early Puritans, as well as to Edmund Spenser and John Bunyan in England, and one that he directly echoed in "The Celestial Railroad." Thus the wife of Young Goodman Brown is named "Faith," and the alluring young woman in "scarlet petticoat," who invites Robin in, rather than helping him to his kinsman Molineux, recognizably echoes the apocalyptic scarlet woman, the "whore of Babylon" in Puritan anti-Catholic propaganda. In the work of the Old Manse period, allegory persists, and the mise-en-scène is less particularized. Hawthorne's abstraction reflects the preference of his transcendentalist neighbors. Aylmer in "The Birth-mark" finds human fleshly imperfection emblematized in his wife's slight blemish, and "Rappaccini's Daughter" bears the name Beatrice from Dante's allegorical *Divine Comedy*.

Yet even if he employs a literary mode associated with his New England ancestors, Hawthorne takes a distance from their positions. The destruction of the maypole of Merry Mount figures the triumph of Puritanic "gloom" over "jollity" in American cultural life, and there is nothing in the description of the Puritans, who take their pleasure in the whipping post, to suggest that Hawthorne was nostalgic for their rule. Hawthorne's allegory is displayed for criticism, even as it is employed for construction. Moreover, established allegorical practice distinguished between conventional allegory and esoteric allegory. Esoteric allegory is farfetched and self-consciously more difficult in order to achieve a "deeper," or more socially suspect, meaning than conventional allegory. For example, the action of "Roger Malvin's Burial" begins and ends at a massive granite rock; nearby is an oak, unexpected in the landscape, which by the end is strangely withered. The heavy emphasis given to these features provokes speculation. Might the blasted oak echo the famous Charter Oak of Connecticut, and the great rock allude to Plymouth Rock? If so, the meaning of the story as a reflection on American patriotic mythology becomes much deeper, but there is no way to establish that such meanings were in fact intended.

A contemporary reviewer faulted "Young Goodman Brown" for its "obscurity of execution," which made its "lesson" incomprehensible to "nine out of ten intelligent readers." It was "an illustration, that needs to be illustrated," an "allegory with crutches." Like Bancroft, Hawthorne recognized in the Puritans the ancestors of still-current ways of living and of understanding life, but he also acknowledged that the political basis of democracy in the nineteenth century was fundamentally different from the religious basis of the seventeenth century.

Hawthorne's difficulty stemmed from another feature of his stylistic practice, his tendency to ellipsis—to saying less than a situation might warrant. "The Gentle Boy" is the longest of Hawthorne's tales except for "Rappaccini's Daughter," and part of its length comes from its dwelling in some detail on the fireside values of domesticity that have no similarly large place in Hawthorne's other tales, although they are frequent in his sketches—and letters. Such domestic values may well be implicit in those other tales too, but they are no more than hinted, and this leaves the tales open to alternative interpretations, especially by modern readers who no longer value domesticity in fiction. Frequently what Hawthorne has left out is precisely the judgment that would allow his readers to be certain which of several alternatives is correct—if indeed correct decision rather than hovering suspension is the goal of his work.

To the extent that Hawthorne's stories provide an emotional impact without a definable meaning, they partake of the aesthetic realm of literature that Poe was struggling to define. Then, too, the thematic resemblances among stories of quite different emotional power suggest that Hawthorne was more concerned to offer a distanced examination of alternatives than either serious moral teaching or deep psychological obsessions. For example, both "Wake-field" and "Young Goodman Brown" take as their action a man's leaving home. He lingers on the threshold as he leaves, and when he returns—after an abortive reunion with his wife amidst a crowd—things have changed for the worse. Wakefield has been too little affected by the intervening years, and the story's tone is satirically externalized. Brown, in contrast, has been too much affected by a single night, and the story is feelingly internalized.

Like Poe's, Hawthorne's work before 1850 is in short forms—another elliptical choice, for a long work usually establishes authorial values more securely than can an unconventional short work. To this day, short prose fictions typically fall into two classes, the highly conventionalized (whether science fiction, crime, western, or "New Yorker") and the radically innovative. Bancroft's extensive narrative with its well-defined shape and its repeated narrative guidance to the reader was clearly coherent with his commitment to the party of the people. In contrast, Hawthorne broke up the national narrative into minutely examined local units, not necessarily of any preestablished significance, and this technique conflicted with his Democratic allegiance. If he resisted the arrogance of the Puritan religious elect, how could he participate in a secular cultural elite?

The primary mark of Hawthorne's political difference from the Whig humorists and his solidarity with Bancroft shows in the seriousness with which Hawthorne treats people of no special social distinction in various everyday situations. The strongest works of the southwestern writers display their social animus, preeminently in George Harris. Hawthorne's most powerful works also convey political implications. These stories are not only somber in moral coloring, but their somber tones are not reserved for the highest social orders. At the same time that Hawthorne and Bancroft were writing, Ralph Waldo Emerson in "The American Scholar" (1837) emphasized the value of "the familiar, the low . . . the meal in the firkin; the milk in the pan; the ballad in the street." To illustrate this concern, he praised the "genius" of such Romantic writers as Wordsworth. Modern readers of Wordsworth, however, more readily admire the "egotistical sublime" of "Tintern Abbey," the Immortality Ode, and above all *The Prelude,* and it takes historical recovery to appreciate Wordsworth's more radically democratic attempts like "Michael," which present the "literature of the poor," the "meaning of household life" that Emerson praised. In the case of Hawthorne, however, the culturally and socially secure first-person narrator of the sketches now compels far less attention than his third-person tales of what Bancroft, or Hawthorne himself in his occasional political writings, would call "the people."

The equal and opposite fanaticisms of Puritans and Quakers in "The Gentle Boy" could make for bleak comedy in the hands of someone like Simon Sugg's Hooper, but Hawthorne treated them respectfully, even while not identifying himself with, or urging readers to side with, either. Not only for modern readers but also for Duyckinck and Melville, "Young Goodman Brown" represented a high point of Hawthorne's accomplishment, which they compared to *King Lear,* although Brown was very much a commoner. So, too, did the kind of popular, mass political activity satirized in southwestern writing become the partially humorous, but finally painfully moving, experience of "My Kinsman, Major Molineux." And when Hawthorne treated the subject of Indian fighting and the frontier in "Roger Malvin's Burial," there is none of the energy of tall talk and high spirits that mark the Davy Crockett kind of writing. Hawthorne's story begins after the fight is over and the Indians—for several years at least—are out of the picture; the action returns to the frontier only for a scene of somnambulistic violence between the members of the pioneer family.

In their treatment of common life the southwestern writers reduced the actions they related to superficiality by their externalized comic renderings and lack of concern for consequences. Hawthorne, in contrast, reduced the actions he treated to feelings by his internalized psychological rendering and obsessive concern for individual consequences. Thus Hawthorne resembles Cooper and Bancroft in acknowledging the dignity of everyday life, in the forests or settlements rather than in the courts or capitals. But he does not resemble them in finding any active ideal in the everyday, either as a heroic individual like Cooper's Leatherstocking or as a political community such as those with which Bancroft populated his American history.

The characteristic situation toward which many of Hawthorne's most effective stories move involves an isolated figure and a crowd. Robin Molineux searches for his kinsman while everyone he meets is involved in a conspiracy against the major, unknown to him until the punitive procession at the end. Young Goodman Brown sneaks off for a meeting in the woods and discovers everyone of high or low repute from Salem to be there. Wakefield goes around the corner from his home and hides for twenty years concealed by the crowd of London. If the crowds are not treated dismissively as mobs, neither are they hailed as the will of the people incarnate. They are powerful and frightening, whether as the community of evil into which Brown refuses induction or as the Puritan vigilantes that the Lord and Lady of May are left to face after their maypole has been cut down.

The problem of crowds, mobs, and riots came to sharp attention in the American 1830s. At the time that Hawthorne had drafted "Provincial Tales," in which his strongest crowd scenes occur, the public issue had not yet arisen, but from 1834 through 1837, there was a tremendous increase in the number of crowd disturbances becoming known through news, and much concern about its significance. The single greatest provocation for these mob activities was abolitionism, and those who participated in group actions against abolitionists were typically respectable people, "gentlemen of property and standing." Hawthorne's meditations on the Puritan crowd as the basis for American politics form a sober counterpoint to the controversies in the popular press.

Antiabolition mobs often self-consciously modeled themselves on the group actions of revolutionary America. In Philadelphia in 1835 and Cincinnati in 1836 mobs specifically invoked the example of the Boston Tea Party, an illegal but righteous action. The only way many Americans of the 1830s could understand abolitionism was as a British conspiracy against the American way of life. Thus in 1837, after the concerted mob action in Alton, Illinois, against Elijah Lovejoy, the abolitionist editor, culminating in his murder, the attorney general of Massachusetts told the multitude at Faneuil Hall that the Alton rioters were following the example of Samuel Adams, Charles Warren, and James Otis. This context does much to explain why Hawthorne might have preferred to forget about "My Kinsman, Major Molineux," which he did not reprint until *The Snow-Image* (1851). He even resisted Duyckinck's suggestion to include "Young Goodman Brown" in *Mosses,* although he finally yielded. Stories of mobs had become highly topical. What might originally have been a historically appropriate, complex, and sober attitude toward prerevolutionary mob activity could scarcely avoid being transformed into apparent approval of either abolitionism or antiabolitionism—neither of which Hawthorne supported.

The characteristic situation of heightened individual subjectivity set against the crowd bears an obvious and important resemblance to certain aspects of Hawthorne's personal situation. The case of Young Goodman Brown may illustrate this resemblance. The story shows what it might have been like for an individual who held the Puritan theological beliefs, in the third generation of the Massachusetts colony, that led to the witchcraft persecutions. As opposed to Bancroft's suggestion that the clergy led the persecution as a means to negotiate a difficult political and ideological moment, Hawthorne locates the problem in the holier-than-thou psychology of a perfectly ordinary member of the community. Young "Brown," wedded to "Faith," seems intended as a generic, typical figure. Yet he proves capable of believing (he is not and need not be certain)— even heroically capable, insofar as the belief greatly pains and shocks him—that everyone except himself is secretly in league with the devil. The last paragraph of the story, however, in depicting the dreary end to which such suspicions doom Brown, makes an eccentric out of him. No longer typical, he is an isolated individual.

The very methods of Hawthorne's art are intensely individualizing and, in this respect, alienating. Popular historiography had made Cotton Mather the villain of the witchcraft scandal. Hawthorne, in contrast, has fixed critical attention on someone who did not wield great power. Mather could have been responsible for leading communal action; Brown could not have been. So Hawthorne's attempt to show the psychological basis for a historical event makes it increasingly difficult to imagine how any event at all could have occurred; the very technique of closely analyzing a single person cuts that person off from any community. Hawthorne dreaded the power to isolate of Calvinist theology in the New England Puritan past and of idealist philosophy in the transcendentalist present, and yet his own mode of writing, like his own situation as a writer, seems to insist upon an isolation that contradicts his commitment to the communally shared world of everyday. Hawthorne's writing reenacts the contradiction of Jacksonianism, which honored the common people but also promised every white, male, native-born Protestant the chance to make of himself something better and special, something no longer common.

Edgar Allan Poe

Unlike Hawthorne and the southwestern humorists, Edgar Allan Poe did not have a well-established regional residence, nor do his writings draw upon local history, lore, and customs. Yet the controversies surrounding his life and reputation testified to the continued absence of any national literary culture. Poe strove to make his art a world of its own, a place beyond locality or even nationality, but his success began only after his death. While he lived, his problems exemplified the fragmentation of cultural life in the United States. As James Russell Lowell explained in a favorable review of Poe in 1845,

> The situation of American literature is anomalous. It has no center. . . . It is divided into many systems, each revolving round its several suns, and often presenting to the rest only the faint glimmer of a milk-and-watery way. Our capital city, unlike London or Paris, is not a great central heart. . . . Boston, New York, Philadelphia, each has its literature almost more distinct than those of the different dialects of Germany.

Poe's life is a tale of five cities: Boston, Richmond, Baltimore, Philadelphia, and New York. He was born in Boston in 1809 and raised in Richmond, Virginia (except for five years spent in London) until 1826, when he entered the newly founded University of Virginia. Leaving the university because of gambling debts, he enlisted in the army under a pseudonym, serving in Boston, where he privately published his first book, *Tamerlane and Other Poems,* "by a Bostonian" (1827). While seeking entry to West Point, he lived in Baltimore and published there a second volume of poems, *Al Aaraaf, Tamerlane and Minor Poems* (1829). After a brief period at West Point, he paused in New York to publish *Poems: Second Edition* (1831) and then returned to Baltimore. From 1831 through 1834 Poe tried to make a place for himself in the world of periodical writing. He submitted stories to prize competitions for the Philadelphia *Sunday Courier* and Baltimore *Saturday Visiter,* leading to publication and a prize in 1833 for "MS. Found in a Bottle."

In 1835, with the recommendation of John Pendleton Kennedy, a Baltimore man of letters, Poe began writing for the *Southern Liter-*

ary Messenger, founded in Richmond the year before. His first story in this journal was "Berenice," and soon he went to Richmond to serve as the *Messenger's* editorial assistant and principal reviewer. Over the next year and a half, Poe published more than eighty reviews in the *Messenger,* notable for their early appreciation of Charles Dickens and of Longstreet's *Georgia Scenes,* as well as for their advocacy of Samuel Taylor Coleridge and Percy Bysshe Shelley, still little known in the United States. He increased the journal's circulation but won notoriety for the "tomahawk" he swung in his savage reviews of many current American productions. For example, reviewing *Paul Ulric: Or the Adventures of an Enthusiast* (1835), by Morris Mattson, Poe began,

> When we called Norman Leslie the silliest book in the world [2 months earlier] we had certainly never seen Paul Ulric. . . . In itself, the book before us is too purely imbecile to merit an extended critique—but as a portion of our daily literary food—as an American work published by the Harpers—as one of a class of absurdities with an inundation of which our country is grievously threatened—we shall have no hesitation, and shall spare no pains, in exposing fully before the public eye its four hundred and forty-three pages of utter folly, bombast, and inanity.

Meanwhile Poe had himself compiled some sixteen tales framed by "The Folio Club," a set of comic characters each of whom in turn tells one of the tales, and he sent them to the same Harper that had published *Paul Ulric.* Harper's letter of rejection says much about the condition of American publishing. The publisher cited as problems the previous appearance of the tales in magazines; the general public's feeling against collections (readers preferred one "single and connected story" to fill "the whole volume, or number of volumes"); and the particular character of the tales, which were "too learned and mystical": "They would be understood and relished only by a very few." As a southerner trying to publish in

New York, Poe encountered discouragement similar to that met by Hawthorne in New England when he was attempting to publish his first planned books. Poe, however, took immediate steps to follow Harper's advice. Having left Richmond and the *Messenger* and settled in New York in early 1837, he completed a volume-length pseudofactual sea story, *The Narrative of Arthur Gordon Pym*. By the time Harper published this work, with Poe listed as its editor rather than its author, in July 1838, his possibilities in New York seemed exhausted, and he moved to Philadelphia.

From 1838 into 1844 Poe remained in Philadelphia. Here he succeeded in publishing, with Lea and Blanchard, his two-volume *Tales of the Grotesque and Arabesque* (1839), which included all twenty-five of the pieces he had already published in periodicals. Included in this collection, among many pieces that even Poe's greatest admirers do not much care for, are "William Wilson" and "The Fall of the House of Usher," both reprinted from the *Gentleman's Magazine,* where from 1839 Poe had editorial responsibilities. When in 1840 *Graham's Magazine* incorporated the *Gentleman's,* Poe went along, publishing "The Man of the Crowd" in December, and in April 1841 he became the magazine's editor. Sales *of Graham's* flourished, spurred by Poe's invention of the detective story in "The Murders in the Rue Morgue" and by his powerful reviewing, including his famous piece on Hawthorne's *Twice-told Tales.* Conflicts with the owner, however, led Poe to resign in 1842. In 1843, Poe won a cash prize for "The Gold Bug," which was widely reprinted and began to make him famous enough for a publisher to venture a pamphlet series, reissuing *The Prose Romances of Edgar A. Poe*—but only one number appeared.

Poe's troubles with owners and editors at the *Southern Literary Messenger* and the *Gentleman's Magazine* had already led him by 1840 to plan a journal under his own control, the *Penn Magazine.* After his further frustrations with *Graham's,* he renewed his plans for a journal, to be called *The Stylus,* the earlier name being "somewhat too local in its suggestions." Poe imagined that he might reach the intellectually most worthy audience if he produced a journal in "mechanical appearance . . . typography, paper and binding" superior to anything produced in the United States. The so-called "*cheap* literature" of the day was to be combated by something at once valuable and costly. The connection of the economic and the spiritual was further underlined in Poe's insistence that he required "proprietary right," an "interest . . . not merely editorial," in the magazine, if he were to "stamp" on the journal that "*individuality*" that only a "single mind" can give. A proper journal must be his sole property, with no split between ownership and editorship; intellectual integrity required no division of labor (a logic that would dictate Poe's writing the entire contents). On this basis, as a proprietor supported by subscribers, Poe could bring the work into "the Republic of Letters" and "insist upon regarding the world at large as the sole proper audience for the author," bending to the whims of neither readers nor owner by pursuing "a criticism self-sustained; guiding itself only by the purest rules of Art."

This plan never succeeded, and when Poe came to New York in 1844, he found himself once more enmeshed in local turbulences. He joined the staff of the *Evening Mirror,* for which he wrote on the literary scene, and he also published a series of reflective "Marginalia" in the *Democratic Review,* the nationalist organ. Evert Duyckinck, as he had with Hawthorne, recruited Poe for the Library of American Books of Wiley and Putnam. In justifying his republication of periodical pieces, Duyckinck explained (not wholly accurately) that they had "hitherto been scattered over the newspapers and magazines of the country, chiefly of the South, and have been scarcely, if at all, known to Northern and Eastern readers." Selected by Duyckinck, *Tales* was published in 1845 and did well enough to encourage the publication *of The Raven and Other Poems* a few months later. Finally, in July 1845, Poe got control of a paper of his own, the *Broadway Journal,* but beyond publishing revised versions of most of his earlier poems and tales he did little distinctive in the months before he had to abandon the project. In 1846 he published a series of pieces on the "Literati of New York" in *Godey's Lady's Book,* and in 1848 he resumed reviewing for the *Southern Literary Messenger,* while also publishing *Eureka: A Prose Poem,* a cosmogonical—aesthetic speculation. The last year of Poe's life resumed the threads of his whole entangled career. While still living in New York, Poe was writing for the Boston weekly *Flag of Our Union* and still hoping to realize *The Stylus.* To raise money for his project, he traveled to Richmond, on the way stopping with friends in Philadelphia. After a happy late summer in Virginia, he traveled north again, but he died, delirious and in mysterious circumstances, in Baltimore, in October 1849.

Poe's successor as editor *of Graham's,* Rufus Griswold, became his literary executor. Griswold published versions of Poe's life that made Poe anathema to respectable literary culture, until modern scholarship restored the facts. Although many who had known Poe protested, Griswold's version still captures much of the feeling that his memory has provoked:

> He walked the streets, in madness or melancholy, with lips moving in indistinct curses, or with eyes upturned in passionate prayers (never for himself, for he felt, or professed to feel, that he was already damned), but for their happiness who at that moment were objects of his idolatry; or with his glance introverted to a heart gnawed with anguish, and with a face shrouded in gloom, he would brave the wildest storms; and all night, with drenched garments and arms wildly beating the wind and rain, he would speak as if to spirits.

This shabby-genteel, urban successor to the aristocratic, Byronic hero alone with the wild elements helped define the *poète maudit* for his younger French contemporary, and posthumous admirer, Charles Baudelaire, through whose translations Poe has powerfully affected European literature. Within the culture of the United

States, Poe served as an early exemplar of what has become a commonplace. As Duyckinck put it, "Our most neglected and best [*sic*] abused authors, are generally our best authors." This was not obviously true in the England of Dickens, Macaulay, and Tennyson, but it had powerful relevance for the America of Poe, Hawthorne, Emerson, and Whitman.

In his own time, and for readers since, Poe's work has posed above all problems of tone. It has never been certain quite how to take any piece written by him. In an anonymous review of the 1845 *Tales,* largely written by Poe himself, his style is praised as "strictly . . . earnest," but this earnestness need not actually derive from the writer's "belief in his statements"; rather it comes from a "power of simulation" that allows "high genius" to produce its chosen effects. Was this pseudoearnestness the narrator's self-delusion, the author's wish to delude the reader, or play in which all parties shared? Readers were confident in laughing at southwestern humor, and Hawthorne's complex ironies only emphasized his thoughtfulness, but Poe's work provoked fundamental uncertainty in response. Was he serious? Should his readers be serious? The problem is one of genre: What kind of work is this?

As early as 1835, Poe faced this problem in a letter to the editor of the *Southern Literary Messenger,* where he had just published "Berenice." In this tale, the eccentric first-person narrator explains his obsession with the teeth of his cousin Berenice, which he endows with spiritual value: "tous ses dents etaient des idées" ("all her teeth were ideas," a neoplatonic figure known in the English metaphysical poetry of the seventeenth century, as in John Donne's famous phrase "her body thought"). Poe's story turns on the narrator's drive to possess the teeth after his cousin's death, a possibly comic reduction of the ideal to its material base. He removes them from her entombed corpse; but she had been buried alive, which turns the bizarre into torture.

Poe's editor complained that the story was "by far too horrible," and Poe replied that he had written the story against a friend's "bet" that it would be impossible to write anything "effective" on a "subject so singular" if treated "seriously." Against the claims of purest art, Poe went on to insist that "the history of all Magazines" shows that just this kind of story is the basis of their success, and then he defined the kind: "the ludicrous heightened into the grotesque: the fearful coloured into the horrible: the witty exaggerated into the burlesque: the singular wrought out into the strange and mystical." Poe denied that such excess was a matter of "bad taste," for such stories, far more than "simplicity," were what was actually *"read."* Nor were these stories easy to write: they required both "originality" and also "much labour spent in their composition." Although Poe invoked British magazines, the work of Coleridge, and Thomas De Quincey's *Confessions of an English Opium-Eater,* (1822), the aesthetic principles he set out were known as those of German Romanticism—so much so that in his preface to *Tales of the Grotesque and Arabesque,* he felt compelled to insist that "terror is not of Germany, it is of the soul." These Romantic premises held that the traditional generic categories and divisions between high and low, serious and comic modes, no longer pertained, and through the mixture of these levels, or tones, the strongest, and most appropriately modern, effects could be achieved.

Many contemporary reviews, however, did not find Poe Romantic. For them his writing was of quite a different kind. They compared him to a lawyer, a type widely recognized as characteristic and important in America. Both Edmund Burke, in warning Britain to seek reconciliation with the colonies, and Alexis de Tocqueville, in his study of American democracy, had emphasized that lawyers gave a distinctive tone to American culture. The lawyer addresses a case professionally rather than from any personal commitment to the issues or individuals involved; both nature and custom yield to analytic power. The lawyer is public, formal, cold, and insincere, even though also often inventive and mystifying. Thus Poe was criticized for shunning the "homely," with its familiar sentiments and comfort. (The "most wild, yet most homely narrative" of "The Black Cat" evidently did not count.) The legal profession seemed to many readers to be the cultural source of the pseudoearnestness so striking in Poe. And legal skills were associated with self-promotion, which, in contrast to the obscurity Hawthorne feared, offered the publicity Poe sought.

The lawyer was the first great American model of the professional, and Poe strove to develop two further models, which might or might not prove reconcilable: the professional writer and the "artist." He had defended "Berenice" as highly skilled magazine writing, and as late as 1844, he proclaimed that he was "essentially a magazinist." On the other hand, in discussing with Duyckinck the selection of tales for the 1845 collection, Poe expressed a wish for something "*representing* my mind in its various phases." He claimed that even though he had written the pieces for specific occasions over many years, he had, nonetheless, kept "the book-unity always in mind" and that each piece was to serve "as part of a *whole*." For this reason, Poe always sought the greatest possible "*diversity and variety*," not only of "subject" and "thought" but also of "*tone*." His stories offered "a vast variety of kinds," with the kinds varying in their value, but "each tale is equally good *of its kind*." Poe claimed in effect that Duyckinck's "Library of American Books" was too partial, compared to the "Republic of Letters." Yet a contradiction remained. Having proclaimed the unity of mind that his works revealed, Poe then explained that this unity was achieved only at the level of craft. The professional model prevailed over the wholeness that art promised, the local occasion over the world at large. Poe may have been more honest than those who held that literature could achieve a unity that overcame the social and economic conditions of modern life.

Poe's career depended on a primary fact of modern American life:

the growth of cities. New York, Philadelphia, and Baltimore were the nation's three largest cities, and from 1820 to 1860 their population increased some sixfold. In the United States only 6 percent of the population lived in cities in 1810 and 1820, but by 1860, nearly 20 percent did. Urban population increased over 90 percent in the 1840s, growing almost three times as fast as total population. Cities were still less industrial than they were commercial, places of exchange and transfer more than of primary production. This period also saw the growth of office work, as the economic functions of cities became separated from people's residences, and the split between men's and women's "spheres" became a marked fact of social, economic, and cultural life. In Hawthorne's fiction the split between a male world of science and a female world of spirit could figure directly in a story like "The Birth-mark." In Poe's work, however, such social effects were displaced and transformed. In this respect, Poe's work may be related to an important tendency in English Romanticism.

When in 1800 William Wordsworth wrote his preface to *Lyrical Ballads,* England had already begun to live through the transformations that would come later to the United States. In defining the social significance of his poetic experiments, Wordsworth emphasized that "a multitude of causes, unknown to former times, are now acting with a combined force" to change the character of the human mind. He included the democratic excitements provoked by the French Revolution and the "increasing accumulation of men in cities." As opposed to the seasonal variation of labor in the country, the "uniformity of their occupations" provokes city dwellers to a "craving for extraordinary incident," which the new mass journalism of the day "hourly gratifies." Wordsworth thus wrote against his age; his poetry set in the country depends upon an analysis and a rejection of his experience of London. Wordsworth hoped to oppose the "gross and violent stimulants" offered, in differing ways, by gothic fiction and by the news.

Poe, in contrast to Wordsworth, allied himself with the powers of journalism. He achieved several successful new hoaxes (notably, stories of a transatlantic balloon journey in 1844), and his fiction relies upon the gothic trappings that Wordsworth found degrading. Wordsworth offered a poetic memory that stabilized and harmonized experience; Poe's characteristic first-person narrators are focuses of disturbance and overstimulation. Yet reviewers noted less the sensational elements of Poe's work than its coldness. "The Fall of the House of Usher" was judged to be like "a finely sculptured statue, beautiful to the eye, but without an immortal spirit" and, by another reviewer, to lack "any link of feeling or sympathy." Poe's writing made the reader feel that it came from a lawyer's office, not from a home (even when it was dealing with a "House"). Readers placed Poe's work in the masculine "sphere," while the delicacy that Wordsworth had sought was placed with "female," sentimental writing.

Poe's cunningly elaborate prose sought to awaken powerful emotions through reorienting his readers' perception of such sensational topics as murder, entombment, and decay. He explained that the effect of "The Fall of the House of Usher" was to derive from "discovering that for a long period of time we have been mistaking sounds of agony, for those of mirth or indifference." This formulation perfectly echoed the journalism of urban social exposé: the poor were starving, they were not happy wastrels. Wordsworth found in the country the opposite of the city, and sentimental writing turned from the streets to the hearth, but Poe reversed them. He transposed the elements of urban experience into the imagined unrealities of his artistic world elsewhere. Yet his earnestness involved such mastery of detail that reviewers frequently compared him to Daniel Defoe rather than to the Romantics.

Poe is obviously a city writer in the London of "The Man of the Crowd," which fully matches the urban sketches of Dickens's London and Gogol's St. Petersburg, which were also written in the 1830s. Poe's imagined Paris in "The Murders in the Rue Morgue" and "The Purloined Letter" defines the genre of urban crime writing more sharply than Balzac in *Splendors and Miseries of Courtesans*. Even where the setting is not urban, however, the models of city life prevail. "The Fall of the House of Usher," despite its back-country setting, shows the power of an "environment" to determine physical and spiritual characteristics alike. This same concern with environment organizes much of Balzac's most characteristic and powerful writing about Paris, as in the evocation of the Pension Vauquer at the opening *of Old Goriot.*

In America as abroad, new conditions of life produced new forms of experience. The pressure of urban crowds and the split between home and work both helped to establish a heightened sense of personal interiority and a need to define and cherish particularity. Shared, public circumstances produced a new form of privacy and offered new media through which to communicate privacy— whether privacy that one owned as a "self," in personal sketch writing, or privacy that one owned as another's, in news and fiction. Poe established a characteristic form of writing. A person defined by a great trauma confesses the event. His first-person narrative is as precise in its homely details as Defoe and yet Romantically strange in its feelings, which it coldly analyzes. This combination defines a moment in the making of the modern individual.

A comparison with Wordsworth may make this point clear. In *The Prelude,* published only in 1850 and therefore unknown to Poe, Wordsworth writes of the "spots of time" that stand as "memorials" permitting the "restoration" of "our minds" when they are "depressed." The power of these moments comes from their revelation that "The mind is lord and master—outward sense / The obedient servant of her will." One such moment for Wordsworth was in his childhood when, lost in the hills, he came upon

> A naked pool that lay beneath the hills,
> The beacon on the summit, and, more near,
> A girl who bore a pitcher on her head,

>   And seemed with difficult steps to force her way
>   Against the blowing wind.

This "ordinary sight" took on a power of "visionary dreariness" that the poem conveys by a differentiated verbal repetition, which, in turn, models the recurrence-with-change of the scene in his memory and later life. So, in the next lines, the "naked pool" that first had headed the scene is recombined with its different elements, the "moorland waste and naked pool" and "the naked pool and dreary crags."

"The Fall of the House of Usher" hinges on questions of self-identity and the powers of the mind for restoration, but Poe is much less hopeful than Wordsworth. Roderick Usher believes that his ancestral dwelling has developed an "atmosphere" that gives it a "terrible influence" that has long "moulded the destinies of his family." The narrator sees here only madness that "need[s] no comment"; not only does the ending of the tale, however, support Roderick's belief—the whole edifice collapsing as Madeline and Roderick die together—but the narrator has himself expressed similar beliefs in the opening paragraph. His first sight of the House fills him with "insufferable gloom," a "dreariness" that "no goading of the imagination could torture into aught of the sublime." (In German Romantic theory, the sublime derived precisely from the power of the mind over nature.) This "utter depression" allows no sense of the "visionary" in dreariness that so powerfully moved Wordsworth, for "combinations of very simple natural objects . . . have the power of thus affecting us," although we cannot analyze the reasons. Having thus taken in "the bleak walls . . . the vacant eye-like windows . . . a few rank sedges . . . a few white trunks of decayed trees," the narrator tries to assert mastery by imposing a "different arrangement of the . . . details," but when he looks in the lake, he is even more chilled by "the remodelled and inverted images of the gray sedge, and the ghastly tree-stems, and the vacant and eye-like windows." In this story the pattern of differentiated repetition shows the power of things, the consciousness of urban fragmentation against which Wordsworth was writing, but from within which Poe writes.

It makes no more sense to judge Poe's work from the standpoint of a socially and historically different sense of the self than it does to judge the organization of political and cultural life in the United States during Poe's lifetime by the standards that came to reign after the Civil War and that largely prevail in the United States now. Despite the establishment of national narrative by Cooper and Bancroft, the Union was still not wholly integrated as a nation. During the period from 1830 to 1850, sectional and local differences increased at least as much as they were overcome through the proliferation of new means of communication and transportation. Only after the Civil War could the South properly be called repressed, and only in relation to the monstrous new energies of nation building that the Secession had provoked and the Civil War had channeled. Split between his five cities, Poe shared neither in a national culture nor in the Republic of Letters; he was an engineer of sensations, his craft neither the "purest art" to which it aspired nor the "literature" against which modern readers judge it.

3

Personal Narratives

Local narratives partake of place; personal narratives arise from and depend on displacement: Pacific voyages, overland journeys to the frontier, slaves' escapes, or even a displacement as small as Thoreau's within Concord. This displacement is physical, but it also defines the fundamental rhetorical situation of the narratives: their intelligibility and force depend on the difference between the world that the reader knows, and reads within, and the world that the narrator has experienced. Etymologically, the Latin word from which "narrative" derives is closely related to the adjective *gnarus*, "knowing." The relation of narrative to individual life-knowledge is sharper in this kind of narrative than in any of the others studied here. In the terminology of classical oratory, the "narration" was the plain and manifest setting forth of the facts of the case. Such an emphasis on plainness and focus on externals typify these narratives. They pay much less attention to the shifting nuances of personal, and especially interpersonal, feeling, than would be expected in a novel.

As reports of activity on the margins of national life, these personal narratives are more like the genre of captivity narrative stemming from Mary Rowlandson's account of her life among the Indians (1682) than they resemble the narratives of inner religious experience, which Jonathan Edwards's "personal narrative," dating

76

from around 1740, exemplifies. For the more privileged white authors, personal narratives characteristically have the circular shape of descent and return—a touching of ground, even a humiliation before the return to the elevation of ordinary civilized life; for slave narrators, the more usual pattern is that of an ascent to freedom. A generic appeal of personal narratives in their time and since is their registration of what seems a more archaic way of life, a virtual past achieved by travel in space rather than in time, but from the perspective of a narrator who is, like the readership, part of a modern world, making contact with that "other" world and transforming it while integrating it. Personal narratives may act thereby to colonize places and kinds of experience, which are then appropriated into national narrative.

Two Years Before the Mast

Published by Harper Brothers in 1840, *Two Years before the Mast: A Personal Narrative of Life at Sea,* by Richard Henry Dana, Jr., made for its publishers some ten thousand dollars (at forty-five cents a copy) in its first two years. Dana came from a distinguished family of Cambridge, Massachusetts (his father had founded the important quarterly, the *North American Review*), but there were money troubles by the time he was at Harvard, and when his studies were interrupted by eye troubles in 1834, he decided to relieve his family's financial burden by going to work. His choice to sail as a common sailor was unusual. He joined a ship that carried cowhides from California to Boston, where it helped make possible the booming Massachusetts shoe industry. Much of Dana's trip, and much of the book, involved his work on land in California, treating and loading the hides. When California became part of the United States in 1848 and a center of world attention with the 1849 Gold Rush, Dana's was one of the very few books that could give any information about it, and the book received an immense second wind of popularity. By the turn of the century Dana's narrative had become a classic of a bygone age, before steamers had replaced sailing ships. It was so widely admired for the clarity and simplicity of its prose that oculists used passages for their eye charts.

Dana wrote against the predominant literature of the sea, derived from Lord Byron and from James Fenimore Cooper's maritime romances. He asserted that there was "no romance" in the "every-day life" of sailing, but "plain, matter of fact drudgery and hardship." Yet Dana also shared a major concern of Romanticism, associated more with William Wordsworth than with Byron—the attempt to purify written language by putting it back in touch with the speech and experiences of people in simpler conditions of life. Dana sought to present "as it really is" the perspective of the "common" sailor, even if this meant using language that would be judged "coarse": for example, "To work hard, live hard, die hard, and to go to hell after all, would be hard indeed!" Equally rooted in the temporal rhythms of work, but more poetic, is another sailors' saying, "In coming home from round Cape Horn, and the Cape of Good Hope, the north star is the first land you make." Dana judged that the sailors' "hard" life exacted emotional costs: "An overstrained sense of manliness is the characteristic of seafaring men." To give "sympathy" even to a sick shipmate would seem "sisterly," and the men's relations with each other are therefore "cruel": "Whatever your feelings may be, you must make a joke of everything at sea"—especially of a close brush with death. The result makes of sea-life a "frigid routine."

This routine was in the first instance physical rather than moral or psychological. Dana devoted pages to establishing the routine of "a day's work" and emphasizing that the whole voyage is marked by the "unvarying repetition of these duties," which include not only the strenuous athletics and fine technical detail of work among the sails and the endless chores of cleaning and carpentry upkeep but also the ceaseless production out of "old junk" of the various fabrics used for innumerable functions aboard ship. Once California is reached and the new routines of work begin, Dana narrates "the whole history of a hide," from its being taken off the bullock to its being taken on to Boston. By 1840 much work was becoming increasingly specialized. The development of factory labor was much noticed. More people, however, were affected by the integration of farms into national market-patterns that encouraged farmers to raise specialized crops for sale and to buy their necessities rather than practice subsistence farming and domestic production. In this context, sailors were interesting because their work still required them to perform many different tasks. The forecastle "looked like the workshop of what a sailor is,—a Jack at all trades." Even the sailors' songs were closely integrated into the work process. When several new members join the crew, their new songs are a great "windfall," because the old ones "had got nearly worn out by six weeks' constant use," and this "timely reinforcement of songs" helped work get finished several days faster.

Its variety, and its movement to vocal rather than mechanical rhythms, made sailors' work, however strenuous, seem an image of residual fullness, but their work also partook of the newly emerging patterns of "discipline and system." Thus "three minutes and a half" were allowed for dressing in the morning, and similar precision ruled every other duty. Over history, prisons and factories have been closely linked, and, in the nineteenth century, techniques of human organization were often tried out in prisons before being generalized to the management of labor. The practice of work on board a ship carried this process to its peak: "In no state prison are the convicts more regularly set to work, and more closely watched. No conversation is allowed among the men at their duty."

The sailors are held to their rigorous routine by the ship's officers, among whom the captain is "lord paramount," source of all power. The extreme stratifications of life on board echoes the sailors' views of class divisions on shore: "Sailors call every man rich who does not work with his hands, and wears a long coat and cravat." There is no easy gradation between the more and the less well off, as in imagined American equality, but a stark division between rich and poor. The captain's authority extends to the power of administering corporal punishment without appeal, and one of the strongest sequences in Dana's book details the flogging of one hapless crew member, and then of the most respected of the sailors, who had questioned the reason for the flogging. Dana is horrified to see "a man . . . whom I had lived with and eaten with for months, and knew almost as well as a brother . . . a man—a human being, made in God's likeness—fastened up and flogged like a beast!" By asserting his human dignity, the victim had provoked the captain's determination to flog him:

> "I'm no negro slave," said Sam.
> "Then I'll make you one," said the captain. . . . "Seize him up! Make a spread eagle of him! I'll teach you all who is master aboard!"

The captain concludes by threatening all of the men, "I'll see who'll tell me he isn't a negro slave." ("Who ain't a slave?" Ishmael asks, more metaphysically, in *Moby-Dick*.) Dana went on to devote his career to maritime law, with special concern for the rights of sailors, and in 1848 he was one of the first from his social group to ally himself with the Free Soil party.

The experience of shipboard life intensely focused the meaning of life in the United States, and it did not show it in the best light. Dana's narrative demonstrates a licensed tyranny that produces frustrations in the politics of daily life that are assuaged only pseudopolitically. When shore leave is finally granted him, Dana will "never forget the delightful sensation . . . of being once more in my life, though only for a day, my own master." Despite his patriotic upbringing, only at this moment "for the first time, I may truly say, in my whole life" did Dana feel "the meaning of a term which I had often heard—the sweets of liberty." He and a shipmate on leave discuss "the times past, when we were free and in midst of friends, in America, and of the prospect of our return." Yet the book registers no consciousness that it is the laws of the United States that empower the captain and permit slavery. "America" stands as the alternative to the lack of liberty that it in fact legitimates. What most recalls to Dana his lost America is the chance to read a copy of the *Boston Daily Advertiser:* "Nothing carries you so entirely to a place, and makes you feel so perfectly at home, as a newspaper." Such a passage at once makes the mundanity of home dearer to all who read it and defuses completely the sense that any changes are needed there.

Dana himself shared the work ethic that subjected the sailors to their regretted toughness. From his first impression through to the end of the book, he reiterates the judgment that "there are no people to whom the newly-invented Yankee word of 'loafer' [this is the earliest *Oxford English Dictionary* citation] is more applicable than to the Spanish Americans." Of California, he speculates, "In the hands of an enterprising people, what a country this might be!" Yet he also fears that the Spanish cultural model will ruin even the children of "Americans (as those from the United States are called) and Englishmen" who might be born there. Dana himself remained the "son of a gentleman," one of the "rich," and recognized that to the sailors he could never seem entirely "one of them."

This ambiguity in Dana's social position affects some of the most significant moments in the shaping of his book. In thinking about a lost opportunity to find out the life story of a suddenly departed shipmate, Dana reflects,

We must come down from our heights, and leave our straight paths, for the byways and low places of life, if we would learn truths by

strong contrasts; and in hovels, forecastles, and among our own outcasts in foreign lands, see what has been wrought upon our fellow-
creatures by accident, hardship, or vice.

This movement of descent, a chastening humiliation, resonated
powerfully with American democratic ideals, and yet it rests only
upon an improved power to "see." There is no hint offered of more
intimate involvement, of actual solidarity. In this respect, Dana
does not prove a clear alternative to the overview offered in British
novels of social exploration by Charles Dickens. Dickens called for
the imaginative power to rise above the city and "take the house-
tops off," to reveal to his readers the unknown vice and poverty
they live amidst. He believed that the knowledge gained from this
vision would lead people to "apply themselves, like creatures of one
common origin . . . tending to one common end, to make the world
a better place!" Dana has actually been among the sailors; nonetheless, Dickens offers the more activist stance in his writing.

A less programmatic passage in Dana acknowledges the distance
that might be needed for seeing, or understanding, a large whole
and, at the same time, acknowledges that even being there with a
common sailor does not mean that a gentleman sees things the same
way. The passage begins in the mode of anti-Romantic deflation:
"Notwithstanding all that has been said about the beauty of a ship
under full sail, there are very few who have ever seen a ship, liter-
ally, under all her sail." For those who see a ship only near shore, "a
ship coming in or going out of port, with her ordinary sails, and
perhaps two or three studding-sails, is commonly said to be under
full sail." Only far from shore, however, does a ship ever have up all
her sail, "when she has a light, steady breeze, very nearly, but not
quite dead aft, and so regular that it can be trusted." Then indeed,
"she is the most glorious moving object in the world." Even among
sailors, however, this sight is rare: "Such a sight, very few . . . have
ever beheld." The reason for this apparent paradox is that "from

the deck of your own vessel you cannot see her, as you would a separate object." But one night, on duty "out to the end of the flying jib-boom," upon turning around Dana realized that he was distant enough to "look at the ship, as at a separate vessel" and see "a pyramid of canvass, spreading far out beyond the hull, and towering up almost, as it seemed in the indistinct night air, to the clouds." The perfectly quiet sea and steady breeze filled the sails so continuously that "if these sails had been sculptured marble, they could not have been more motionless."

All through his rapt contemplation of this spectacle, Dana has forgotten that there was another man out with him—a "rough old man-of-war's man"—who has also been looking. Dana closes the scene with the words of his fellow sailor, which are poetic enough to dignify him and yet different enough from Dana's to mark their divergent perspectives, the gentleman's aesthetic contemplation against the laborer's assessment: "How quietly they do their work!"

Narrative of Frederick Douglass

Dana's earnest exposure of the brutalities of maritime labor was read nostalgically within a few decades of its writing: sailing ships and Spanish California were irrevocably distanced by the mechanization of seafaring and the Americanization of California. No less strange has been the history of the *Narrative of the Life of Frederick Douglass, an American Slave, Written by Himself.* When it originally appeared in Boston under the imprint of the Anti-Slavery Office (1845), the narrative made a powerful impact, fostered by the reputation Douglass had achieved as an abolitionist speaker. Within five years, it had sold over thirty thousand copies. When Douglass revised and expanded his life story in *My Bondage and My Freedom* (1855), the introduction by James McCune Smith hailed Douglass as "a Representative American man—a type of his countrymen." During the Civil War, Douglass advised President Lincoln, and he held many prominent public positions before writing *Life and Times of Frederick Douglass* (final version, 1892). Yet in the first *Cambridge History of American Literature* (1917), Douglass merits one half of one line, and in the *Literary History of the United States* (1948) he is not mentioned at all. Since the Civil Rights movement of the 1960s, Douglass has regained a place in American consciousness, and the *Narrative* in particular has become more widely read than it was even in its first days of currency.

Douglass's work and career, like those of his fellow escaped slaves and abolition workers, pose deep questions about the meaning of "America" for freedom and equality. Solomon Northrup, a free black of upstate New York, was kidnapped, drugged, and spent *Twelve Years a Slave* (1853). From the slave quarters where he was sold in Washington D.C., he caught his first glimpse of the Capitol. The *Narrative* (1847) of William Wells Brown emphasized the irony of terrified slaves fleeing the United States, the "land of whips, chains, and Bibles," in order to reach, in the words of one slave song, "Victoria's Domain," British Canada, where they would be free and safe from seizure and extradition. The same North Star that meant America and home to Dana's mariners was the beacon leading out of America for the slaves, and it gave a title to Douglass's abolition newspaper, published from Rochester, New York, after his freedom had been bought, and he was no longer vulnerable to capture and reenslavement. The searing experience of witnessing a whipping—for Dana the climax of his voyage out, marking the farthest point of his removal from the freedoms enjoyed by a white American—was for Douglass the "blood-stained gate" through which he entered the "hell of slavery." The first knowledge of the world Douglass recalls is the screaming of his aunt while she was flogged.

Douglass's *Narrative* now figures as a culturally valued work of writing, but it stands at some distance from what usually counts as "literature." For even so marginal a literary genre as autobiography, it has seemed aberrant, because Douglass's most valued experiences were not those of the self, as would be expected in autobiography, but rather were moments of social solidarity. When he was about sixteen, Douglass secretly ran a Sunday school in which he taught fellow slaves how to read:

> I look back to those Sundays with an amount of pleasure not to be expressed. They were great days to my soul. The work of instructing my dear fellow-slaves was the sweetest engagement with which I ever was blessed. We loved each other. . . . Every moment they spent in that school, they were liable to be taken up and given thirty-nine lashes. They came because they wished to learn. . . . I taught them, because it was the delight of my soul to be doing something that looked like bettering the condition of my race. . . . We were linked and interlinked with each other. I loved them with a love stronger than any thing I have experienced since.

Thus Douglass's strongest love—and in the *Narrative* he also mentions his marriage—arose from this collective activity of resistance. We may understand this in part because of the condition of deprivation from which he started. His individual identity was restricted by the ignorance that was part of being a slave. Like all the other slaves of his acquaintance, he had "no accurate knowledge" of his age, knowing as little of it "as horses do." The passage of a slave's life was marked by collective approximation: "planting-time, harvest-time, cherry-time." The "means of knowing" the identity of his father, widely believed to be a white man, "was withheld from me." Although he knew his mother's name, "I never saw my mother, to know her as such, more than four or five times in my life." Douglass could not "recollect of ever seeing my mother by the light of day," for she could visit him only by travelling twelve miles from the plantation where she had already put in a day's work.

Yet if Douglass was incapacitated from forming what is considered a normal individual identity, such as an autobiography recounts, and instead formed deeply meaningful group ties, he nonetheless left his fellow slaves and escaped north to freedom. It was the masters, however, who destroyed the Sunday-school community, "with sticks and stones," preferring to see their slaves spend Sundays in "boxing and drinking" rather than in learning to "read the will of God." And, later, it was Douglass's owner who brought him to Baltimore to work in the shipyards, at the risk of his life amidst racist whites rather than amidst other slaves. And every such wrenching from his community brought Douglass closer to freedom. Even so, the point of Douglass's escape deeply challenges the usual standards for "literature." Douglass refused to rest with the spiritual, but sought instead the material. It was not enough for him to be free internally; he must possess his freedom also really, physically, in the world.

In Douglass's account, "a slave was made a man" by his protracted physical resistance in a fight with the man entrusted with breaking the slave's spirit. Douglass's success in this fight marked for him "a glorious resurrection, from the tomb of slavery, to the heaven of freedom," based on the demonstration that any white man who might expect to flog Douglass "must also succeed in killing" him. This "freedom," at once existential in its wager with death and Christian in its sense of "resurrection," would be enough in any number of twentieth-century first-person narratives; nevertheless, Douglass insists on escape north. Having escaped, however, Douglass then breaches the usual contract between writer and reader by refusing to narrate his actual escape. His reason is soundly practical, but hardly literary: the same route might well be used again by others, who would be imperiled if anything about it were revealed. In *My Bondage and My Freedom*, Douglass specifically criticized fugitive slave narratives that detailed techniques of escape. Yet Douglass also violates literary expectations at a more local level. In an allegorical story, it would be no surprise to encounter an overseer who is strict named "Severe" or one named "Gore" who is famous for shooting out the brains of a stubborn slave; but historical documents show that these were the names of actual people.

The final problem that Douglass's *Narrative* poses for "literature" is in its language. Instead of a personalized shaping of experience, Douglass's language is rather conventional. In evoking the sufferings of his grandmother, whom he believes was abandoned by her owners to die in a hut, after decades in which she had served and cared for them, Douglass quotes a stanza from John Greenleaf Whittier's abolitionist verse. Rather than speak for himself, he turns to a Yankee. Or again, while serving with the slave breaker, Douglass has moments by Chesapeake Bay, where he sees sailboats moving freely, and moving toward freedom, and he contrasts their state with his own:

> I would pour out my soul's complaint, in my rude way, with an apostrophe to the moving multitude of ships:—"You are loosed from your moorings, and are free; I am fast in my chains, and am a slave! . . . You are freedom's swift-winged angels, that fly round the world; I am confined in bands of iron! O that I were free! . . . Alas! betwixt me and you, the turbid waters roll.

This is self-conscious, traditional rhetoric, an avowed "apostrophe," highly antithetical and exclamatory, with time-worn epithets. In his preface to the *Narrative,* the abolitionist leader William Lloyd Garrison singled out this passage for special praise, as the book's most "thrilling," irresistible in its "sublimity": "Compressed into it is a whole Alexandrian library of thought, feeling, and sentiment." By twentieth-century American standards of literature, such antiquarian bookishness no longer works, yet Garrison rightly recognized Douglass's "Alexandrian" learning. Douglass had studied the traditional forms of oratory. When he was about twelve, Douglass had "got hold of a book entitled *The Columbian Orator,*" first published in 1797 by Caleb Bingham of Massachusetts and almost as inevitable in American education as *Webster's Speller* was and McGuffey's *Eclectic Readers* later would be.

In *The Columbian Orator,* a work of republican education, Douglass found arguments against slavery and arguments, in the words of the Anglo-Irish Richard Brinsley Sheridan, for emancipation (of Catholics). Through this work, "the silver trump of freedom had roused my soul to eternal wakefulness." Thus, the slave writes and speaks in the language of American Fourth of July speeches. Such oratory had become conventional by this time, reinforcing but not directing American politics and values. Yet Douglass's work was not even in this sense literary, for it had a precise practical purpose. It meant to explain how he came to be so capable an abolitionist spokesperson—at once to authenticate his own experience as a slave and to explain why he did not talk the way a slave was expected to.

Douglass's goal, which he shared with his fellow writers of slave narratives, was much less to recover the language and experience of slavery than to end them. Scarcely a word of direct speech by slaves appears in his narrative; the only extended sequence of vernacular registers the chaotically competing voices of white workers calling for Douglass while he worked as an assistant in the shipyards. Early in the narrative, Douglass recalls the slaves' "wild songs," of which he quotes only a chorus, "I am going away to the Great House Farm! / O, yea! O, yea! O!" The words of the songs, he explains, "to many would seem unmeaning jargon" but to the slaves "were full of meaning." Douglass expresses his belief that "the mere hearing of those songs would do more to impress some minds with the horrible character of slavery, than the reading of whole volumes of philosophy on the subject could do." Yet he confesses that "I did not, when a slave, understand the deep meaning of those rude and apparently incoherent songs," for he was himself "within the circle." Even though all along the songs have the emotional power to move him to tears, only through the distance of his own freedom can he grasp their rational sense. Against any northern misconceptions, he must insist that slave songs are no evidence of contentment, any more than might be "the singing of a man cast away up on a desolate island." Nevertheless, this extended meditation on the meaning of the songs makes no attempt to put them on the page. Douglass's goal is to rescue the castaways, not immortalize the products of their exile.

In one significant respect, however, Douglass's *Narrative* is as self-consciously "literary" as any work could be, for its guiding thread is the story of how it came to be written, that is, the story of how Douglass gained the intellectual and moral power that fit him for his work as an abolitionist orator and thus made it necessary for him to explain his origins. The "new and special revelation" that guided Douglass's life dated from the moment his master instructed his mistress to stop teaching Frederick how to read, on the grounds that this knowledge could have no result except to make the slave disobedient. From this admonition, Douglass "understood what had been . . . a most perplexing difficulty—to wit, the white man's power to enslave the black man," and he determined to gain this power for himself. What he had valued as part of the "kindly aid" of his mistress, he now valued even more because of the "bitter opposition" of his master, to whom he opposed himself. Echoing the Satan of Milton's *Paradise Lost*, who declared, "Evil, be thou my good," Douglass decided that what to his master "was a great evil" would be to him "a great good."

In later learning to write, Douglass devised means of tricking his white playmates into instructing him, and finally he perfected his skills by working over the abandoned copybooks with which his young master had learned his letters. The result was that by the time he had learned to write, it was with the hand of Master Thomas (even as earlier he had learned to speak like young Master Daniel, as he explained in *Life and Times*). The role of *The Columbian Orator* has already been noted, but there is one more extraordinary function of established white culture in the making of Frederick Douglass. Born Frederick Bailey (his mother's name) in Maryland, he took as a fugitive an alias—Johnson—to help prevent his detection, but he discovered that there were so many by this name that it was confusing, so he needed a new name. This name he took at the suggestion of a friend from a book that the friend was reading, the poetic romance *The Lady of the Lake* by Walter Scott (in its Gaelic etymology, "douglas" connotates blackness). Thus Douglass's narrative tells of taking on the powers of white culture in order to oppose that culture, of learning the republican arguments of freedom in order to extend that freedom beyond the limits the United States had set for it.

The same double-sidedness marks many features of slaves' experiences as recounted in other narratives. Christianity was used hegemonically to teach slaves that God meant them to serve their masters, although it was also taken up by slaves as a tool of resistance, as in Douglass's Sunday school. The technical and bureaucratic means by which white society extended its power, thus promoting the exchanges of messages and goods on which the expansion of the slave economy depended, also provided slaves the means to escape. After years on a cotton plantation in Louisiana, Solomon Northrup finally gained writing materials and found a white man he could trust to mail a letter for him, back home to those who knew him. The national postal service did its work, and friends came South to release him. As Douglass revealed in his *Life and Times,* he himself had escaped by the recently opened railroad that linked Baltimore with Philadelphia. Its bustle and crowds let him board the train unnoticed; a borrowed sailor's documentation certified his right to travel; and the train's speed meant that before he was even expected home from his workday in the shipyards, he had already reached freedom.

The Oregon Trail

Neither Richard Henry Dana's displacement from land to sea nor Frederick Douglass's displacement from south to north was the major direction of American history in the 1840s. By 1845 the "manifest destiny" of the United States to spread over the whole continent had been proclaimed by John O'Sullivan in the *Democratic Review,* and in that same year Texas was annexed to the United States. In 1846, the Mexican War began, which allowed the acquisition of almost all of what is now the southwestern United States. Likewise in 1846, its dispute with Great Britain over the Oregon Territory resolved, the United States reached its present boundary in the northwest. Meanwhile, the "Bear Flag" rebellion in California began the process that made California a state in 1850. By 1840, overland migration to the west coast had begun along the Oregon Trail; and in 1846 nearly three thousand emigrants took that route.

This context gave timeliness to a series of pieces by Francis Parkman that was published in New York's genteel *Knickerbocker Magazine* from 1847 into 1849 entitled "The Oregon Trail. Or a Summer's Journey out of Bounds. By a Bostonian." With revision and addition, the work appeared as a book from G. P. Putnam and Company in 1849: *The California and Oregon Trail: Being Sketches of Prairie and Rocky Mountain Life.* Parkman was already launched on the large project of historical writing that would run from *The Conspiracy of Pontiac* (1851) through the seven volumes of *France and England in North America* that appeared after the Civil War, yet *The Oregon Trail* is not directly a national narrative. Parkman recognized in the movement of transcontinental migration a force like the one that had "impelled" the barbarians "from the German forests," the "ancestors" of those now on the move, "to inundate Europe, and break to pieces the Roman empire." That is, he saw a modern version of the theme that had moved his great historiographic model Edward Gibbon. But this is not Parkman's topic, even as he momentarily poses a tableau in which the "slow, heavy procession" of the settlers' wagon train passes an encampment of Indians, "whom they and their descendants, in the space of a century, are to sweep from the face of the earth."

Parkman undertook his trip on the Oregon Trail as part of his historical research. Born in 1823 of a long-established and financially comfortable Boston family, Parkman became in his early teens "enamored of the woods." While studying at Harvard, he took long, arduous journeys into the wilderness that still existed in New England. These became the field trips that he carried over into upstate New York and then the Ohio Valley and Great Lakes for his chosen project. At first he planned to write the history of "the Old French War" (the Seven Years, or French and Indian, War) but soon he was aiming to go back to the beginnings of that conflict and take in the whole "history of the American forest" (by which he meant, its history from the first arrival of Europeans). Parkman was "haunted with wilderness images day and night." He determined to rely as little as possible on books and as much as possible on "personal experience" as the basis from which he would write. The goal of his western travels in 1846 was to gain an "inside view of Indian life," to study "the manners and characters of Indians in their primitive state."

Along with most of his contemporaries, Parkman believed that in studying currently existing Indian communities on the Great Plains or on the edges of the Rocky Mountains he was encountering the past, for it was the essence of primitives to be, and to remain, at an earlier stage of cultural development than that of "civilized" white Europeans and Americans. Thus, although himself located on the cutting edge of contemporary history as he encountered individuals and groups, both private and military, that played key roles in the events of 1846 and in the history of the westward expansion of the United States, Parkman preferred to devote his attention to the living past, to which he brought himself with great pains and extraordinary will. For several weeks he lived in a settlement of Oglala Sioux, and from this experience he believed that he knew "the Indian"—in particular, the forest-dwellers of the seventeenth and eighteenth centuries.

Parkman had long been fascinated by Indians, but he was frustrated by his reading on the subject, and so he "resolved to have recourse to observation." To accomplish this purpose, "it was necessary to live in the midst of them, and become, as it were, one of them." As with Dana among sailors, but to a much greater degree, Parkman shows in his book the impossibility of becoming "one of them," and yet he does not acknowledge any consequence of this failure. He does not puzzle over the tension between knowledge through observation and knowledge through the experience of living "in the midst," which Dana noted in discussing the image of a ship "under full sail," and which so disturbed Douglass as he thought about the meaning of slave songs. Having been "domesticated for several weeks among one of the wildest of the wild hordes that roam over the remote prairies," Parkman is certain that "these men were thorough savages," wholly unmodified by contact with white civilization. All that they do has come down "from immemorial time." The fruit of Parkman's hard-won experience is the same basic understanding that his culture already held. Himself a historian and engaged in historical research, Parkman is so thrilled at reaching this long-sought living archive that he does not reckon with the changes that history has worked there too. For example, the horses that are so crucial in the lives of these Sioux were introduced to the Americas by the Spaniards, and thus the way of life that Parkman observes results from the interaction of cultures, not from aboriginality.

Parkman asserts that there are almost no "points of sympathy" between the "nature" of a "civilized white man" and "that of an Indian": an "impassable gulf lies between." To the extent that the desired inward knowledge thus is not available, the Indians come to seem so "alien" that one "begins to look upon them as a troublesome and dangerous species of wild beast, and if expedient, he could shoot them with as little compunction as they themselves would experience after performing the same office upon him." (Presumably, this is one of the few "points of sympathy.") For Parkman, the act of shooting has a special relation to the movements of the mind. In an expository set piece describing the "easiest and laziest" method of killing buffalo, he describes the climax, "Quick as thought the spiteful crack of the rifle responds to his slight touch, and instantly in the bare spot appears a small red dot." As opposed to the Indians' arrows, the rifle shot is as invisible and instantaneous as thought; civilization proceeds by such spiritualization.

Parkman's narrative repeatedly charts the movement from observation to revulsion to aggression: "'You are too ugly to live,' thought I; and aiming at the ugliest, I shot three of them in succession." This time it is buffaloes, but the language and feeling are much the same as those that he had expressed toward Indians. Moreover, so intimately linked is the life of the Plains Indians with the buffaloes that "when the buffalo are extinct, [the Indians] too must dwindle away." Buffalo bulls are so "ugly and ferocious" that "at first sight . . . every feeling of sympathy vanishes." This may shock our pieties, but every person who has "experienced it" knows "with what keen relish one inflicts his death wound, with what profound contentment of mind [one] beholds him fall." Observing an old Indian with "hard, emaciated face and gaunt ribs," Parkman thinks,

> He would have made a capital shot. A rifle bullet, skilfully planted, would have brought him tumbling to the ground. Surely, I thought, there could be no more harm in shooting such a hideous old villain, to see how ugly he would look when he was dead, than in shooting the detestable vulture which he resembled.

In John Keats's "Hyperion," the dispossessed Titans speculate that it is only right that they be replaced by the Olympian gods, "for 'tis the eternal law / That first in beauty should be first in might." In Parkman this aesthetic ideology means that to call others ugly gives one rights over their lives. Yet in Parkman's narrative, even beauty is no defense. Having first mistaken an antelope for a wolf, he prepares to shoot it, and does so even after realizing his error. When he examines the kill: "The antelope turned his expiring eye upward. It was like a beautiful woman's, dark and rich. 'Fortunate that I am in a hurry,' thought I; 'I might be troubled with remorse, if I had time for it.'" This moment is characteristic of Parkman's effects. His remorse is registered but only under negation; he gives us the very words with which to specify our discomfort. Yet there is no remorse, because Parkman is absolutely confident that he can do no real wrong. Later, when he sees an antelope "like some lovely young girl" coming close to some buffaloes like "bearded pirates," which, therefore, look "uglier than ever," he draws a bead on them as if buffaloes were the killers of antelope. Any remorse has turned into aggression.

At one moment Parkman exercises greater modesty than elsewhere. Encountering an Indian "immovable as a statue, among the rocks and trees," his eyes "turned upward," Parkman surmises that he is communing with a pine tree that is "swaying to and fro in the wind . . . as if the tree had life." (Parkman's sense of his difference from the Indian is so powerful as to obscure for him the fact that trees do have life.) Parkman "long[s] to penetrate his thoughts" but recognizes that he can "do nothing more than conjecture and speculate": "Among those mountains not a wild beast was prowling, a bird singing, or a leaf fluttering, that might not tend to direct his destiny, or give warning of what was in store for him." Having reached this sense of the intensely aware participation in the world that another person, from another culture, might experience, Parkman has the "delicacy" not to disturb the Indian. As he leaves the scene, he sees a peak, which "something impelled me to climb." After a long, arduous ascent, he reaches "the very summit" and, seated "on its extreme point," looks over the prairie "stretching to the farthest horizon." Parkman's momentary, respectful self-restraint fuels an action that overgoes the Indian's contemplation. The Indian, in the midst of the scene, looks up; Parkman, from his extremity, looks down. Parkman believes that everything that the Indian sees carries meaning for him, but for Parkman himself, only the fact of the apparently endless expanse, and no particular of the scene, carries meaning.

In this overreaching, this drive for mastery, this movement from observation to revulsion to aggression, Parkman was living out the energies that were winning the West. However much he might look down on the overland emigrants and even though his social peers in Boston did not support the Mexican War, he was joining in the emigrants' expansionism and ethnic chauvinism. The knowledge Parkman gained of what Indians were really like empowered him to begin his massive history. This work rested on the claim that the Indians of North America had been doomed by the triumph of the British—committed to establishing settlements and thus to civilization—over the French, who merely exploited the products of the wilderness, while letting the Indians live. Thus, according to Parkman, the whole history of crimes against Indians by the United States need cause no remorse, for the Indians were for all practical purposes already dead long ago. From the "cannibal warfare" of little fishes, eating each other in a pool in the Rockies, Parkman had learned that although "soft-hearted philanthropists . . . may sigh long for their peaceful millennium," nonetheless, "from minnows up to men, life is an incessant battle."

Narrative of Arthur Gordon Pym

The encounter with savagism that motivated Parkman's journey figures climactically in Edgar Allan Poe's *Narrative of Arthur Gordon*

Pym of Nantucket, published in 1838, roughly a decade earlier. For the verisimilitude of this fictional narrative, Poe drew upon the large body of writings about disaster at sea and upon reports of exploration in the South Seas (immediately before the first sections of *Pym* appeared in the *Southern Literary Messenger,* Poe wrote articles on the grand plans of J. N. Reynolds for a South Seas expedition). In presentation, *Pym* takes its form from the procedures of personal narratives like those discussed in this chapter, and it also joins a tradition of fiction that includes Daniel Defoe's *Robinson Crusoe* (1719) and Jonathan Swift's *Gulliver's Travels* (1726). Yet Defoe, in adapting the conventions of religious narrative, helped establish conventions for creating fictional character, and Swift's increasingly complex satirical allegories obviously related to life in the England of his time. Poe's narrative neither establishes a complex interior history for its protagonist nor presents fictional worlds that offer lessons for the contemporary world of its readers. Within this particular imitation of personal narrative, Poe begins to fashion a world of his own, an imaginative space of writing to stand apart from the space of the nation.

Pym's elaborate subtitle gives some feel for its contents:

Comprising the details of a mutiny and atrocious butchery on board the American brig *Grampus,* on her way to the South Seas, in the month of June, 1827[;] with an account of the recapture of the vessel by the survivers; their shipwreck and subsequent horrible sufferings from famine; their deliverance by means of the British schooner *Jane Guy;* the brief cruise of this latter vessel in the Antarctic Ocean; her capture and the massacre of her crew among a group of islands in the *EIGHTY-FOURTH PARALLEL OF SOUTHERN LATITUDE; together with the incredible adventures and discoveries* STILL FARTHER SOUTH to which that distressing calamity gave rise.

And there is much more than this: Pym's delirium and near-starvation while he is hidden in a chest within a ship's hold; his nearly being eaten alive by his own maddened Labrador dog; cannibalism among the famine-struck "survivers"; and life among black "savages," whose "apparent kindness" concealed for a time their "most barbarous, subtle, and bloodthirsty" nature.

The reader is propelled with Pym from one catastrophe to the next, but there is neither any rationalized speaker to figure as a fictional character in the usual sense nor any organized plot. In the earlier pages of the work, Pym refers to events that fall between those being narrated and the later time of writing, but by the book's end, nothing has come of these hints. They even prove misleading, suggesting, for instance, that Pym and his initial companion—who dies of starvation halfway through the story—discussed the narrated events years later. Pym himself as good as dies in the opening pages of the book. A high-spirited boat trip turns into a nightmare after Pym's little vessel is run over in the stormy night by a much larger ship. According to accounts of the ship's crew, "The body of a man was seen to be affixed" to the ship's bottom and was finally rescued, "although life seemed to be totally extinct." Pym explains, "The body proved to be my own," which had been "fastened" to the bottom of the ship by a protruding bolt that "made its way through the back part of my neck, forcing itself out between two sinews and just below the right ear."

Returned to life, Pym thrills to visions "of shipwreck and famine; of death or captivity among barbarian hordes," and he acknowledges that such "visions" actually "amounted to desires." If the narrative thus functions as wish fulfillment, responsibility for those wishes has been displaced from Poe to his protagonist. From this situational basis, however, no further interrelation is established between character and action; the episodes that follow present a disconnected array of dreadful sensations, of "anticipative horror," like the "longing to fall" that overwhelms Pym while he is trying to descend a cliff. Like Poe's briefer local narratives *Pym* may register the shock of city experience, and it projects that shock from its metropolitan origin onto the far-flung oceanic periphery upon which urban economic growth depends.

As the narrative ends, Pym and a companion, having escaped from the savages, float southward in a canoe amidst the increasingly warm and milky waters of the Antarctic Ocean, until finally they

> rushed into the embraces of the cataract, where a chasm threw itself open to receive us. But there arose in our pathway a shrouded human figure, very far larger in its proportions than any dweller among men. And the hue of the skin of the figure was of the perfect whiteness of the snow.

This cliff-hanging conclusion is justified by a final note, explaining that Pym had died before he finished writing. Thus the completion of his life substitutes for the completion of his narrative. This fractured and truncated form partakes of what Aristotle would have judged the randomness of biography rather than the shaping of plot, and it stands as rhetorical evidence that the account is truth rather than fiction. Pym's companion may supposedly be found in Illinois.

This concluding note resumes the concerns of the preface, in which the book represents itself as an exercise in the rhetoric of verisimilitude. The preface begins with Pym's fear that he cannot write effectively enough to give his narrative "the *appearance* of that truth it would really possess." Pym's imperfect memory combined with the "marvellous" character of the events; the result made his narrative seem "merely an impudent and ingenious fiction." Pym explains that "Mr. Poe," then of the *Southern Literary Messenger*, encouraged him to trust to the "shrewdness and common sense of the public," for any "uncouthness" in the narrative would only enhance its credibility. Pym, however, still swayed by "distrust in my own abilities as a writer," does not act until Poe offers to present the narrative in his journal *"under the garb of fiction.*" This extraordinary twist accounts for the appearance of the first chapters of Pym's narrative as Poe's "pretended fiction," and Pym professes himself sufficiently heartened by readers' responses to conclude that "the facts of my narrative would prove of such a nature as to carry with them sufficient evidence of their own authenticity." Finally he can offer them to the public himself, and as the truth that they are.

The preface and final note, which frame the book, suggest that its narrative may be interpreted in relation to conditions of writing as well as to the social or political conditions of American life. The journey southward that leads to a fantastic interplay of white and black, not only in human conflict but also in the very fauna and landscape, may have as much to do with black ink and white pages as with slavery or ethnology. When Poe claimed that "terror is not of Germany, but of the soul," he defined his intricate, "arabesque" works as effectively structured stimulants. Through the chaotic sequence of sensations in *Pym,* Poe manipulates the form of personal narrative to produce feelings rather than to communicate experience. Despite its emphatic claim to truth, the book's character as a fictional production was clear to its reviewers. Nonetheless, through the 1840s, Harper and Brothers still advertised the Pym narrative among its works of travel. So important did the claim to truth remain as a criterion for personal narrative, that when in 1845 Harper was offered a sailor's narrative of four months among the cannibals of the Marquesas Islands, an editorial "council" decided that "it was impossible that it could be true and therefore was without real value" and so rejected the manuscript for *Typee.*

Herman Melville

Although suspicious that this sailor's manuscript by Herman Melville was the work of a "practised writer," John Murray of London nonetheless published in his nonfictional Home and Colonial Library series the *Narrative of a Four Months' Residence among the Natives of a Valley of the Marquesas Islands: or, A Peep at Polynesian Life*. Then, with the endorsement of Washington Irving, it was picked up by Wiley and Putnam in New York for their Library of American Books series and published in 1846 under its author's preferred title, *Typee* (with the Murray subtitle). Poe could only claim an authenticating companion for Pym's narrative, but Melville's companion, known as "Toby," actually came to light to vouch for the book after reading about it, and Toby's narrative appeared as a supplement to the book's second edition. Even with this good luck, however, and even with the example of Dana, invoked by several of the first reviewers, it remained especially hard for English readers to credit that *Typee* was really written by a "poor outcast working seaman," rather than by an "educated literary man."

The opening chapter of *Typee*, the pages by which Herman Melville first became known to the reading public, immediately show an impressive power in evoking "Six months at sea!" There is no fresh food, salt water around is matched by salt fare aboard. Ordinary, middle-class "state-room sailors" complain even of a brief transatlantic voyage. Melville's more extreme experience contrasts the privileged leisure of tourists to sailors' exploited labor. The book takes its stand on the democratic, and the extraordinary, side. Against the sensory deprivation of maritime routine rise "strange visions," conjured by the very name of the Marquesas: "Naked houris—cannibal banquets—groves of cocoa-nut—coral reefs—tatooed chiefs—. . . *heathenish rites and human sacrifices*." These purely conventional images come to life through the play of assonance and rhythm. Each phrase begins with a stressed syllable, and the sequence of items without conjunctions enforces a higher level of stress than is usual in prose, yet without the metronomic regularity that would sound merely like poetry. Likewise, the rhyme of "reefs" and "chiefs" prepares for the more distant echo between "rites" and "sacrifices."

Melville's evocation introduces expository background about the islands; the chapter ends with a vivid personal anecdote, drawn from a second Marquesan visit several years later. France had taken possession of the islands, and the French navy was presenting the king and queen of the islands to an American commodore. The queen was fascinated by the tattooing of an old seaman, much to the embarrassment of her French sponsors, and

> all at once the royal lady, eager to display the hieroglyphics on her own sweet form, bent forward for a moment, and turning sharply round, threw up the skirts of her mantle, and revealed a sight from which the aghast Frenchmen retreated precipitately, and tumbling into their boat, fled the scene of so shocking a catastrophe.

Like much satire, the passage risks racism and misogyny in order to attack those in power. The Shakespearean wordplay, by which the emphasized second syllable of "catastrophe" signals an unmentionable physical part, shows the "freedom" that reviewers always found, for better or worse, in Melville's work, and the anecdote takes a further freedom in stripping from French imperialism its pretensions to a civilizing mission.

From its very beginning, *Typee* stood as an impressively, and suspiciously, powerful piece of writing; yet it was true enough. Herman Melville had actually lived among the Typee. He had arrived among them in just the way the book describes: he jumped ship with a companion, and they made their way through the surprisingly difficult island terrain until they reached the wrong valley, for the Typee were believed to be fierce cannibals, unlike the Happars, who dwelt in the neighboring valley. Melville's sojourn lasted only four weeks, rather than the four months he claimed, and he required the aid of other books of travel and exploration to supplement his memories, but the force of this personal narrative rests on experience. The high cultural skills shown by a sailor, so unsettling to some readers, have a simple explanation: the notorious social mobility of the nineteenth century allowed Americans to fall in life as well as to rise.

Melville was born in 1819 into great financial comfort, with parents whose fathers were both revolutionary heroes. At first the family lived in New York, away from his father's Boston family; in 1830, when the father's business began to fail, they moved to Albany, his mother's base, and in 1832 the family's ruin was sealed by Melville's father's death. For the next dozen years, Melville was adrift, working as a clerk, a farmer, and a teacher before his first experiment as a sailor, a trip to Liverpool in 1839. After an unsuccessful search for work in the Mississippi Valley in 1840, he sailed with the whaler *Acushnet* from New Bedford, Massachusetts, in 1841. This was the ship he abandoned in the Marquesas. After escaping from the Typee, he signed on with an Australian whaler, which he soon left in Tahiti under nearly mutinous circumstances. Another American whaler brought him to Hawaii, and after several months of various jobs there, he returned home as a sailor on an American naval vessel, the *United States*.

Almost at once upon his return, Melville began writing up the stories of his travels, stories with which he had fascinated his family, and the success of *Typee* encouraged a sequel. *Omoo: A Narrative of Adventures in the South Seas,* centers on Melville's time in Tahiti (expanding two weeks into two months). *Omoo* (a Polynesian word for "wanderer") confirmed the reputation won by the author with *Typee*. Melville was again praised for his vigorous, skillful narrative, and his social standing still seemed anomalous. One British journal found "Herman Melville" obviously like "the harmonious and carefully selected appellation of an imaginary hero of romance." Moreover, aspects of Melville's work provoked not just social suspicion, but moral disapproval. Already in *Typee*, Melville's commentary on missionaries caused so much discomfort that he removed nearly thirty pages from the second American edition, and even so, he had to change publishers for *Omoo,* this time successfully persuading Harpers.

An evangelical, abolitionist journal had complained of *Typee* that it was written "not for Americans," but for the London circles familiar with "theaters, opera-dancers, and voluptuous prints," and a reviewer of *Omoo* found himself driven in "recoil" from the book's "reckless spirit," its "cool, sneering wit," and "perfect want of *heart.*" These exaggerated responses register that *Omoo* is more comic than earnest (it portrays vagabondage rather than a movement to settle down) but, above all, they show that Melville continued to offend the interests of missionary piety. In recounting the dreadful depopulation of Tahiti through the transmission of European diseases, Melville quotes the cry of the islanders to the missionaries, "Lies, lies! you tell us of salvation; and, behold, we are dying. We want no other salvation than to live in this world."

What a reviewer called *Typee*'s "paradisiacal barbarism" powerfully suggests, in the form of credible personal experience, that there might actually exist in the South Seas a heaven on earth. Unlike Parkman and Dana, but like Douglass, Melville drew on his time outside what was considered the normal life of the United States in order to challenge the values of that life. Yet Melville could not fully commit himself to this position, and therefore *Typee* is at once fascinating and incoherent. Despite its biographical basis, no more than in *Pym* can a narrative identity be firmly defined for Melville's pseudonymous "Tommo." The large narrative cycle of entry into and exit from the valley of the Typee contains not only smaller cycles of daily rhythms but also an oscillation of feelings—from bliss to revulsion—that seems governed by no law beyond that of change.

In *Typee,* drawing on his life in the South Seas as well as on his reading, Melville works through a series of commonplaces, each of which becomes vivid through rhetorical elaboration. Melville's distrust of what may lie "beneath the . . . fair appearances" of native hospitality is no different from Pym's concern with the horrors beneath the "apparent kindness" of the "savages." Melville's experience is at every moment qualified by the sense that he is among "after all, nothing better than a set of cannibals," just as Parkman diminishes an "Apollo"-like Sioux brave with the reflection, "after all, he was but an Indian." Yet Melville can also reflect that the term "savage" is improperly applied to the islanders, when one considers the "civilized barbarity" of western culture—which reveals "white civilized man as the most ferocious animal on the face of the earth"—without adding the approval that Parkman's survivalist ethic would dictate. Among the Typee, Melville observed, and to some degree himself enjoyed, not only a negative freedom from all the "thousand sources of irritation that the ingenuity of civilized man has created to mar his own felicity" but also a positive "happiness" arising from an "all-pervading sensation" described by Jean-Jacques Rousseau as "the mere buoyant sense of a healthful physical existence."

As his reference to Rousseau suggests, Melville most powerfully responded to elements of Typee life that matched subordinated or repressed elements within his own culture. His most acute registration of real difference comes in his description of the Typee way of making fire, a lengthy and exhausting, almost orgasmic, process that is in contrast to both the ascetic sobriety of the Romans, who preserved a sacred flame with the Vestal virgins, and the casual comfort of modern America, where a match can be struck in an instant. This contrast suggests relations among temporality, sexuality, and economics that set Typee apart from Western models of simplicity and complexity alike. Yet despite his criticisms and explorations, Melville bears the marks of his culture so deeply that he chooses to return, making an escape from the Typee against considerable resistance. He explains his wish to escape by invoking his fears of either of two fates: tattooing or cannibalism. These clichés of Polynesia represent alternative forms of total incorporation into an alien way of life, necessitating that his body be worked over either by human teeth or by the shark teeth used as tattooing needles. At one point, the narrative explains that even if cannibalism does exist among the Typee—as it does also among the supposedly more civilized Happar—it is not the indiscriminate eating of humans but a part of a very specific ritual. Yet Tommo's departure is shadowed by his increasing anxiety lest he be eaten. Likewise, his reflections show the innumerable ways in which American life disfigures those who live it, and yet, for no reason that is rationally explained, he dreads tattooing as irremediably separating him from his life back home. The American sailor whose tattoos provoked the rivalry of the Typee queen is forgotten.

After *Omoo,* Melville married and settled in Manhattan as a professional author. His next book, *Mardi* (1849), went further than Poe's *Pym* in trying to stake a claim beyond that of personal experience, but its disastrous reception brought his work back to this safer narrative form. In five months of 1849, Melville wrote both *Redburn: His First Voyage* and *White-Jacket; or, The World in a Man-of-War. Redburn* approaches the socially and personally explosive materials of Melville's own adolescence, the family's financial fall and the author's consequent sea voyage to Liverpool. It does so, however, in a more overtly fictionalized form than does either *Typee* or *Omoo,* even though *Redburn's* subtitle, "Being the Sailor-Boy Confessions and Reminiscences of the Son-of-a-Gentleman, in the Merchant Service," works to neutralize the problems of credibility provoked by those earlier works.

By locating the book's experiences in a "boy" several crucial years younger than he himself had been, Melville gains both intensity and distance, for, by convention, youthful perception and feeling are more acute and less reliable than those of adults. No matter how powerful, then, they need not be fully credited. Melville asserts this distance through the use of formal, third-person chapter titles, which show the control of the narrative persona (an older Redburn) over the youthful protagonist (e.g., the first chapter, "How Wellingborough Redburn's Taste for the Sea Was Born and Bred in Him"). The boy's perspective at once suggests, selects, and controls the topics that can emerge. The effect is not so complex as that of Dickens's *Great Expectations* (1861) or even of his *David Copperfield* (1848–50), but it does make possible Melville's first direct approach to the materials of contemporary American life, especially poverty and social conflict.

Even before he gets to sea, Redburn appears as a social victim, who is aggressive against those more fortunate or less sensitive than himself. Traveling down the Hudson from his family home to New York City, Redburn feels marked by the "scent and savor of poverty." He is excluded from the other passengers' sociability, and when he discovers that the fare has been raised so that he lacks the funds, he makes a surly scene, which leaves "every eye fastened" upon him. Staring back proves insufficient retaliation, and finally he levels his gun at one "gazer"; after this action has provoked a stir, Redburn spends the rest of the trip cold and wet on the deck in the rain. The chapter concludes, "Such is boyhood." This deflation does not put the problem to rest. In New York, Redburn's poverty marks him like Cain: while waiting to board a ship, he rests in "a mean liquor shop"; lacking the right clothes and "not looking very gentlemanly," he feared that from "any better place," he would be "driven out."

This social animus allows Melville to bring to life on shipboard the problem that Dana for himself had defined only as his not being "one of them." The insistent hard manliness of sailors that Dana described means that no special concern is shown for a young newcomer, and Redburn, because he is also a "gentleman with white hands," becomes a special butt. Yet he is no innocent victim either, for his own priggish condescension to the other sailors provokes them. He believes he feels "compassion" for their "sad conditions as amiable outcasts," deep in "ignorance" and lacking "proper views of religion," but when he tries to share his proper views, the sailors turn against him with abusive laughter. The chapter's ending again acts to control and to defuse the situation: "my being so angry prevented me from feeling foolish, which is very lucky for people in a passion." The anger is not denied, but it is placed as youthful folly rather than explored as part of a constellation in which habit, expectation, and upbringing had distanced Redburn from the social role that his economic condition requires him to fill. This distance leads Redburn to feel himself an "Ishmael," "without a single friend or companion." A fearful "hatred . . . against the whole crew" is growing up in him.

Redburn's complicated and bitter social comedy culminates with a chapter in which Redburn "contemplates making a social call on the captain in his cabin." The chapter strikes a norm of democratic sociability against which the captain, Redburn, and the crew are all found wanting. The sailors mock Redburn as they see him doing his best to put together a decently clean outfit for his proposed visit. Discovering that his hands are stained yellow from a morning's work tarring, and lacking the kid gloves dictated by social decorum, Redburn "slipped on a pair of woolen mittens" knit by his mother. To the reader too, Redburn looks quite a clown. Obstructed by the mate from making his call, Redburn tries the next day to address the captain, who flies into a rage against him. This provokes a series of reflections by Redburn that conclude, "Yes, Captain Riga, thought I, you are no gentleman, and you know it!" For Redburn can imagine no reason, whatever the customs of rank at sea, for a captain to be so intemperate in response to a sailor's attempt at civility, however ignorant and misguided. Resentment and justice could hardly be more perfectly mixed. This painful episode of greenhorn humor was the only excerpt from Melville's works included in the massive *Cyclopaedia of American Literature* (1855), compiled by George and Evert Duyckinck, who had in the late 1840s been among Melville's closest associates.

Redburn is beset by high and low alike for his violations of the ship's social code, but he is not himself even a quixotic version of the golden mean between high and low. He snobbishly trusts that the captain "could not fail to appreciate the difference between me and the rude sailors among whom I was thrown." If he disavows solidarity with the crew, why should the captain avow fraternity with him? Yet to judge these transactions requires that readers learn to stand apart from the positions of all the characters represented in the book. That is, in training readers to make democratic judgments, the book exercises a troubling exclusiveness.

Redburn's shipboard experience of social displacement unsettling social norms is reenacted when he lands: his father's guidebook proves useless for finding his way around Liverpool. This old English city has been so transformed that it is effectively no older than New York. In England, Redburn encounters poverty and misery far more desperate than his own, and the book's mode shifts to emphasize other characters more prominently than Redburn himself. Redburn meets the improbably handsome Harry Bolton, who has lost his money gambling and is going to sea. In a glamorized style that reviewers found "melodramatic," Harry echoes Redburn's own condition, and Melville further hints at this link by Harry's choice to go whaling after landing with Redburn in New York. This good angel is set against the "diabolic" sailor Jackson, whose wasting disease makes him look "seamed and blasted by lightning," a premonition of Ahab. Their deaths are the major interests of the book's ending, leaving Redburn alone in a world that has been shorn of its extremes.

The relatively limited focus of *Redburn* opens up to an astonishingly ambitious scope in *White-Jacket*, subtitled "The World in a Man-of-War." Its most obvious relation is to Dana's narrative, and in fact Dana, who had become an acquaintance through his family's connection with that of Melville's wife, had helped encourage Melville to work up his naval experiences. The book is powerfully disciplined in restricting itself to life aboard ship; even when the ship is in harbor, any time on shore is rigorously excluded. Thus in Melville's book the life on board functions quite differently from the way it does in Dana. In Dana life before the mast is contrasted to the shore life of a free American, but in Melville the emphasis is on their similarities—at times allegorically precise, at others symbolically suggestive. Yet in fictionalizing his own service aboard the *United States*—and entrusting the narrative to a semifictional sailor known by his strange white jacket—Melville changes the name of the ship itself to the *Neversink* and thereby further generalizes his procedure.

It is emphatically not the United States that is being microcosmically represented by the ship and its life, but the "world." Thus American values can still offer a new world that opposes the way of the world aboard the ship. The "world" of the *Neversink*, moreover, is that of men without women, of men at work; this world utterly excludes the domestic life of home relations and feminine values, as if that sphere were wholly otherworldly. These alternative values appear almost uniquely in a moment that also echoes Dana, but with a difference: "To be efficacious, Virtue must come down from aloft, even as our blessed Redeemer came down to redeem our whole man-of-war world; to that end, mixing with its sailors and sinners as equals." Against the distanced knowledge of "seeing" that Dana sought, the goal here is a full "mixing," which carries with it the pain of intimacy and even possibly death.

As opposed to such a humanistic hope, however, the world of *White-Jacket* is strenuously modern. The *Neversink* is not a knowable community, but an endlessly subdivided society. The men who work among the "water-tanks, casks, and cables" in the hold below decks are scarcely ever seen, and "after a three years' voyage . . . still remain a stranger to you." Living on board ship "is like living in a market," in its lack of privacy and constant crowding. At the rare moments of leisure, when sailors can walk freely on deck, the effect is like that of promenaders "on Broadway." And like a large city, the ship has street crime; when a *"gang"* learns that a shipmate has three or four gold pieces in a bag hidden under his shirt, they will lie in wait for him, knock him down, and carry off the cash. The result is a perverse primitive communism, as a constant series of robberies establishes a rough equality of poverty among all the sailors.

The ship is thus highly disordered, but it is no less highly ordered. In its regimentation, it is "like life in a large manufactory": "the bell strikes to dinner, and hungry or not, you must dine." The figure of speech by which a worker's hands are made to stand for his whole person, so familiar in the dehumanizing industrial discourse of the nineteenth century, had already in the seventeenth century begun to dominate the way in which sailors were spoken of, and to. Unlike the specialization of a factory worker, each sailor has so many different functions to perform, under various circumstances both regular and extraordinary, that the routines can only be known by numbers: "White-Jacket was given the *number of his mess;* then, his *ship's number,* or the number to which he must answer when the watch-roll is called; then the number of his hammock; then, the number of the gun to which he was assigned." These numbers must be memorized by a sailor immediately upon his coming on board, and severe penalties follow if they should be forgotten. The minute, arithmetical detail that organizes the man-of-war annihilates all previous maritime experience a sailor may have accumulated: "Well-nigh useless to him now, all previous circumnavigations of this terraqueous globe . . . his gales off Beachy Head, or his dismastings off Hatteras. He must begin anew; he knows nothing; Greek and Hebrew could not help him, for the language he must learn has neither grammar nor lexicon," but only a disconnected sequence of numerals.

The modern social arrangements of this world contrast with its archaic politics. Life on board is a "despotism," extending from the captain down through his chain of command: "The captain's word is law; he never speaks but in the imperative mood." He is even "lord and master of the sun," for when the functionary responsible for the solar observation at noon has done his work, it is reported to the captain, who orders, "*Make* it so." Only then is the bell struck, "and twelve o'clock it is." Against this system, Melville invokes "the common dignity of manhood," which the sailors possess despite all their other failings. The common seamen are known to the officers as "*the people,*" and the democratic political suggestions of this term are important to Melville's overall shaping of the book.

The officers exercise such total control that they can even order carnival. When the ship is becalmed in frigid weather off Cape Horn and it is necessary to stir the men's blood, the order comes down, "*all hands skylark!*" At once there erupts "a Babel here, a Bedlam there, and a Pandemonium everywhere." This scene from Breughel, however, soon produces ugly consequences; a fight breaks out, and its instigator is flogged the next day, while the officers look on with imperial impassivity. As Melville observes of a similar incident later, "Of all insults, the temporary condescension of a master to a slave is the most outrageous and galling." Like masters and slaves, the people and their officers form two "essentially antagonist classes," with wholly different interests. The officers' glory, pay, and promotion may depend on the "slaughtering of their fellow-men," and they can rise only "over the buried heads of killed comrades and mess-mates." Yet the officer class is "immeasurably the stronger" and enforces its will; therefore, "tyranny" must prevail as the political norm.

In some respects, Melville's portraits of modern society and archaic governance run in parallel in *White-Jacket,* but they are sharply connected in his consideration of flogging, an even more essential feature of shipboard discipline in the military than in the merchant service in Dana's book. In a little over a year on the *United States,* Melville was required to witness the flogging of some one hundred and sixty-three of his shipmates, about one-third of the crew. In questioning the justice of flogging, Melville recalls St. Paul's claim of privilege as a Roman citizen. Eighteen hundred years later, Melville asks, "Is it lawful for you, my countrymen, to scourge a man that is an American?" Even if on the ships of some nations flogging may "conform to the spirit of the political institutions of the country," America is different, and, therefore, its navy should not "convert into slaves" any of its citizens. In the current state of affairs, for an American sailor "our Revolution was in vain; to him our Declaration of Independence is a lie."

One of Frederick Douglass's most famous speeches, entitled "What to the Slave is the Fourth of July?" (1852), explored a similar contradiction. Douglass charged that the Fourth of July "reveals to [the slave], more than all other days of the year, the gross injustice and cruelty to which he is the constant victim." And Douglass added that the appropriate rhetorical decorum for dealing with such facts was not "argument," but "scorching irony." Thus Melville, in seeking his different goal of "abolition," notes the fact that naval laws and customs combine to assure that officers "are exempted from a law" that terrorizes the people; officers are never punished for the sort of minor violations that lead to sailors being flogged. He then asks, "What would landsmen think, were the State of New York to pass a law against some offence, affixing a fine as a penalty, and then add to that law a section restricting its penal operation to mechanics and day laborers, exempting all gentlemen with an income of one thousand dollars?" The political inequality on board ship is brought back home to the social inequalities of the modern city. Melville's ironic question first provokes outrage at the contrast of sea to land: in New York the laws make no allowance for social rank. But then the question provokes a second thought:

on land economic inequality does affect one's relation to the law. (The law impartially forbids rich and poor alike to spend the night on park benches, but only the poor are likely to do so.)

Melville's main argument against flogging relies on the American political rhetoric of equal rights. Such rhetoric is not merely a past heritage for White-Jacket; it is also a future force for change. Even if flogging has always been considered necessary, it must be so no longer: "The world has arrived at a period which renders it the part of Wisdom to pay homage to the prospective precedents of the Future in preference to those of the Past. . . . The Past is the text-book of tyrants; the Future the Bible of the Free." Even while calling on America to march in the "advance-guard" of nations, freed from the "lumbering baggage-wagons of old precedents," Melville invokes as precedent the biblical Exodus that had inspired so much Puritan rhetoric and been refashioned as a model for the nation by George Bancroft: "we Americans are the peculiar chosen people— the Israel of our time; we bear the ark of the liberties of the world." Therefore, because "the political Messiah . . . has come in *us*," American "national selfishness is unbounded philanthropy . . . to the world."

This panegyric echoes the political rhetoric of manifest destiny that had justified the Mexican War, which had ended only the year before, and it resonates as well with the claims of American literary nationalism that were prevalent in the Duyckincks' circle in New York, which Melville frequented. Moreover, it precedes the debates that led to the Compromise of 1850. These debates strove to cool the apocalyptic strain of American national self-conception on the grounds that such liberationist rhetoric threatened the Union, which was resanctified as a stabilizing rather than a transformative power. As a result, the compromise sickened many Americans who loved the values of freedom and loathed the Fugitive Slave Law, which subordinated freedom to national unity. The fervors of White-Jacket are themselves nonviolent. They serve a rhetorical strategy that aims to persuade America to overcome a national flaw—the arbitrary flogging of free men—and their author makes clear his contempt for martial glory. Melville makes the language employed by the bloody jingoist War Hawks against Mexico work instead in the cause of a modest, liberal reform. The problem is to decide whether such a strategy does more for the good cause, or for a morally dubious nationalism.

Melville's treatment of flogging does not depend wholly on such rhetorical utopianism, for the book's climax comes in a powerful moment of fictional Utopia. White-Jacket is himself about to be flogged. He had never been assigned one of the necessary numbers when he joined the ship, and, by relying on his merchant-sailor's experience, he is consequently out of place at a key moment, for which he must be punished. His assertion that he had never been told the number means nothing against the officer's assertion that he must have received it. The book focuses closely on the mind of White-Jacket as he prepares for the flogging. Even though he feels his "soul's manhood so bottomless" that nothing the captain could do would reach and degrade it, he yields to an "instinct diffused through all animated nature . . . that prompts even a worm to turn under the heel." He will seize the occasion to "rush" the captain and "pitch him headforemost into the ocean," even though he would drown as well. Nature has given him "the privilege, inborn and inalienable, that every man has, of dying himself and inflicting death upon another." Here the social bond is powerfully reduced to its minimal elements of pure, conflicting individualities.

No less powerful, however, is the imagination that recalls White-Jacket to the world. The corporal of marines and the best of the sailors join in vouching for White-Jacket's character, and he is spared by the captain. Both archaic political authority and modern, rationalized details of labor organization are overcome through the human respect that the captain suddenly feels for the calm judgment of his subordinates, and the sense of justice that moves them to speak out, at risk to themselves (as Dana shows) and with no individual interests to serve. At the very moment that the "world" threatens to dissolve into warring, individual atoms, it is socially redeemed. This hope is quite different from that of the American apocalypse, but it is no less present, even in the world's current state, and perhaps it is both more possible and more worthy of realization.

White-Jacket was widely and warmly reviewed, but one reviewer complained that the book had been discussed "in a literary light only." Readers had praised the "power and vividness of its descriptions, of its wit, its humor, its character-painting," as if it were simply another "new novel." This critic, however, judged that "the literary feature" of the book was trivial beside its "didactic" concerns. For the book was no "romance of fiction" but aimed instead at "great practical subjects," like the Articles of War and flogging. Here, however, the reviewer found the book severely flawed, for a successful literary writer, however gifted with "theories, fancies and enthusiasm," lacks the necessary "character, wisdom and experience" to discuss serious matters. In criticizing the navy, Melville repeats the errors of the cobbler in the story, who successfully criticized "the foot" of a new statue but made a fool of himself when he presumed to judge any of the higher parts.

The reviewer draws the lesson that "the mind as well as the body is subject to the "Division of Labor."" In drawing this lesson, he was himself helping bring about a very important division of labor. This review is quite an early use of the term "literary" in the limited, modern sense that confines it to fiction, romance, and novels. The relation of Melville's work to the category of the "literary" would prove crucial, and explosive, in his next two works, *Moby-Dick* (1851) and *Pierre* (1852). The marketing problems of these "literary" narratives drove Melville to writing periodical fiction (republished in book form, *Israel Potter* [1855] and *Piazza Tales* [1856]) before trying literary narrative again in *The Confidence-Man* (1857). After the failure of this work, Melville published no further prose, but at his death in 1891 he left nearly completed a long story, "Billy Budd," published in 1924 as part of the revival of Melville's reputation as a "literary" figure.

The defense of "poetry" (which included fiction and drama) from Sidney in the Renaissance to Shelley in the earlier nineteenth century had emphasized the capacity of poets to address the weightiest issues of their times. Poets might guide statesmen more effectively than could historians or philosophers. By the middle of the nineteenth century, however, it seemed common sense to confine the power and vividness of "literature" to a realm of fiction that has no impact on the governance of life. Like the cobbler, the literary writer was unquestioned in a delimited realm and was out of place anywhere else.

Walden

No more than Melville could Henry David Thoreau embrace such a division of literature from life. Both writers were literary in the sense of their aiming for a wide range of impressive stylistic effects as well as in their fabricating shapes that gave unity to their works; yet both also were writing from their own experiences and with the wish to change the experiences and actions of their readers. No one could be more "local" than Thoreau, the man of Concord, who carried out his most notable exploration within the limits of his native town. It was also Thoreau's goal to define what the "only true America" might be, that is, to provide an alternative national narrative. Moreover, there is an immense, a comic, gap between what the titles promise in Dana's *Two Years before the Mast* and Thoreau's *A Week on the Concord and Merrimack Rivers* (1849). Nonetheless, Thoreau, both in *A Week,* his first book, and in *Walden, or Life in the Woods* (1854), set the genre of personal narrative as the norm from which he was departing.

Walden begins by striking the note of personal narrative. Thoreau explains that any egotism of the prose merely acknowledges that "it is always the first person speaking," and he states as his aim to offer a "simple and sincere account" of his experiences. In the opening chapter, a key articulation hinges on the simple narrative sentence which begins, "Near the end of March, 1845, I borrowed an axe and went down to the woods by Walden Pond." Likewise in the second chapter, "When first I took up my abode in the woods, that is, began to spend my nights as well as days there, which, by accident, was on Independence Day, or the Fourth of July, 1845, my house was not finished for winter." In the Conclusion, Thoreau defines what he has done as going "before the mast and on the deck of the world"; that is, like Dana and Melville, Thoreau claims to be learning from and reporting about work that he has done with his own hands, contrary to society's conventional expectations of polite writers. If one were really to go west, he argues, one better have something to do there (a reader might think of Cooper's Natty Bumppo). Hunters or trappers have better reason than any touristic traveler for paying serious attention to what they might encounter in the wild. The hunter, therefore, despite slaughtering animals, may provide more "true *humanity*" than the conventionally humane tourist, for what Thoreau means by "humanity" is "account of human experience."

Yet in placing himself in the woods, "out of bounds," Thoreau works very differently from Parkman. Having lived wild, he seeks a writing to match: "*Extra vagance!* it depends on how you are yarded. The migrating buffalo, which seeks new pastures in another latitude, is not extravagant like the cow which kicks over the pail, leaps the cow-yard fence, and runs after her calf, in milking time." Thoreau wishes his discourse likewise to be homely, comic, and passionately surprising: "I desire to speak somewhere *without* bounds; like a man in a waking moment, to men in their waking moments." At his very moment of extremity, Thoreau catches and bridles himself: he echoes one of the most important formulations of nineteenth-century poetic theory, Wordsworth's definition of the poet as a "man speaking to men." Like Wordsworth, Thoreau works with the tension between the model of direct orality and the actual condition of writing, in which he fears that the "volatile truth" of words will always escape from their "residual statement."

Like White-Jacket on the *Neversink*, Thoreau recognizes the modernity of his world. He pitilessly insists that "the old have no very important advice to give the young, their own experience has been so partial," and any "experience which I think valuable" proves to be something about which the elders were silent. The railroad has disciplined Americans to live like William Tell's son, fearlessly indifferent to the metal bolts of death that shoot by. In order to write his book, Thoreau must share his bookkeeping. His "account" proves to be that of an accountant, as he fills pages with the petty arithmetic of dollars and cents for boards and nails and beans, as many numbers as those White-Jacket had to learn. To triumph over life, Thoreau explains, one must "rout it in detail."

In this world, accounts need pondering, and the difficult labor of reading is more important than the effortless skill of hearing. The language that is "spoken" and "heard" is learned "unconsciously," but the language of writing and reading comes from "maturity and experience," which require being "born again." Formal oratory and racy vernacular and intimate conversation all fall short of this power: "If we would enjoy the most intimate society . . . we must not only be silent, but commonly so far apart that we cannot possibly hear each other's voice in any case." Thomas Carlyle had praised Shakespeare in "The Hero as Poet" by proclaiming, "Speech is great; but Silence is greater." In the early twentieth century Joyce summarized the literary vocation as "silence, exile, and cunning." Thoreau shares in this history.

Thoreau complained of modern life, "Where is this division of labor to end? and what object does it finally serve?" Yet he himself depended on such divisions. The opposition of conscious writing to

unconscious speech, Thoreau's constant search for the inner meaning, participate in the social separation of the sphere of literature.
The exhortation to be "a Columbus to whole new continents and
worlds within you, opening new channels, not of trade, but of
thought" takes its point and value only in a world that has devalued
outer action and set a privilege upon the spiritual, with which literature is allied. This privilege drives Thoreau to reverse the values he
most typically avows. Instead, he urges that "we should oftener
look over the tafferel of our craft, like curious passengers, and not
make the voyage like stupid sailors picking oakum." The mind and
eye pull away from the hands, as personal narrative becomes literary narrative.

4

Literary Narrative

Romance, Romanticism, and the Literary

In his extended works from *The Scarlet Letter* (1850) through *The House of the Seven Gables* (1851), *The Blithedale Romance* (1852), and *The Marble Faun* (1860), Nathaniel Hawthorne was the writer of prose narrative most important in establishing the kind of writing now recognized as "literary." Spurred by the success of *The Scarlet Letter,* Hawthorne's publishers moved to consolidate his position by reissuing *Twice-told Tales* (1851), collecting several of his recent sketches and tales along with some dozen previously unrepublished pieces in *The Snow-Image* (1851), and commissioning from him a book of mythological narratives for children, *A Wonder-Book for Girls and Boys* (1851–2, followed by *Tanglewood Tales* in 1853). The first year in which Hawthorne's writing provided enough income for his family to live on was 1851. Nevertheless, the gap in his career as a writer of fiction—seven years to *The Marble Faun* after only three years of high activity—indicates that even Hawthorne was not fully or clearly established in the role of a professional writer. His *Life of Franklin Pierce* (1852), written for the successful presidential campaign of his college friend, gave him access to a lucrative patronage position as American consul in Liverpool (1853–7), and with the financial security he earned from this position Hawthorne spent further years in France and Italy. These biographical facts emphasize the fragility of the newly emergent literary narrative.

Along with his college acquaintance and friend Henry Wadsworth Longfellow, Hawthorne was the figure around whom the recognition of "literature" was established in the United States. Hawthorne best combines recognition in his own time with recognition in later discussions of American national literature, but Edgar Allan Poe did more to put into place the theories and perspectives that have formed the twentieth-century notion of literature. I have noted that a review of Melville's *White-Jacket* sharply distinguished between the work's "literary" and "didactic" qualities. Poe vigorously promoted this newly specialized sense of the word "literary." In his "Literati of New York" series, for example, he observed of Catharine Maria Sedgwick (whose *Hope Leslie* [1827] had been a notable predecessor of Hawthorne in the fiction of colonial Massachusetts), "As the author of many *books*—of several absolutely bound volumes in the ordinary 'novel' form of auld lang syne, Miss Sedgwick has a certain adventitious hold upon the attention of the public, a species of tenure that has nothing to do with literature proper."

By appealing to "literature proper," Poe was establishing a distinction between the mere fact of book publication and higher values that are essential rather than "adventitious." These values depend on spiritual facts rather than just on physical appearance in a familiar format. In fact, the familiar, "ordinary . . . form of auld lang syne" is suspect. Literature proper apparently will be innovative, recognizable by its difference from, rather than its resemblance to, what has gone before. Yet there will necessarily be some problem with new work. It may require special talents to acknowledge it, to understand that the work in question is not a failed example of an old form but rather a uniquely innovative accomplishment. In his major review of the second edition (1842) of Hawthorne's *Twice-told Tales,* Poe emphasized, therefore, that

Hawthorne was the "example, par excellence, of the privately-admired and publicly unappreciated man of genius." Even though his work represented the "highest regions of Art," indeed, precisely for that reason, Hawthorne did not attract the public that Poe found Cooper to have won with his predictably popular thematic material.

I use the term "literary narrative" to characterize the work of which Hawthorne is the great exemplar, because "literature" and the "literary" are words still in use and because they begin to achieve their present meanings in Hawthorne's time. The term most closely associated with this body of fiction in its own time, however, was not "literature" (despite Poe's advocacy) but "romance." This is especially the case because in the prefaces he wrote to his long fictional works, Hawthorne himself made extensive and significant use of this term, and through his usage the term became important again in mid-twentieth-century claims for a tradition of fiction that might be specifically American.

The term "romance" takes its meaning both positively and negatively. Negatively, the main idea of romance is as a contrast to everyday life. Thus in the preface to *The Marble Faun,* Hawthorne explains his choice of Italy "as the site of his Romance," because it offered "a poetic or fairy precinct, whose actualities would not be so terribly insisted upon as they are, and must needs be, in America." He gave much the same explanation in the preface to *The Blithedale Romance,* in which he explains that his concern with a "socialist community" related to Brook Farm (where he had a decade earlier involved himself) was "merely to establish a theatre, a little removed from the highway of ordinary travel," in order to avoid "exposing" his work to "too close a comparison with the actual events of real lives." This language of terrible insistence and of exposure sounds a note of defensiveness that is a major feature of Hawthorne's prefaces. More important than any consistent theory may be Hawthorne's attempt to escape the hostility of those in his native Salem who resented the critiques of named or recognizable local personalities in *The Scarlet Letter* and *The House of the Seven Gables*. Even in these earlier works, Hawthorne had already tried to mark his distance from the local. In the "Custom-House" sketch introducing *The Scarlet Letter*, he defined "neutral territory" as the proper ground for the "romance-writer." In "appropriating" for *The House of the Seven Gables* a "lot of land which had no visible owner," Hawthorne sought a space secure from "inflexible" and "dangerous" criticism, insisting that his romance had "a great deal more to do with the clouds overhead" than with "the actual soil" of his home county.

The second major negative sense of "romance" functions not as part of a distinction between writing and life, but within the realm of writing. "Romance" as a kind of fiction is distinguished from the "novel." Hawthorne begins his preface to *The House of the Seven Gables*, subtitled "A Romance": "When a writer calls his work a Romance, it need hardly be observed that he wishes to claim a certain latitude, both as to its fashion and material, which he would not have felt himself entitled to assume had he professed to be writing a Novel." The novel seeks "a very minute fidelity . . . to the probable and ordinary course of man's experience," whereas the choice of "circumstances" for the romance is much more greatly "of the writer's own choosing or creation."

Hawthorne was adapting a distinction that had had some currency in the eighteenth century and more recent support from Walter Scott, yet Hawthorne's distinction was not uniformly observed, even by those readers and writers closely linked to him in their taste and character. In reviewing *The Scarlet Letter*, Evert Duyckinck proclaimed it a "psychological romance": "the veriest Mrs. Malaprop would never venture to call it a novel." The review by Edwin Percy Whipple, however, quite calmly and without any second thought did call it a novel. Whipple was himself deeply involved in the Boston literary society that Hawthorne had joined with the publication of this book, and he became one of Hawthorne's closest literary advisers, so he can hardly be considered inept. In *The House of the Seven Gables* Hawthorne himself blurs any distinction between "novel" and "romance." He writes that "a romance on the plan of Gil Blas, adapted to American society and manners, would cease to be a romance." "Romance" here has the sense of "fiction," for the French work *Gil Blas* (1715) by Alain-René Lesage is a prototypical picaresque novel of wanderings across the whole range of society. Hawthorne's point is that such great social movement could not really happen in the Old World, but in America it is "the experience of many individuals among us." American social mobility makes possible for some an "ultimate success" that "may be incomparably higher than any that a novelist would imagine for his hero." America is too improbable for a novel, and too true for a romance, and Hawthorne's generic distinctions are occasional tools used for polemical contrasts.

When used less as a contrastive term and more positively, "romance" continues to have much the same range. Its primary meaning is not much different from "fiction." As Herman Melville was at work on his third book, *Mardi,* he found that he wanted to make it different from *Typee* and *Omoo*. In these first two books he had taken some liberties with literal truth and had relied on travel writing to supplement gaps in his own knowledge or memory, but *Typee* and *Omoo* could still safely appear as nonfiction. In the months that he was working on *Mardi* and meditating a change of direction, Melville also changed the tenor of his reading. No longer were the books that he bought so heavily oriented toward travel narrative. His reading included Shakespeare, Montaigne, and the *Biographia Literaria* (1817) of Samuel Taylor Coleridge, the most important critical book of English Romanticism and crucial for the emergence of "literature" in that national culture.

In the winter months of 1848, Melville had decided, as he wrote to his publisher John Murray, to "change" his mode of writing to

"Romance," "downright and out," "real" romance as opposed to the relative factuality of his earlier books. He explained that *Mardi* "opens like a true narrative," but from there "the romance and poetry" would "grow." By this departure from personal narrative, Melville hoped to gain a greater play of "freedom and invention" and to achieve a work that was "original." The result would be "better" and "so essentially different" from *Typee* and *Omoo* as a "literary acheivement [*sic*]." Murray shared the scorn of "fiction" that may, paradoxically, be found also in the new best-selling novels of the 1850s. Ellen, the heroine of Susan Warner's *The Wide, Wide World* (1850), is warned by her mentor, "Read no novels," and she must regretfully put away issues of *Blackwood's* that had inadvertently come into her hands. Ellen's values are those of middle-class evangelicals, but Melville associates his choice of fiction, romance, and the literary with social elevation. He insisted to Murray that an "American" could be a "gentleman," who had read the Waverley novels, even "though every digit may have been in the tar-bucket." As in Poe's claim for "literature proper," the claim for romance is a claim for social status.

In his preface to *Eureka,* which he subtitled a "Prose Poem," Poe addresses himself "to the few" who love and understand him; to them he offers the book for its "Beauty," even while also insisting on its "Truth." For these elite readers—his chosen audience for whom he is their chosen writer—he asks that the book be considered not as a work of scientific truth but rather "as an Art-Product alone," "let us say as a Romance" or even as a "Poem." In "The Philosophy of Composition," where he discusses the principles that he claims to have applied in his writing of "The Raven," Poe defines "unity of effect or impression" as the necessary goal of a poem, the same goal he claimed for the tale in his earlier review of Hawthorne. *Eureka* raises this goal to its highest pitch. In *Eureka,* Poe offers the reader the possibility of "an individual impression" of the universe. From the top of a mountain, he points out, the *"extent and diversity"* of the scene are more impressive than its oneness. Only by the improbable, somewhat comic, expedient of "rapid[ly] whirling on his heel" could a viewer grasp "the panorama in the sublimity of its *oneness.*" To tell the story of the universe in an analytic narrative that has a hypothesized beginning, a middle in which we live, and an imagined end, Poe uses a mixed form that combines the intensity of a poem with the commitment to truth of prose.

In calling such a work "a romance," Poe recalls the debates over the "romantic" in German literary theory around 1800, where the mixture of modes, the breakdown of "classical" genres helped to define the modern, "Romantic" product of verbal art. The "novel" (*Roman* in German, *roman* in French) was the name given to this genre to end genre. The novel was the epic of the modern world, but it was not in verse, and as prose it could include both the disorienting clownery of spinning round on one's heels and the sublime mysticism of the secret of the universe. The emphasis on "romance" and the rise of the literary in mid-nineteenth-century America also connect in other ways to the Romanticism of earlier generations in Germany and Britain. In both of these cultures, the basis for what is now understood as "literature" was laid through the sharp sense of an absent public sphere. The French Revolution seemed to promise free speech among equals, but the promise failed, and in England, Wordsworth and Coleridge turned from public life. *The Prelude,* Wordsworth's great poem of vocation, demands epic scale and length, only to recount "the growth of a poet's mind." Deprived of an acceptable world of political exchange and no longer in a position to enjoy patronage, the Romantic writers had to develop their work in relation to market concerns. The relation they chose was opposition.

Wordsworth and Coleridge expressed their democratic hopes in a sturdy commitment to the idea of writing for "the people," but they found no actual audience to which they would give that honored name, only a degraded "public"—like those eager for the "gross and violent stimulants." In *White-Jacket,* Melville catches this tension in an exchange about the poems written by one of the men on board. The poet denounces the "public," and his shipmate objects that, after all, he is himself part of the public. The poet replies that the shipmate is a member of "the people" (the name, recall, also given to the sailors on the ship), and the two agree to maintain a sharp distinction between the public and the people, always to "hate the one [the public] and cleave to the other [the people]."

Shakespeare was above all others the writer of the past to whom the English and German Romantics turned to explore the concerns they felt most strongly. In the political frustrations of Hamlet, who was forced into dissimulation and soliloquy by the constraints of the deadly court in which he lived, the Romantics found a model for the interiorization that they both suffered and valued. They recognized, too, in Shakespeare a writer who had had to deal with a market system. In his sonnets—first beginning to be widely appreciated and discussed only in the Romantic period—Shakespeare shows strong self-pride together with a pained awareness of his low position in the social scale. In England, the theory of "literature" can hardly be separated from the attempt to pry Shakespeare from the theater and make his existence most vivid in books. Charles Lamb's essay "On the Tragedies of Shakespeare" (1811) determined that these plays could be appreciated only in the study, not on the stage. In the next generation, Thomas Carlyle, in *On Heroes, Hero-worship, and the Heroic in History* (1841), treated Shakespeare as an example of "The Hero as Poet." Carlyle lamented Shakespeare's subjugation to "cramping circumstances," which had forced him to dilute his tremendous insights into passable crowd-pleasers that showed their greatness only in "bursts of radiance." Melville's "Hawthorne and His Mosses" (1850) almost echoes Carlyle. Melville deprecates the "popularizing noise and show" of "Richard-the-Third humps and Macbeth daggers." Shakespeare's greatness, he proclaims, comes in "occasional flashings-forth," in "short, quick probings at the very axis of reality," through his mad characters such as Timon and Lear. The plot of the drama becomes a sop to the audience, and the characters become the test of greatness, characters known through their soliloquies and tirades rather than through their actions and dialogue.

In the 1790s, Wordsworth's engagement with the French Revolution—his disillusion with both the French course of terror and the British refusal to democratize—fueled his neo-Shakespearean drama, *The Borderers*, which was not published until 1842 but was quoted by Coleridge in his 1813 Bristol lecture on Hamlet. The most powerful lines in the play are spoken by the villain, but this did not diminish their influence:

> Action is transitory—a step, a blow—
> The motion of a muscle this way or that.
> 'Tis done, and in the after-vacancy
> We wonder at ourselves like men betrayed.
> Suffering is permanent, obscure, and dark,
> And shares the nature of infinity.

Character no longer reveals itself in action but forms a mute, dark concretion to be known. This Romantic turn to the inner world served some of Hawthorne's best and most sympathetic critics in characterizing his work. In reviewing *The Scarlet Letter* as a psychological romance, Duyckinck (a devoted reader of Coleridge) quoted a tag from these lines, and in his review of *The Marble Faun*, looking back in summary of the whole of Hawthorne's career, Whipple quoted the full passage that I have just cited.

In the United States, as in England, "literature" emerged in relation to the market. The moment at which "literature" took shape was the very same moment in which the "best-seller" also arose. Eighteen fifty, the year of *The Scarlet Letter*, was also the year in which Susan Warner's *The Wide, Wide World* established sales figures that two years later were topped by Harriet Beecher Stowe's *Uncle Tom's Cabin* but by few other books of the nineteenth century. The very moment Hawthorne reached a substantial public was the moment in which his rivalry began with what he called the "damned mob of scribbling women," who reached a much larger public. Having a potential readership greater than that in any European nation because of its high literacy rates, the United States, by 1850, had become available as a national market because of both the improved transportation that railroads permitted and the new steps in the technical organization of publishing and bookselling that made this audience actual.

After the Panic of 1837 (which had damaged Hawthorne's career by stopping sales of *Twice-told Tales*), from 1843 into the middle 1850s, economic expansion was uninterrupted in the United States. James Fields, a partner in the Boston publishers Ticknor and Fields, had worked for years to establish New England literature in a national market, and, at this point, his efforts started to reap their reward. Under Ticknor's imprint, Hawthorne's *Scarlet Letter* began to establish the basis for the cultural leadership that was exercised through the *Atlantic Monthly* (founded in 1857, taken over by Ticknor and Fields in 1859, and edited by Fields from 1861 to 1871, when William Dean Howells took over) and that made Boston for several generations a publishing center of greater cultural weight than New York. Part of the process at work here was a stratification of audiences, so that by 1851 Hawthorne could make a living through publishing his kind of fiction, while publishers could do well financially with the work of more popular authors like Warner.

This market situation illuminates the complexities of a letter that Melville wrote to his father-in-law, Lemuel Shaw (chief justice of the Massachusetts Supreme Court), in October 1849, just after publication of *Redburn* and shortly before he went abroad to negotiate the sale of *White-Jacket*. Having just spent the summer writing these two books after *Mardi*, published in March, had met a hostile reception, he wrote:

> For Redburn I anticipate no particular reception of any kind. It may be deemed a book of tolerable entertainment;—& may be accounted dull.—As for the other book [*White-Jacket*], it will be sure to be attacked in some quarters. But no reputation that is gratifying to me, can possibly be achieved by either of these books. They are two *jobs,* which I have done for money—being forced to it, as other men are to sawing wood. And while I have felt obliged to refrain from writing the kind of book I would wish to; yet, in writing these two books, I have not repressed myself much—so far as *they* are concerned; but have spoken pretty much as I feel.—Being books, then, written in this way, my only desire for their "success" (as it is called) springs from my pocket, & not from my heart. So far as I am individually concerned, & independent of my pocket, it is my earnest desire to write those sort of books which are said to "fail."—Pardon this egotism.

Here the literary is set firmly against the economic: only one kind of writing is done for "money"; it is a "job." A double scale registers success and failure in a way that uses the same words to mean totally opposed things. For many nineteenth-century writers at moments of risk, whether Douglass determining to gain the powers of literacy or Melville reckoning the costs of the literary, the model for this doubleness was Satan's "Evil, be thou my good." Melville, accordingly, defines failure as success. Against the mere "desire" that stems from the "pocket," there is the "earnest desire" that comes from the "heart": an inner "individual" essence against the adventitious garb of society. Melville needed money to support his wife and child, but his necessary "egotism" as a writer ambitious of literary fame dictated his prose. Even writing to his father-in-law, Melville does not name as motives his wife, Shaw's daughter, or his eight-month-old son, Shaw's grandson. To the "individually concerned" writer, these intimate others are reduced to his pocket, from which he wishes he were "independent." The writer's activity is set in counterpoint to the obscured agency of the marketplace world, in which things may be "deemed," "accounted," "attacked," "called," or "said" without the apparent intervention of people. Even the writer is "forced" and "obliged," barely able to assert that he is not wholly "repressed."

Throughout the history of Western vernacular writing of high ambition, almost all of its practitioners either had lived on patronage, or had been persons of independent means, or had been members of the learned professions in positions of some comfort. Melville had no profession, no means, and no patronage. Only the existence of a market for his writing had drawn Melville into authorship in the first place, but he found that, once it had been entered, the world of literature opened horizons that he could not reach. Having drawn him in by its positive attractions, it protracted his relation in a negative way, in experiments to see how much he could speak "as I feel" and still make a living, experiments to see how much failure he could survive.

In describing transatlantic Romanticism, I mentioned the political problems of public speech in England and Germany. The United States should have posed no such problems. Its founding allowed the possibility of, and seemed to demand, public speech of a sort that was impossible elsewhere. Just at the moment he received a large advance payment on *Mardi*, in March 1849, Melville wrote to Duyckinck: "I would to God Shakespeare had lived later, & promenaded in Broadway." Then he would have been free of "the muzzle" imposed by Elizabethan restrictions. Even if no one can be "a frank man to the uttermost" in his writing, still, Melville believed, "the Declaration of Independence makes a difference." Shakespeare on Broadway soon proved more explosive than Melville imagined.

In May 1849, two rival actors were in New York playing Macbeth: the English tragedian William Macready at the Astor Place Opera House and the popular American actor Edwin Forrest at the Broadway Theatre. The tensions between a more fashionable audience at the Astor and a more popular audience at the Broadway, exacerbated by nationalist rivalries, led to a mob's closing down Macready's performance. Cultivated public opinion, including Melville, petitioned Macready to perform again, promising him protection. Hundreds of police and militia tried to control the protesters without success, and the militia fired directly into the crowd. Twenty-two people were killed. The shocking outcome of the Astor Place Riot cast doubt on the difference the Declaration of Independence had made. Over the years, from the founding of the United States until the middle of the nineteenth century, changes occurred in the nation's political culture that provoked the emergence of a literature surprisingly like that which elsewhere had grown from the frustration of democratic hopes.

By 1850, the United States was at once more intensely national and more intensely sectional than it had been when Cooper began to write. The expansion to the Pacific, the Mexican War, the whole apparatus of manifest destiny, sealed by the astonishing growth of overland railroad connections, strengthened the nation as a whole and brought it to a new level of power. Yet the tensions that developed over the future of slavery tremendously enhanced both solidarity within sections and antagonism between sections. The Old South and the new Southwest fused into the "South" that soon became the Confederacy, while New England, New York, Pennsylvania, and the Old Northwest were fusing into the "North" that became the "Union" of the newly formed Republican party. Moreover, the demands of entrepreneurs in the new industrial system that was becoming increasingly important in national economic life required a thorough transformation of the grounding of American law. The law shifted from its basis in English common law into elaborate codifications that required a much higher level of professional expertise than before. Economic issues that once would have been matters for public debate and legislative activity were channeled into the courts, and political questions of the utmost consequence were shunted away from the forums of debate, on the grounds that they threatened the sacred Union.

Politics was displaced into two different venues. In the courts, issues that seemed to be too difficult or explosively dangerous to debate publicly could be resolved ad hoc, as individual cases, through an adversarial but nonpartisan proceeding. In the characters of separate individuals, matters could be resolved silently and privately. Emerson wrote in "Politics" that the "antidote" to the "abuse of formal government" is "the influence of private character, the growth of the Individual." In *Mardi* an enigmatic document is discovered that reproaches the nationalistic oratory of a figure who transposes the rhetoric of "Young America" into this South Sea fiction. The document powerfully claims that "freedom is more social than political." Freedom's "real felicity is not to be shared," but is rather of "a man's own individual getting and holding." Standing against the republican principles of the American Revolution, this claim rehearses the analysis Tocqueville had made of American "individualism."

"Individualism," Tocqueville had argued, was a new word for a new thing; it was not merely selfishness, which is a passion, but a "mature and calm feeling, which disposes each member of the community to sever himself from the mass of his fellows." Selfishness corrupts all virtue, but individualism, at least at first, "only saps the virtues of public life." Yet the solitary powers of the literary writer, the romancer, were very much individual. Looking back to Shakespeare's great individualist Coriolanus, who turned against the republican freedoms of his native Rome to find a "world elsewhere," the English critic William Hazlitt worried that the "power" of the greatest writing might be at one with the "power" of autocratic politics. For "the imagination is an exaggerating and exclusive faculty," a thoroughly "anti-levelling principle." As the imagination formed its elite among those who hoped to make a career in literature, the more intensely specialized legal profession generated its own elite; both opposed everyday plain thought, speech, and sense. The new systems of courts and character both required education as a prerequisite and then a process of interpretation in order to make the system work.

By midcentury, national narratives like that of George Bancroft came to seem sectional in their necessary emphasis on one side or another of issues that were increasingly contested; local narratives, like those of the southwestern humorists, could seem increasingly divisive in a nation that feared splitting apart into antagonistic sectional cultures; and even "personal" narratives—not just that of Frederick Douglass—proved intensely ideological. In this situation, "literature" could fill a special function that had not had a place before. It offered an internalized psychology that had not been part of "personal" narrative, and it took place in a "neutral territory" that was neither here nor there, neither national nor local, with regard to the intensely debated political issues of the day. It proposed eternal questions of "the human heart," rather than discuss more immediate and controversial issues.

The great speeches of political oratory, for which such senators as Henry Clay, John Calhoun, and Daniel Webster were known throughout the United States, became a less important form than they had been. The "Compromise" of 1850, which occupied Congress for almost the entire year, was meant to end once and for all the debate over the issues surrounding slavery, and in their speeches Clay, Webster, and Calhoun had all emphasized that political oratory was itself a divisive mode, creating problems where none would exist if one only would trust to the loyalty of the American people.

The case of Webster was the most crucial for the figures who became associated with literature, for they were northerners, like Webster, while Clay represented the West and Calhoun the South. To accept Webster's position in his famous speech of March 7, 1850, was to opt for silence (as against dangerously divisive debate); while to reject his position could well mean to reject both oratory and politics as the corrupt means by which Webster had compromised morality in order to preserve the Union. In his speaking tour of the southern states in 1847, part of his continuing presidential ambitions, Webster had already begun to lay the basis for this position. He had explained there, "I desire to see an attachment to the Union existing among the people, not as a deduction of political economy, nor as a result of philosophical reasoning, but cherished as a heartfelt sentiment."

The opposition of heart to head that was to be so crucial in Hawthorne's romances is in Webster's statement presented as a formula for political harmony, and the heart's sentiments are seen as the stable ground on which political tranquillity may be established. In his moralizing, exemplary biography of George Washington, Parson Weems had maintained that "Private Life is always *real* life," and Hawthorne's romances emphasize the private as the reality that public life either mocks or conceals. In the "Custom-House" preface to *The Scarlet Letter,* the documents about Hester Prynne left by Surveyor Pue are available for Hawthorne's imaginative use because they were "not official, but of a private nature." Only the popular female writers of the time are now known as "sentimental" novelists, but Hawthorne's fiction is no less committed to sentiment. The hearth replaced the great natural landscapes of James Fenimore Cooper as the locus of a "natural" moral virtue on which the preservation of America depended. This was the tendency of Hawthorne's fiction as much as it was that of the women writers. Despite his fascination with the protracted agonies of moral guilt, Hawthorne's positive position was no different from that of Edmund Burke. It was a position that became increasingly important for mid-nineteenth-century American culture: the "normal instincts of mankind" are valuable because they make up the "conservative principle of society." In 1856 the American critic Henry T. Tuckerman wrote, concerning George Washington, that "sentiment is the great conservative principle of society." Tuckerman had earlier argued in a review of *The Scarlet Letter* that Hawthorne's "psychological" writings served to rectify the nation's sentiments. Hawthorne thanked Tuckerman for this "beautiful" review, which "understood what I meant."

Webster, in emphasizing the importance of unreflective loyalty and commitment, had already contributed to a reinterpretation of the American Revolution in line with Burke. In his speech at the completion of the Bunker Hill Monument (1843), Webster explained that the American Revolution had not been a violent innovation, but a development from the previous two centuries of American life. Bancroft also believed in the developmental character of the Revolution, but he did not deny, as Webster's claim for sentiment tended to, that logic, analysis, and argument had gone into justifying, motivating, and waging the Revolution.

The week after Webster's speech on compromise, *The Scarlet Letter* appeared, on March 16, 1850, and its sales were surprisingly strong, requiring a second edition within weeks. The book obviously could not have been directly influenced by the compromise debates, but it was written out of the same national situation. In ending the Missouri Compromise of 1820, which had established a specific geographical boundary north of which slavery would not be permitted in federal territories, the Compromise of 1850 replaced something that had been clear-cut, arbitrary, and arithmetical with a set of possibilities that left much open for interpretation. Hawthorne's concern with interpretation, his fiction of the possible and the potential, was not new at this time. As early as the *Twice-told Tales*, a review in the *Church Examiner* contrasted Hawthorne's stories to more highly mimetic fictions, which "usurp the realm of real fact" and thereby "disturb and displace the fabric of things as they are." As an example of "higher fiction," Hawthorne's work, like "true poetry," "leaves things as they are." Yet this preservative function enhances what is left in place, for it "breathes into them a vital glow."

When the Union had to be cherished and fostered rather than shaken up and tampered with, Hawthorne's long-standing mode of writing became newly relevant. The essence of its relevance, however, lay in its not being recognized as relevant. It provided a welcome alternative to politics, but it also kept in play, in displaced form, certain elements of the political scene. The long period of relative tranquillity over the slavery issue had been based upon a principle of strict segregation: slavery was uniquely a matter for state decision and not for national discussion. But the sudden accession of new national land forced the question of slavery out into the territories and made it a matter at once of fantasy—might there be slaves there?—and of principle—should there be slaves there?—rather than of fact: there were actually almost no slaves there.

Hawthorne's "neutral territory" for the romance writer's imagination had a strange relation to the imaginative spaces of the West that were being peopled with slaves or free farmers in the minds of ideologists. Purist logic held, as Lincoln would remark, that the nation must be either all slave or all free. The corollary was usually unspoken, except by Garrisonian abolitionists and, increasingly, by southern "fire-eaters," namely, that if Americans remained divided by slavery there would no longer be a Union. The "moderate" position tried to reconcile the claims of slavery (or freedom) and union. Such reconciliation of opposites was the specific task of the imagination, as Coleridge had defined it in the *Biographia Literaria,* and the imaginary resolution of these real problems was one of the means by which romance in Hawthorne's hands helped to negotiate the moment of political crisis in the middle of the nineteenth century. Nevertheless, in "The Custom-House" Hawthorne explained his spiritual dejection by claiming that "imagination" was incompatible with receiving "public gold." Thus he established his own literary authority on grounds that discredited the speeches of Senator Webster and the history of Ambassador Bancroft, both of which for the previous two decades had been more widely sold, read, and admired than the fictional oeuvre of any author. To the question, in 1850, what was the greatest American literature? Bancroft's *History* and Webster's speeches might have proven likely answers; less than a century later, they had been wholly displaced, not merely by a shift in taste or evaluation, but by a radical and thoroughgoing redefinition of literature.

That the imagination was held to make possible creativity, the primary feature of the new idea of literature, was clearly seen in the claims made by mid-nineteenth century writers for "romance." The power of originating from nothing, which had been God's, was now available to humans. The first English usage of "original" had been in the theological phrase "Original Sin," but Adam's, or Eve's, assertion of freedom was now revalued. The imagination achieved its creative capacity through a process of growth and development. The romance of Hawthorne's that most explicitly focuses on the issue of development is *The House of the Seven Gables*, in which the artist-figure is a photographer. In the 1840s the sense of "development" as a biological process of transformation became prominent—when Charles Darwin published *Origin of Species* in 1859, what is now called evolution was usually referred to as the "development hypothesis"—at the same time that the word began to be applied to the processing of photographs (the term still used now). Also at this moment, the English clergyman John Henry Newman published his *Essay on the Development of Christian Doctrine* (1845) and became a convert to the Roman Catholic church. Newman's *Essay on Development*, as it was called, made available a sense of development as the process by which truth is revealed gradually through history.

Because the process occurs over time, it will necessarily be imperfect at earlier points in a writer's career. Thus Poe explained in his review of Hawthorne that those most capable of judging, that is, those using these new criteria, the "few," judge differently from "the public." Maintaining the older criteria of literary criticism as a judgment of the skills of craft shown in the performance of a composition, the public judges a writer on the basis of action, "by what he does"; but the new standards emphasize character instead, "what he evinces the capability of doing." Melville made the same point in "Hawthorne and His Mosses," writing of Shakespeare: "The immediate products of a great mind are not so great, as that undeveloped, (and sometimes undevelopable) yet dimly-discernable greatness, to which these immediate products are but the infallible indices." The criterion is not achievement but potential, "indices" to be interpreted. This distinction illuminates a crucial difference between two notions of "character" in the narratives of the mid-nineteenth century. In the most popular narratives, such as *The Wide, Wide World,* the character of the heroine is shown as produced by the didactic ministrations of those who love her, and her character is judged from her actions. Character in Hawthorne is instead a given, not to be formed but to be found out, as if a natural fact that the writer explored rather than produced.

The result of successful imaginative activity is the literary creation of a world that stands free from the world of everyday life as an independent whole. In Melville's *Mardi* (1849), the "romance" that takes over from the narrative of shipwreck and sailing adventure is initiated through the chapter title as the voyagers come upon the new islands of Mardi: "World Ho!" A crew of European and South Sea sailors yields to a new group of characters. Conversations among a half-divine king, a philosopher, a historian, and a poet allow Melville to launch into both speculative and satirical reflections on his world through the shape of this new world. This voyage not only narrates fictional discoveries; it also enacts the writer's discoveries in the resources of fiction as a high mode of literary ambition.

In Chapter 169, the writer addresses the reader: if he has "chartless voyaged," it has been in order to reach a "new world," the "world of mind." Melville's language in this chapter seems attuned to that of John Keats's poetry. In his "Ode to Psyche" (1819), Keats had charted a similar internalization, in honoring the heroine of a fiction of late antiquity, Psyche, the "soul": "Yes, I will be thy priest, and build a fane / in some untrodden region of my mind."

Mardi includes within its fiction a chapter on the literature of the fictional world of Mardi. The great author "Lombardo" supposedly emulates the old blind bard who, it is said, proclaimed, "I will build another world." The bard's model for Lombardo proves identical to one marked out by the models of Romanticism, such as Keats's formulation, "That which is creative must create itself." As Lombardo works on his poem, he goes "deeper and deeper into himself," working through a fearsome interior landscape, until he emerges into a pastoral pleasance, at which point he can rejoice, "I have created the creative." Here the inner struggle of the author to transform his own soul into a beautiful, productive world provides the basis from which it may be reproduced in the world of the imaginative poem.

This interiority where imagination works and growth develops, where character is known and formed, is the privileged space of the literary, both in authors and in their characters. In the great Shakespearean prototype, Hamlet has "that within which passes show." Yet this creative originality was not supposed to diverge utterly from common life. Hawthorne, in the preface to *The House of the Seven Gables,* had emphasized that the romancer—even while freed from ordinary probabilities—remained bound to observe "the truth of the human heart." William Hazlitt had defined "originality" as "seeing nature differently from others, and yet as it is in itself"; that is, "originality" had not only the now usual sense of uniqueness, but it also maintained an etymological connection with "origins." The "original" is more in touch with the primary source of things— for Hawthorne, precisely the human heart.

The effect of such work, Poe observed in reviewing Hawthorne, was "totality." This term had been put into current usage by Coleridge in his lectures on Shakespeare. Addressing the old "unities" of neoclassical dramatic criticism, Coleridge suggested a change: "instead of unity of action, I should greatly prefer the more appropriate, though scholastic and uncouth words, homogeneity, proportionateness, and totality of interest." These new terms, Coleridge believed, involve the "essential difference" between the "shaping skill of mechanical talent," a lower form of accomplishment, and "the creative, productive life-power of inspired genius." The "harmony that strikes us" in even the "wildest natural landscapes" is effected by a "single energy modified *ab intra* [from within] in each component part." This energy is the "particular excellence" of Shakespeare's plays and gives them their unique power of harmony. Reviewing Coleridge's work in 1836, Poe had praised his "gigantic mind" and recommended that the *Biographia Literaria* be published in the United States, which had much to learn from its "psychological science."

The harmonious, interactive power that Coleridge admired in natural landscape and found in Shakespeare, Poe in *Eureka* calls "mutuality of adaptation," and from it he argues an aesthetic point comparable to Coleridge's: "The pleasure which we derive from any display of human ingenuity is in the ratio of *the approach* to this species of reciprocity." In a crucial difference from Coleridge, Poe does not so readily assume that even Shakespeare actually achieved the level of full integration; and Poe resists Coleridge's distinction between the merely mechanical skill of craft and the purely organic growth of genius. Nonetheless, he continues,

In the construction of plot, for example, in fictitious literature, we should aim at so arranging the incidents that we shall not be able to determine, of any one of them, whether it depends from any one other or upholds it. In this sense, of course, *perfection* of plot is really, or practically, unattainable—but only because it is a finite intelligence that constructs.

In contrast, however, "the plots of God are perfect."

Poe then reverses the usual direction of comparison between human and divine. He takes a term from aesthetics and transposes it into cosmotheology: "The Universe is a plot of God." The purpose of *Eureka* is to analyze, and narrate, that plot: "Oneness is a principle abundantly sufficient to account for the constitution, the existing phaenomena, and the plainly inevitable annihilation of at least the material Universe." The "arms and the man" of this modern epic will then be, *"In the Original Unity of the first Thing lies the Secondary Cause of All Things, with the Germ of their Inevitable Annihilation."* In using the principles of literary criticism to understand the universe, Poe relies on the convertibility of truth and beauty. The world he has created through his argument, he asserts, must be identical to the world that God has created, for otherwise the universe would be less perfect than this critical construction.

Hawthorne's Romances

However perfect the universe as a whole might be, it was clear to the romance writers of the middle nineteenth century that their daily experience was flawed and fragmentary. This split is acknowledged in Melville's letter to Lemuel Shaw or in Hawthorne's contrast between the deadness of his work in the customhouse and the liveness of imagination that he sought. This experience had been with Hawthorne for a long time. As early as his first patronage work, the place Bancroft had gotten him in the Boston Custom

House from 1839 to 1841, Hawthorne's letters to his fiancée, later his wife, emphasize his sense of there being two distinct worlds, one of which is "the" world and is much inferior to the world of the hearth, love, and imagination. So he wrote from work to Sophia,

> My Dove is at home . . . in the midst of true affections; and she can live a spiritual life, spiritual and intellectual. Now, my intellect, and my heart and soul, have no share in my present mode of life—they find neither labor nor food in it; every thing that I do here might be better done by a machine. I *am* a machine, and am surrounded by hundreds of similar machines;—or, rather, all of the business people are so many wheels of one great machine—and we have no more love or sympathy for one another than if we were made of wood, brass, or iron, like the wheels of other pieces of complicated machinery.

The "home" and the "spiritual" are set against the "machinery" of "business." Although the United States was indeed becoming a more industrial economy at this point, Hawthorne's "mechanical" does not stigmatize the industrial so much as the bureaucratic and commercial, the middle-class male sphere. Hawthorne's terms of analysis were widely shared, even beyond the use in Coleridge that has already been noted. In his great essay of 1829, Thomas Carlyle had read the "Signs of the Times" and proclaimed this age "not an Heroical, Devotional, Philosophical, or Moral Age, but, above all others, the Mechanical Age . . . in every outward and inward sense of that word."

The problems that afflict Hawthorne reach out to Sophia. Because he finds in Sophia's leisured home life the values that he misses, he joins that life to his to serve a compensatory function. In another letter he explains that Sophia "must listen to the notes of the birds," because "the rumbling of wheels will be always in my ears." Yet this demand transforms Sophia's life from one of leisure to one of responsibility. He enjoins her: "thy spirit must enjoy a double share of freedom, because thy husband is doomed to be a captive." Sophia's "enjoyment" becomes part of an arithmetical, ledger-keeping process in which it is her "office" to register "the additions" to "our common stock." This quantification of enjoyment is part of what Carlyle meant by "Mechanical."

Carlyle referred in his essay not only to the literal machinery of industrialism but also to the spiritual machinery of commercial organization, which, he argued (like Wordsworth condemning "gross and violent stimulants") had affected even the writing and reading of poetry. When Hawthorne has escaped from the machinery of the city and party patronage, to join in the socialist experiment of Brook Farm, he finds not an integration of his being, but only another split, this time between his true self—the sensitive writer—and the physical demands of agricultural labor. To work in nature is not automatically to achieve an "organic" escape from the mechanical.

To Hawthorne the experience of Brook Farm was "unreal": "The real Me was never an associate of the community; there has been a spectral Appearance there, sounding the horn at day-break, or milking the cows, and hoeing potatoes, and raking hay, toiling and sweating in the sun." He evokes a situation that echoes the world of "Young Goodman Brown," a world in which it was believed that the Devil had power to display "spectres" of those he controlled. The putatively ennobling activities of the farm become demonic. Hawthorne finally discounts as joking his claim that "this Spectre was not thy husband," but Coverdale's narrative of *The Blithedale Romance* depends upon a similar distance from shared communal life, a split between poetic sensibility and daily activity that is a further part of what Carlyle meant by mechanization. The problem is the same at Brook Farm as it was in the customhouse, where Hawthorne wrote to Sophia that a journal of his "whole external life" would be "dry" and "dull," in contrast to what he could also write, a "journal of my inward life throughout the self-same day." The gap between the accounts would challenge belief: "Nobody would think that the same man could live two such different lives simultaneously."

Imagination asserts a wholeness that may be purely imaginary, a fictive compensation for the real fractures that provoke it. The question remains, Is it the same person, or is there no integral identity, only a dispersion among roles that define a self through their relations of difference rather than of similarity? The search in literature for "character" is one response to this problem. So in *The House of the Seven Gables* the daguerrotypist Holgrave, the "artist," has by the age of twenty-two been a country schoolmaster, a salesman in a country store, the political editor of a country newspaper, a peddler, a dentist among factory workers, a supernumerary on a merchant ship, a Fourierist, and a mesmerist. Yet through all these roles, each "taken up with the careless alacrity of an adventurer" and then "thrown aside as carelessly," Holgrave, Hawthorne asserts, "had never lost his identity," and he possesses "his law," which is different from what governs other characters. As opposed to the pain of Hawthorne's split between inner and outer, Holgrave represents a pure triumph of the spiritual, of inner essence over external accident.

If the character Holgrave is a contrast to Hawthorne, Hawthorne's own experience is exacerbated in *The Scarlet Letter*, where Dimmesdale leads a "life of ghastly emptiness" because he has become wholly caught in a split between his "official" role as spiritual leader in the Boston community and the private facts of his responsibility for Hester's adultery. He is unaware of Chillingworth's true relation to him, as the wronged husband of Hester exercising a long, terrible vengeance in the role of physician to Dimmesdale's sick body and soul, and his concealment has been so rigid that he does not know that Hester may still love him, as he discovers he loves her. A community that represses the emotional bases of life by allowing them to be known only within its "iron framework" of law nonetheless responds with excitement and yearning to Dimmesdale's election sermon, which he has achieved through his emotional reintegration. Yet his prophecy of America's future is belied by the customhouse from which Hawthorne begins the book. Once again—in the actual nineteenth century as in the imagined seventeenth century—American politics have disconnected real feeling from public life; the "sentiment" that Webster had summoned to preserve the Union must remain in the heart rather than fuel public debate. *The Scarlet Letter* carries out this agenda by transposing its "psychological romance" into a faraway time, fulfilling the political commandment not to speak of politics. The separate, and better, world of romance helps to support the fragmented world of everyday life, as it also depends on it. This might have been the plot of God to preserve the Union, but it proved otherwise.

This interdependence of romance and everyday marks the relation of "The Custom-House" to "The Scarlet Letter," that is, of the introductory sketch of modern life to the long tale of the seventeenth century with which it shares a book. Because the phrase "the scarlet letter" names both the whole book and one of its parts, "The Custom-House" occupies a space that in its absence would not be recognized as vacant. It adds something that was not required and so complicates the tale that follows. For example, it offers to prove the "authenticity" of the narrative, but it does so by invoking "literary propriety," an appeal to convention rather than a warrant of authenticity. By taking possession through "The Custom-House" of the (physical) scarlet letter as his property, the author of "The Custom-House" personalizes the narrative.

There are many correspondences between the authorial figure of "The Custom-House" and the characters of "The Scarlet Letter." Both Hester in the tale's opening and Hawthorne in the sketch are subjected to disapproval by an imagined crowd of Puritan authorities. Both Dimmesdale in the tale and Hawthorne in the sketch are split by a passionate inner life that is wholly at odds with their "of-

ficial" public position. Both Chillingworth in the tale and Hawthorne in the sketch display prowess as critical analysts of character. These and other resemblances allow readers to justify the
presence of "The Custom-House" by integrating it thematically
with "The Scarlet Letter." Such resemblances, however, also under-
mine the self-sufficiency of "The Scarlet Letter," making the tale an
allegory of the writer's situation in 1850. "The Custom-House"
concludes that the public figure of the "decapitated surveyor"—
Hawthorne in the newspapers—is only "figurative" and that Hawthorne's "real human being" is a "literary man." By the same logic,
the public life of Hester—in the tale—is also only figurative, and its
reality is Hawthorne's literary life.

A recurrent mood of "The Custom-House," emphatic near its
end, is harried dejection, which leads Hawthorne to welcome his
"execution" in the change of political administrations that costs
him his patronage job. It is as if, he explains, a man planning suicide had "the good hap to be murdered." From this mood issues
forth "The Scarlet Letter," only to end where it began, in the mood
of the questions the heartsick women of Massachusetts ask Hester:
"why they were so wretched and what the remedy." From the man
alone in 1850 to the women alone in the seventeenth century, there
is no action that will bring happiness. With luck one will be decapitated, or else, as Hester envisions, "the angel and apostle of the
coming revelation" will appear. The only remedy is patient trust in
the future. "The Scarlet Letter" does, however, propose a specific
source for the misery: Hester's past action, which both found her a
child and lost her its father. Action lies only in the past, feeling in
the present, and hope in the future.

Here *The Scarlet Letter* shows its consonance with the politics of
sentiment that Webster and others proposed as the means to negotiate the threat of disunion over the issue of slavery. Politics is internalized and personalized, and issues are removed from consideration in the public world in which Hawthorne wrote just as they are

in the private world that he wrote about. Hawthorne's critique of the emptiness of life under the eagle of "Uncle Sam" in the custom-house is accurate. "Official" politics have been cut off from anything that might seem real.

Consider a major rhetorical motif of "The Custom-House," the insistence that the gloom of "The Scarlet Letter" stems in part from an act of revolutionary victimization. Hawthorne's loss of his political appointment has "decapitated" him and he now writes as a "politically dead man." This joke hinges on a common hyperbole of the age, that of likening patronage dismissals to acts of French revolutionary terror. Even Franklin Pierce, a man of no linguistic originality, had used the figure in a speech of 1841 that Hawthorne quotes in his *Life*. What makes the phrase jocular is that patronage changes are not "revolution," but carry out the etymologically related action of "rotation" in office: revolutionary principle becomes rotatory patronage. Whether one is in office or out, one is as good as politically dead, for the officeholder, Hawthorne argues, "does not share in the united effort of mankind." Paradoxically then, public office is private. In a polity that allows for no significant action, politics can be only the corrupting hunt for spoils or else a noble, inert, and silent love for the Union.

As mid-nineteenth-century politics became merely office holding and patronage brokering, articulated, speculative passionate intelligence withdrew from the ranks of the Democrats and Whigs. The sketches of "official" character that occupy Hawthorne in the avowedly antipolitical literary practice of "The Custom-House" correspond to his occupation during his maximal political involvement, when after Pierce's election he devoted great energy to helping Pierce assign patronage positions. In the *Life of Pierce*, Hawthorne's claim to authority is his knowledge of "the individual," his capacity to read Pierce's "character" and judge his "motives." This emphasis on character is not the idiosyncrasy of a "literary man." The Whigs on their side ran exactly the same kind of campaign. The

1852 election allowed no issue between the major parties, only personality, although the marginalized Free Soil candidate, John P. Hale, had in fact strongly acted on principle. In 1845, while serving as a Democratic member of Congress from New Hampshire, Hale wrote that he had been "decapitated" when the regular party establishment, led by Pierce, denied him renomination because he opposed the extension of slavery into Texas.

The 1850s proved a turning point in American political history: the Whig party disappeared; the long-time Democratic majority, begun by Andrew Jackson, became a sectionalized and ethnicized minority; the Republicans emerged and ruled for three generations. The Union would shortly split and be reunited by bloody conquest. Slavery was crucial in this transformation, but such changes were unthinkable for the still-dominant established parties, especially during the period between the Compromise of 1850 and the renewal of trouble over the Kansas—Nebraska Act in 1854. This interlude of paralytic calm was the moment of Hawthorne's greatest commitment to writing.

Consensus reigned between the two major parties. The *Life of Pierce* declared that no "great and radical principles are at present in dispute" between the Democrats and the Whigs, but both are "united in one common purpose," that of "preserving our sacred Union." In the politics of the early 1850s, character offered a ground for choice when there were no issues at stake, for Pierce did not undertake to do anything if elected. Hawthorne recognized slavery as potentially divisive: he did not favor slavery; he urged only that nothing be done about it. In the *Life of Pierce* he explained that slavery was

one of those evils which divine Providence does not leave to be remedied by human contrivances, but which, in its own good time, by some means impossible to be anticipated, but of the simplest and easiest operation, when all its uses shall have been fulfilled, it causes to vanish like a dream.

Such a fantasy of evanescence recalls the extinction of Chillingworth after Dimmesdale has escaped him in *The Scarlet Letter*, but it comes even closer to the death of the villain Jaffrey Pyncheon in *The House of the Seven Gables*, like a "defunct nightmare." The key to redemption in *The House of the Seven Gables* is the replacing of all human action, which is guilt ridden, with the beneficent process of nature—in particular, a nature that has been domesticated, in keeping with the book's intense household focus. The dreadful pattern of stasis in the house and repetition in the crimes of its inhabitants is undone by the natural development of Phoebe at her moment of transition from girl to woman.

The point of the plot in *The House of the Seven Gables*, in a drastic transformation of Aristotle, is to erase and undo all action. Just as Holgrave is about to repeat his ancestor's mesmeric possession of a Pyncheon woman, he holds back; instead, he will be united with Phoebe through the natural course of love. So too, the apparent murder of Jaffrey proves to be death by natural causes, and so likewise the death thirty years earlier for which Clifford had been imprisoned. In both cases "a terrible event has, indeed, happened . . . but not through any agency." Even Jaffrey, we learn, had not actively committed any crime in allowing Clifford to be convicted. The long-standing class conflict between owners and workers, Pyncheons and Maules, is mediated through modest marriage. The daughter of the Pyncheons, Phoebe, is herself a housewife rather than a lady waited on by servants; the son of the Maules, Holgrave, is both a radical and an entrepreneur. Together they embody a nation where a small business can lose five dollars or gain a million— all without government interference, social motion regulated by Providence alone. Hawthorne envisaged this logic of romance for America in politics as well. As late as 1863, he wrote to his sister-in-law Elizabeth Peabody that the Civil War would achieve only "by a horrible convulsion" what might otherwise have come by "a gradual and peaceful change," and Sophia Hawthorne echoed her husband's judgment in a letter to a Union general, agreeing with his conviction that "God's law" would surely have removed slavery "without this dreadful convulsive action."

Action is intolerable; character takes its place in the Romantic internalization that moved Shakespeare off the stage and into the book. No longer the traditional Aristotelian one who acts, nor, as in many great novels, one who speaks, a character becomes one who is known. Following the technique he developed in writing his tales, Hawthorne, in his longer works, maintains an extremely high proportion of narration to dialogue, while at the same time abandoning most of the materials—that is, the actions—of traditional narration. In certain ways his fiction technically anticipates that of Gustave Flaubert and Henry James in its emphasis on its characters, as narrated.

Such narrative inquisition takes place within those great changes of the nineteenth century that produced vast new amounts of knowledge about individuals in the social sciences and that exercised vast new powers over individuals in their roles as soldiers and workers. Nevertheless, when the narrative is not social science, but literature, its special concern is to represent as personalized what in fact depended on impersonality. In *The Scarlet Letter* the reader does not penetrate the "interior" of Dimmesdale's "heart" until Chillingworth has led the way there. The relation between the two men more closely anticipates psychoanalysis than it corresponds to any actual medical practice in either the 1850s or the 1640s, and it allows Hawthorne to achieve a powerfully ambivalent fantasy of being perfectly known: the dream of therapeutic intimacy and the nightmare of analytic violation.

Such extremes are no greater than those in "The Custom-House." There Hawthorne's wish to reach "some true relation with his audience" through literature found its demonic counterpart in official life—the stenciled and black-painted name "Hawthorne" that circulates the world on "all kinds of dutiable merchandise." The characters of the name are known and effective, but through no action of Hawthorne's. Yet even as a writer, Hawthorne's signature in the periodical press was valuable to his party, and his appearing in the Democratic-controlled *Salem Advertiser* converted book reviews into political capital. Hawthorne's name circulated in a complex system of exchange that made it worth the party's while to provide him a livelihood and that gave him the character of a Democrat without requiring any act on his part.

Hawthorne's own contradictory situation here may be compared with that of his party, which, in the 1850s, wished to go ahead into the future yet feared losing control over what had already been established. (In contrast to the Democrats' temporal anxiety, the Whigs feared the spatial extension into new territories as a threat to the established Union.) This tension between motion and regulation operates in both the *Life of Pierce* and *The Scarlet Letter.* In the *Life* this tension determines the contradiction between progress and stability that Hawthorne's fiction must resolve. In *The Scarlet Letter* the turn from action to character means that the terms of contradiction emerge in Hawthorne's analysis of what prevents a character from acting—as when Hester tempts Dimmesdale in the forest. Hester's "intellect and heart had their home . . . in desert places, where they roamed as freely as the wild Indian." In contrast, Dimmesdale "had never gone through an experience calculated to lead him beyond the scope of generally received laws," although "in a single instance" he had transgressed one. Hawthorne elaborates, "But this had been a sin of passion, not of principle, nor even purpose." Dimmesdale, "at the head of the social system . . . was only the more trammeled by its regulations, its principles, and even its prejudices." Therefore, "the framework of his order inevitably hemmed him in." Dimmesdale's emotional wavering is structured like Pierce's political trimming: the tension of regulation versus motion that determined the contradiction between stability and the future in the *Life of Pierce* here determines the contradiction between "principle" and "passion" ("e-motion").

The interrelations of principle and passion define a set of possibilities that give meaning to the characters of *The Scarlet Letter* in a way that readers usually expect to be done by the plot. Dimmesdale himself, as noted earlier, is defined by passion without principle; opposed to him is the "iron framework" of Puritanism, principle without passion. Lacking both passion and principle is Chillingworth: he "violated, in cold blood, the sanctity of a human heart" —violation negating principle and cold blood negating passion. At times, however, the text marks Chillingworth with "dark passion," making him a double of Dimmesdale (for they are the two men with claims on Hester). Finally, the combination of passion and principle can be found in the ideal Hester. Readers may construct this figure but then must confront Hawthorne's failure to actualize her in his text, for in most of the book Hester buries her passion and is dominated by ascetic principle, making her a double of the Puritan establishment's "iron framework."

The *Life of Pierce,* in contrast, does not hesitate to offer Pierce as the imaginary mediating figure who combines the future with stability. Pierce's Whig opponent General Winfield Scott shares the value of stability, but he has already done his work; he does not belong to the future. Slavery negates stability, for it threatens the Union, and because slavery is also providentially doomed, the slave South combines the two negatives: instability and no future. Free Soilers and abolitionists point toward a future without slavery, but no less than the slavery they oppose, they too threaten stability.

The organization of (in)action in both romance and biography works through a structure of conflicting values related to the political impasse of the 1850s. The famous ambiguity of Hester's scarlet letter may also be related to the fundamental problems in the 1850s over the meanings of such documents of American life as the Declaration of Independence and the Constitution. The turn to the courts to adjudicate constitutional issues made these documents no less subject to interpretation than was Hester's letter. Recall particularly that "adulterer" or "adultery" is nowhere spelled out in Haw-thorne's text, just as the word "slavery" is nowhere present in the Declaration or in the Constitution. Just as it became necessary for these documents to take on new meanings, and for theories to be developed to justify these meanings, so, as the letter leaves its origi-nal context, it takes on new meanings: "Many people refused to in-terpret the scarlet A by its original significance." Hester plans never to abandon the letter, for while it endures, it will be "transformed into something that should speak a different purport." The letter enters into a career of indeterminacy that allows it to combine the celebratory communal hopes of A for "angel" in the sky after Win-throp's death and the anguished solitary pain of Dimmesdale's *A* in his flesh. The identification of Pearl with the letter further em-phasizes that its meaning must be understood through experience, growth, and development.

Taken back into politics, such an emphasis would follow the de-velopmental conservatism of Edmund Burke and protect the Con-stitution against abolitionists just as Newman had sought to protect Christianity from Protestantism. (Such protection has been a more partisan activity than its authors have intended. Hawthorne himself believed that Protestantism was fundamentally Christian, and good cases have been made that the Constitution is fundamentally anti-slavery.) It denies the need for any tampering innovation and denies also the value of any reductive fixation on the original meaning or intention. The established position during the 1850s was to want things both ways. The Constitution was a document appropriate to guiding America to a better future, for it did not mention slavery; yet in the bad present of the 1850s one had also to recognize the original constitutional "guarantees" of slavery. This double vision preempted action, and in refusing to open itself to the new issues of the day, the system, shared by Jackson and Webster, became a dead letter, even as Hawthorne made it the basis for a new cultural form in the shimmering life of the scarlet *A*.

Hawthorne was aware that his chosen romance writing was a fragile and unreliable mode. Echoing a figure that Coleridge had used in the *Biographia Literaria* to characterize the effect he and Wordsworth had sought in *Lyrical Ballads,* Hawthorne defined the special "medium" of the romance writer as "moonlight, in a familiar room," thus domesticating the emphasis on external nature in Coleridge's "moonlight or sunset diffused over a known and familiar landscape." Yet if his primary tool is the uncanny atmospheric effect—the ordinary made strange by moonshine—nonetheless, the claims for his art are high. I have argued for the attempt to link safely together the present and the future in the *Life of Pierce.* In *The House of Seven Gables,* the task of romance is defined in equally grand and specific terms as "the attempt to connect a bygone time with the very present that is flitting away from us." The persistence of the past and the evanescence of the present teach a lesson that Hawthorne offers while shying away from any too emphatic a "moral" claim. Too obtrusive a moral, like an "iron rod" or a "pin through a butterfly," causes a story to "stiffen in an ungainly and unnatural attitude." Thus between the mobile present of the "novel" and the totally static "moral," the romance again mediates.

These metaphors for his accomplishments and his concerns help to explain some of the major tensions in Hawthorne's long fictions. He focuses on temporal processes: Hester's long penance in *The Scarlet Letter;* the working out over centuries of Maule's curse in *The House of the Seven Gables;* the consequences of bringing together old Moodie's previously separated daughters in *The Blithedale Romance;* the emergence of modern consciousness and conscience in Donatello in *The Marble Faun.* Yet his technique is also strongly oriented to optical presentation, whether of hovering atmospheric, picturesque effects or of allegorical fixities. Hawthorne's temporal concerns emphasize persistence with development. Their effect is not change (although *The Transformation* was the title of the English edition of *The Marble Faun*); rather, it is the unfolding of an essence, in accord with the laws of the human heart. Hawthorne tends to place the decisive moment of origination offstage, away from the main narrative, which itself presents an aftermath. He prefers to stage a "theater," in which things may be contemplated, rather than a drama, in which people do things.

The key figure in Hawthorne's long narratives, in keeping with his theatricality, is the "sensitive spectator," the descendant of his "spiritualized Paul Pry." At times this role is embodied in one of the fictional characters, but more frequently the role names an achievement that the author is implicitly claiming for himself and challenging the reader to match. The "sensitive spectator" is another of the bridging devices by which Hawthorne's romances function. The notion of "sensitive," as referring to sensibility rather than to the physical senses, dates only from the early nineteenth century, with Walter Scott and Washington Irving among the first to use it in this way. By long tradition within its usage, the term had suggested a contrast to the "intellectual" or rational features of humankind. With a force like that of the physical, a force that can leave one "shocked" by some form of powerful "impression" as it acts directly on the "nerves," the psychological aspects of a situation strike the sensitive spectator and provoke response, just as, in a usage beginning in the 1840s, a "sensitive" photographic plate, one that has been properly "prepared," traces the action of something as impalpable as light.

Cooper's Hawkeye looked on a scene to act; in the extreme but exemplary case, for him to see is to kill, by means of his rifle. In the historical panoramas that Bancroft offered in overview of centuries, the act of vision empowers a discriminating judgment that separates the most laudable from the lesser forms of human action. In Douglass's *Narrative*, the vista of boats in the Chesapeake exacerbates the pain of enslavement and further motivates the quest for freedom; and in *The Oregon Trail*, Parkman's acquisitive vision dominates the Indian's mystical vision. Dana and Melville criticized the position of overview in favor of that of the involved participant. Closest to Hawthorne's "sensitive spectator" are the narrators of local sketches and tales, who offer a norm that is shared with the reader and set against the poor, weak, comic, or provincial "others" that so typically are the objects of narration. In Hawthorne's romances, he maintains the sketch's distance from the narrated characters and its closeness to the reader, while the social level of the scene rises somewhat, and the tightly focused vision of the sketch is generalized by its extension over a full-length narrative.

In *The Scarlet Letter* the sensitive spectator is invoked importantly early and late in the book to guide readers' responses to Hester. Within a page of Hester's first appearance in the tale, the narrator describes her and her effect on the assembled viewers as she emerges from prison with her baby and her letter. Those who "had expected to behold her dimmed and obscured by a disastrous cloud" were instead "astonished" by "how her beauty shone out, and made a halo of the misfortune and ignominy in which she was enveloped." Against this outer view, however, "to a sensitive observer, there was something exquisitely painful in it." The sensitive observer grasps the essence of inner experience, unlike the crowd that remains spiritually hostile to Hester even if awed by her beauty and the splendor of her embroidery.

In contrast to the splendor, with its hidden pain, of this opening scene, in the final sequence of the narrative Hester appears "familiar" to the crowd, her coarse gray clothing "making her fade personally out of sight and outline." Her face resembles a "mask," or "the frozen calmness of a dead woman's features," because Hester no longer has any "claim of sympathy" on her world. Against the crowd, a "spiritual seer" might find in Hester the resolve to "convert what had so long been agony into a kind of triumph," as she plans to escape with Dimmesdale. Having "first read the heart," this "preternaturally gifted observer" could then afterwards have "sought a corresponding development in the countenance and mien" and thereby have "detected" in her expression something "unseen before." In an Emersonian movement of compensation, the sensitive spectator responds to the absent and contrary features of a face or context, feeling the pain in bravery and the triumph in humility that together make Hester a reconciliation of opposites, embodying the power Coleridge had attributed to the imagination.

In *The House of the Seven Gables* a similar complexity is established through play on the figure of the sensitive spectator with regard to the House itself. After the long easterly storm, during which Jaffrey Pyncheon has died in the House, the weather finally dawns bright and beautiful. In presenting the House in this new light, Hawthorne first invokes the figure of "any passerby," who might wrongly surmise from the "external appearance" that the history of the House must be "decorous and happy." Even a "person of imaginative temperament," who would give a second look and become "conscious of something deeper than he saw" might still imagine that the House bore an ancestral "blessing," rather than the curse around which the book revolves. One feature in particular would "take root in the imaginative observer's memory"—the great "tuft of flowers" called "Alice's Posies," which "only a week ago" would have seemed "weeds." This image of beneficent natural process suggests that perhaps there is indeed a more positive heritage from the past than the apparently unrelieved evil on which the book has dwelt.

The "common observer," who watches an Italian street organist playing outside the House, expects only an "amusing" scene when the door opens; but "to us," that is, the reader and the narrator, "who know the inner heart of the Seven Gables" as well as its "exterior face," there is a "ghastly effect" in the contrast between the frivolity outside and the corpse within. Yet even stronger than "our" knowledge is the power of imaginative observation, which has perceived the beauty of Alice's Posies and recognized, even in the history of crime, the Utopian potential that motivates the book's end.

The Blithedale Romance highlights the complexities of spectatorship in its narrative structure. Departing from his usual technique, Hawthorne experiments with a first-person narrator. The materials of the narrative are also unusually close to Hawthorne's own life, for "Blithedale" is transparently a version of Brook Farm, and Miles Coverdale, the narrator, is a literary artist. Consequently, some readers have been fascinated by the possible autobiographical dimensions of the work, while others have been eager to argue that the apparent events of the work instead reflect Coverdale's distorted perceptions. The book itself invites this line of analysis, because it delays until its very last words "Miles Coverdale's Confession." Coverdale reveals a secret that puts into a new light all that has gone on and that he has recounted. He has been in love with Priscilla, the mysterious young seamstress. Because the action of the book has involved Priscilla's love for the obsessive philanthropist Hollingsworth and Hollingsworth's rejection of the passionate feminist intellectual Zenobia, who commits suicide, the revelation calls into question all that has gone on before. The "confession" also explains the bitterly ironic tone that at times inflects the narrative, for Coverdale seeks to distance himself from the pain of lost love, which has made his later years increasingly barren and frustrated.

Miles Coverdale himself is the primary sensitive spectator in *The Blithedale Romance*. (Priscilla's special sensitivities are not combined with the spectator's distance but are rather part of a more complex vulnerability.) Coverdale offers contradictory descriptions of his role. At one point he criticizes himself for "making my prey of other people's individualities," which would make him hardly any different from the more assertively egotistic Hollingsworth. But only a few pages earlier, Coverdale observed that he would have done something only "had I been as hard-hearted as I sometimes thought." His spectatorship compromises his relation to the community at Blithedale. He often retreats to his "observatory," a hidden nook up in a tree. Its isolation and secrecy, he thought, "symbolized my individuality." From its aerial distance, however, everything going on at Blithedale "looks ridiculous." Yet his spectatorship also implicates him in the affairs of the others. Returned from Blithedale to Boston, Coverdale finds a post of observation in the third-floor back room of a hotel. Days of watching the "backside of the universe" lead him to reflect that "realities keep in the rear," and soon he sees Zenobia and Priscilla, on the brink of a crucial decision in which he tries to intervene.

Coverdale gives an intricate summary of his position. He reflects that Zenobia

> should have been able to appreciate that quality of the intellect and the heart which impelled me (often against my own will, and to the detriment of my own comfort) to live in other lives, and to endeavor—by generous sympathies, by delicate intuitions, by taking note of things too slight for record, and by bringing my human spirit into manifold accordance with the companions whom God assigned me—to learn the secret which was hidden even from themselves.

In its union of mind and heart, its scrupulous attentiveness, and its quest for the unrevealed, even the unconscious, this self-image presents an ideal of what Hawthorne's narrative and his readers might seek. Yet in *The Blithedale Romance,* this ideal is compromised by its location in a flawed character. Even in this passage, Coverdale's case is obviously exaggerated by the force of defensiveness and desire alike.

Nor in the earlier romances was the "sensitive spectator" a simple matter. In *The Scarlet Letter* Chillingworth is the character who most fully carries out the agenda of penetration into the secrets of others through intimate knowledge, fueled by intuition as much as by science. Still, Chillingworth, however wronged and suffering, is the villain. The covert and malicious, yet institutionally legitimated, surveillance that he carries out on Dimmesdale is echoed, more coarsely, in *The House of Seven Gables,* where Jaffrey Pyncheon searches into "the secrets of your interior" to threaten Clifford with incarceration for lunacy. Although Holgrave is a descendant of the Maules and is implicated in the history of the House, he presents himself only as a "privileged and meet spectator," whose task is to "look on" and "to analyze." Phoebe, however, is distressed that he speaks "as if this old house were a theatre," because "the play costs the performers too much, and the audience is too cold-hearted."

Sensitivity is susceptibility, and such openness may not be part of any warmth. Even "sympathy" may be "nervous," more physiological than spiritual. It does not necessarily convey concern for others, but testifies only to one's capacity to be affected by others' feelings. So Coverdale reflects that his "cold tendency, between instinct and intellect, which made me pry with a speculative interest into people's passions and impulses, appeared to have gone far towards unhumanizing my heart." He fears that "with the power to act in the place of destiny" to help his friends, he has, instead, "resigned them to their fate," as mere "figures on my mental stage."

The power to harm by distance, the uncaring irresponsibility that refuses to act on knowledge, may be distinguished from another dangerous power, what, in *The House of Seven Gables,* Hawthorne calls the power of the "sadly gifted eye" of a "seer." Faced with the "tall and stately edifice" of character presented to the outside world by a hypocrite like Jaffrey, this seer's power of vision causes the "whole structure" to melt "into thin air," until all that remains is the evidence of the original, hidden crime: "the hidden nook, the bolted closet . . . or the deadly hole under the pavement, and the decaying corpse within." Reminiscent of the archeological metaphors so dear to Freud in his theory of unconscious repression, this figurative language also echoes that of the household of the Union so common in the political rhetoric of the 1850s. It seems an extraordinary instance of Hawthorne's own motivated unconsciousness that he never registers an awareness that slavery might be a founding crime that vitiates the glories of the national structure built upon it.

Hawthorne's fiction does not challenge the political order, yet there are respects in which it stands against its age. The power of his hesitant stylistic effects to undo the reality of what they describe, as the seer unsees the reality of the edifice, provoked one reviewer to complain, "We want the result, and not the process. . . . We want *things*." Because a book is a marketable commodity, and therefore itself a thing, are readers entitled to demand that it also contain things? Hawthorne resisted such a demand. Even while he himself was operating within the market system and the whole machinery of business that made half his life seem like no life at all, Hawthorne tried to find a space for freedom in his romances. By highlighting a process of creation that had not yet solidified into things, Hawthorne tried to distinguish imagination from commodity.

The Marble Faun is the book in which these issues are most elaborately turned over, for with three artists among the four main characters, the question of vision and its relation to life is crucial. The mysterious, dark, Miriam displays in a suite of her drawings a "beautiful imagination" that reaches out with "sympathies" of such "force and variety" that she can make art out of the common experiences of womanhood that have, exceptionally, been denied to her. But her sympathetic receptivity is joined with an intimidating acquisitiveness. Faced with the famous painting of Beatrice Cenci (who had been sexually abused by her father and then in retaliation caused his death), Miriam exclaims, "If I only could get within her consciousness!"

The young American Hilda is not an original artist, but a copyist. Nonetheless, the "depth of sympathy" by which Hilda operates allows her to achieve "what the great master had conceived in his imagination" but had failed thoroughly to execute. Other copyists "work . . . entirely from the outside" and "only reproduce the surface." They leave out "that indefinable nothing, that inestimable something, that constitutes the life and soul through which the picture gets its immortality." Hilda, in contrast, is "no such machine." She intuits her way into "following precisely the same process . . . through which the original painter had trodden to the development of his idea."

Fully equal in sensitivity to the artist is the Italian naïf Donatello, whose roots in the countryside link him to both cultural antiquity and natural vitality. He loves Miriam and he hates her persecutor, the mysterious Capuchin; when the Capuchin menaces her, Donatello hurls him off the Tarpeian Rock. He explains, "I did what your eyes bade me do, when I asked them with mine." This dialogue of the eyes proves the true love between the couple, yet it is proved in a surge of hatred and its criminal response. The sensitive spectator, when not an artist but a person of no reflective consciousness, may prove a dangerous agent, as Hawthorne shows in this terrifying fantasia on a cliché of ordinary social exchange, the scornful woman's "killing glance." Hilda accidentally comes upon the scene just as it occurs, and "that look" from Miriam to Donatello, like "a flash of lightning," fixes itself in her memory and shatters her moral repose. The look is not only deadly but also contagious, when it is seen with responsive sympathy.

Finally the whole action of *The Marble Faun* and the fates of its characters are controlled by a system of politically regulated surveillance, a vision more powerful in its effects than even the artists' and lovers' exchanges of glances. The secret police of the Roman government have Miriam under control: "Free and self-controlled as she appeared, her every movement was watched and investigated far more thoroughly by the priestly rulers than by her dearest friends." The artists' exchanges of vision are one figure within the book for the artistic power of the author's imaginative sympathy, but the figure of state control offers an alternative. It acknowledges the writer's total command in shaping form and inventing incident, even while he tries to give the form and the event the spontaneity of nature.

There is a further force at play in this sequence, still another coercive spectator. Hawthorne's "Postscript" explaining the police plot was added to the second English printing of the book, after reviewers had complained about the lack of resolution in the original ending. Hawthorne had hoped to justify his procedure by arguing that narrative is itself a dubious and tenuous enterprise. Narratives require beginnings, ends, causes, and connections; in contrast, "the actual experience of even the most ordinary life is full of events that never explain themselves, either as regards their origin or their tendency." Hawthorne does not deny that things happen ("events"), but they are inexplicable, and therefore "any narrative of human action and adventures—whether we call it history or romance—is certain to be a fragile handiwork." Readers did not accept this excuse. As he acknowledged, "everybody" was dissatisfied, and so he made the change, invoking the quasi-historical narrative of state agency to provide origin and tendency. Yet he also asserted, "For my own part, however, I should prefer the book as it now stands." The romance enacts a compromise. Hawthorne may give the appearance of being "free and self-controlled" as an artist, but his conceptions are under surveillance by a powerful readership whose demands he must meet. Hawthorne's revision attributes to politics (the secret police) responsibility for what is actually a matter of economics (his audience), but elsewhere in the book he does focus attention on the economic conditions of artistic production.

Hawthorne explains that "a sculptor in these days has very little to do" with the "process of actually chiselling the marble," for there are Italian artisans who can take any object placed "before their eyes" and reproduce it in marble with consummate "mechanical skill." If the artist but gives them the model, at the appointed time, "without the necessity of his touching the work with his own finger," he will discover the statue from which his fame will spring: "His creative power has wrought it with a word." Hawthorne becomes sarcastic about the sculptor's fortune in avoiding "the drudgery of actual performance." The sculptor's apparently magical potency actually unmakes him, for his works are "not his work," when they derive from "some nameless machine in human shape."

The Romantic theory of art, by its emphasis on the spiritual, the "creative," has itself become another crippling split, reminiscent of Hawthorne's need for Sophia to double her investments in pleasure while he worked. The image of artistic wholeness does not wholly cover the division of labor on which it depends as a business. The establishment of literary narrative made possible the dream of an autonomous world of art and pleasure, which proved however to depend on economic and political conditions that produced misery at the personal, local, and national levels. Hawthorne's romances powerfully proclaim the separation of art from life and also show that such separation is impossible. Even as it was becoming established as a relatively autonomous practice and institution, literature was at once more powerful than it feared and more responsible than it wished.

Moby-Dick

In dedicating *Moby-Dick* to Nathaniel Hawthorne, "in token of my admiration for his genius," Herman Melville announced that after the failure of *Mardi* and the successes of *Redburn* and *White-Jacket* he was again writing literary narrative. The special power of this particular literary narrative is its voracious capacity to swallow many other forms and kinds, beginning with the learned "Etymology" and "Extracts" that launch the book from the library and place it in a world history stretching back to Genesis. The generic basis of *Moby-Dick* is personal narrative, like so much of Melville's earlier work, but Melville pushed beyond its limits. In a letter to his

English publisher, Bentley, Melville boasted of "the author's own personal experience of two years and more as a harpooneer," but he had never been one. In *Moby-Dick,* as he had done in his earlier personal narratives, Melville freely supplemented his own experience with relevant books, both of whaling and about whales.

As the narrative begins, the most immediate signals are those of local sketch writing. Since 1830, with the "Jack Downing" sketches by Seba Smith, "Down East" humor about Yankees had paralleled the popularity of southwestern humor. One frequent mark of these Yankee characters was an outlandish biblical name. "Call me Ishmael" becomes richly suggestive, but it begins as the name of a grimly comic, self-mocking narrator who introduces the reader to odd happenings in the life of the shoreside whaling community. The "damp drizzly November" in Ishmael's soul joins him to a line of hypochondriac periodical writers. The basic form of *Moby-Dick* follows that of Thorpe's "Big Bear of Arkansas." Each frames a story about the most astonishing hunter of the most amazing animal. Yet the immensely greater size of *Moby-Dick* breaks the generic mold, and its resemblance to two different kinds of local narrative suggests that it can properly belong to neither.

National narrative was the established large form of the time, and it often demonstrated its national scope by taking in the characteristic narratives of various locales, as Prescott suggested that Bancroft did. Melville, in *Moby-Dick,* as he had earlier in *White-Jacket,* strikes key notes from the prevailing rhetoric of America. The claim for human equality helps to justify treating the mates and harpooneers of the whaler the *Pequod* as characters capable of tragedy, even though they are workers, not nobles. The narrative calls upon the "great democratic God," who granted literary immortality to Cervantes the pauper and Bunyan the convict and who placed "Andrew Jackson . . . higher than a throne!" As with Bancroft and Tocqueville, national narrative extends to the global. Playing "Advocate" for the glory of whaling, Ishmael boasts of "the whaleman who first broke through the jealous policy of the Spanish crown" concerning the Pacific colonies of South America. He explains that "from those whalemen at last eventuated the liberation of Peru, Chili, and Bolivia from the yoke of Old Spain," which made possible "the establishment of the eternal democracy."

Without Ahab, *Moby-Dick* would not be a literary narrative. Ahab hijacks national narrative by leading the *Pequod,* which in many ways has been made representative of America, into disaster, disrupting the genre's triumphalism. As a tragic hero, modeled on Shakespeare's, Ahab fulfills the Romantic program for the literary. Yet without Ishmael, Ahab could not achieve his tragic stature. The dramatically styled speeches of Ahab require the narrative contextualization and speculative interpretation provided by Ishmael as sensitive spectator. This suggests a combination of Shakespeare and Hawthorne, which Melville first sketched in "Hawthorne and His Mosses," written in early August 1850, just after he met Hawthorne. By October, Melville had moved from New York to the Berkshires, where he could frequently visit Hawthorne while working on *Moby-Dick*.

The slim documentary evidence indicates that Melville had begun *Moby-Dick* in early 1850, after returning in February from some months abroad. By May he wrote to Dana that he was half done with "the whaling voyage," and in early August, Evert Duyckinck, who was with Melville in the Berkshires, wrote back to New York that the work was "mostly done." Yet *Moby-Dick* was not actually completed for another year. It seems that the experience of meeting Hawthorne provoked Melville to imagine a new level of ambition. He articulated this ambition in "Hawthorne and His Mosses," and he then determined to revise his romance-in-progress to try to reach the goal of matching Shakespeare's tragic power with an American work.

The encounter with Hawthorne may have catalyzed Melville's aspirations, but already in the letter to Dana he anticipated that he was writing "a strange sort of a book." He vowed that he would include not only the "truth" of whaling but also the "poetry." *Truth and Poetry* was the title of Goethe's autobiography, which was one of a cluster of important works of Romantic literature that Melville had bought and read during his trip abroad. It appears that before he met Hawthorne, Melville had been trying to create through his reading an imagined literary community that did not exist in the America of his time. His purchases in England form a catalogue of important Romantic writers and the works that the Romantics admired. Besides the Goethe book, he acquired the works of Charles Lamb, *Confessions of an English Opium-Eater* (1822), by Thomas De Quincey, and Mary Shelley's *Frankenstein* (1818), as well as volumes of Renaissance drama (which Lamb particularly had highlighted), and he read with great excitement Laurence Sterne's strange, innovative *Tristram Shandy* (1760–7). Moreover, on that trip he participated in many intense conversations on "metaphysics," on "Hegel, Schlegel, Kant & c," with George Adler, the German-born philologist, whose philosophy Melville described as "Coleridgean," as he might have recognized from reading the previous year in his then newly acquired copy of the *Biographia Literaria*.

By importing the techniques of Shakespeare into a novel, Melville echoes the ambition and encounters the problems of Goethe's *Wilhelm Meister's Apprenticeship* (1796) which he borrowed while he was writing *Moby-Dick*. Goethe's novel inaugurated the tradition of the *Bildungsroman*, which focuses on the formation of a character. The action that shapes Wilhelm revolves around his aspiration to bring *Hamlet* to the German stage. Goethe deepens the way character figures in the novel by drawing on the play of Shakespeare that had most impressed readers with the mysterious depth of its central character. Within *Wilhelm Meister*, Goethe put forward important speculations about the novel as a genre in contrast to drama. In drama, the emphasis falls on the "deeds" of "characters"; in novels, "it is chiefly sentiments and events that are exhibited." The hero of drama actively presses forward to hasten the end, but "the novel hero must be suffering," or at least "retarding": by whatever means, "the sentiments of the hero . . . must restrain the tendency of the whole to unfold itself and to conclude." This theory justifies Goethe's choice *of Hamlet*, because it makes *Hamlet* seem a novelistic drama. *Moby-Dick*, however, is a dramatically inflected novel. While Ahab actively presses forward, Ishmael's sentiments and reflections keep the book from ending too fast.

Friedrich Schlegel's "Letter on the Novel" (1799) builds from Goethe's work to a somewhat different end. For Schlegel, the difference between drama and novel depends on the place that the work occupies in its social setting: plays are meant to be "viewed," and novels are "for reading." In contrast, then, to Shakespeare's plays, Schelegel defines a novel (in German, *Roman*) as "a romantic book." The key term "romance," discussed earlier, takes some of its force from this context. For Schlegel, a novel gains unity not from its plot, but through a central focus on thematic or conceptual materials. This "higher unity" allows a novel to be formally a "mixture," incorporating "storytelling, song, and other forms." The novel has the privilege that Schlegel in his most famous critical statement reserves to "Romantic poetry" (*romantische Poesie*, which might also be translated "novelistic poesis"): to "mix and fuse" all divergent types so as to become the only "kind of poetry . . . that is more than a kind."

Moby-Dick, as a work of literary narrative that incorporates national, local, and personal generic elements under this dominance, as a "romantic book," is a novel *(Roman)*, and, as a novel, it is liable to problems concerning the status of action in its hero. Ishmael goes to sea to evade suicide by submitting himself to a regimen that frees him from the need for self-regulation. Rich and various as are the activities that engross him throughout the book, they all are therapy rather than action. Ishmael is repeatedly healed or purged. Queequeg cures him of misanthropy; the "Mast-Head" chapter warns against his speculative excess; the "Try-Works" teaches him the danger of gloomy obsession; and at the end of the book, "tossed" overboard, "dropped" astern, and "buoyed" by Queequeg's coffin, he is "picked up." Only insofar as he acts as the book's writer, and insofar as the action of the novel is that it is being written, does Ishmael perform an action. This literary action, however, has precisely the force of its differentiation from all other kinds of action available in the culture. Thomas Carlyle, whose pages on Shakespeare were echoed by Melville in "Hawthorne and His Mosses," had lamented in *Heroes and Hero-Worship* that the modern writer has "importance" only for the book trade. Otherwise, "He is an accident in society. He wanders like a wild Ishmaelite."

In contrast to Ishmael, Ahab is modeled on tragic heroes, and the passionate power of his quest seems an obvious source of action, providing direction rather than wandering. Yet his revenge is really a reaction. "I will dismember my dismemberer," Ahab proclaims. The overall movement of the book seriously compromises the status of his action. In its broadest structure, the plot is a satire on human impotence: St. George comes up to the dragon, and it does him in; there is really no contest. Melville emphasizes this pattern in many ways in the climactic chase sequence. Ahab is presented as the greatest of all whale-hunters; he actually finds the whale by "snuffing" like a dog, rather than requiring all the elaborate paraphernalia of technology that he has ostentatiously stripped away. As the chase begins, in his eagerness to locate the whale that he has already sensed, Ahab cries out after it, "flattening his face to the sky." This image of intensity and eagerness is cast down into humiliation after the whale, without even being harpooned, has caught Ahab's whaleboat by surprise and held it between his jaws, while Ahab, trying to get free, "fell flat-faced upon the sea."

The same reversal of intended agency into passivity occurs between the description of Ahab's initial approach to the whale and the conclusion of the whale's toying with the whaleboat. First, the boats approached the whale, and the "breathless hunter [that is, Ahab] came so nigh his seemingly unsuspecting prey, that his entire dazzling hump was distinctly visible." (Note the transfer that carries "his" over from Ahab to the whale.) But then, after the whale has caught the boat by surprise, "Ripplingly withdrawing from his prey, Moby Dick now lay at a little distance." The same phrase, "his . . . prey," has reversed its direction. Ahab is the whale's prey.

Melville's writing in *Moby-Dick* produces extraordinary entanglements for action, not only on the large scale of genre but also in the local procedure of particular passages. After Ahab first appears to the crew on "The Quarter-Deck" and exhorts them to join his mission of revenge, there follows a series of chapters that in their formal variety and complexity register Ahab's disruptive effect within the texture of the book. "Sunset" trumpets the model of Shakespeare. Its prose is metered to imitate blank verse, and it represents the speech of Ahab to himself alone, a soliloquy. This explodes the personal narrative. How could Ishmael report what Ahab says to himself? The next two chapters play off soliloquies by the mates, earnest Starbuck and jolly Stubb. "Midnight, Forecastle" is written as a stage scene involving all the crew in drunken talk and revelry. It looks back to the "Walpurgisnacht" of Goethe's *Faust* and forward to "night town" in Joyce's *Ulysses*. Following this chaos, Ishmael broods reflectively for two chapters, explaining to the reader what Moby Dick meant to Ahab and then what "The Whiteness of the Whale" meant to Ishmael himself.

"The Chart" follows these chapters. Ahab is poring over the technical charts whale-hunters used to predict where and when to find whales, but the chapter shows that something in Ahab cannot so rationally be accounted for. Ahab's will is a force that breaks apart his individuality, and therefore it is very difficult to determine who, or what, is responsible for things that happen. One extraordinary sentence charts both Ahab's "spiritual" struggle and Ishmael's struggle to grasp what is going on:

> Often, when forced from his hammock by exhausting and intolerably vivid dreams of the night, which, resuming his own intense thoughts through the day, carried them on amid a clashing of phrensies, and whirled them round and round in his blazing brain, till the very throbbing of his life-spot became insufferable anguish; and when, as was sometimes the case, these spiritual throes in him heaved his being up from its base, and a chasm seemed opening in him, from which forked flames and lightnings shot up, and accursed fiends beckoned him to leap down among them; when this hell in himself yawned beneath him, a wild cry would be heard through the ship; and with glaring eyes Ahab would burst from his state room, as though escaping from a bed that was on fire.

Carrying "hell in himself" like Satan in Milton's *Paradise Lost,* Ahab's interior is a broken landscape. He does not securely possess himself; he is "forced" by "dreams of the night," which usurp his "own intense thoughts." He proves even more complex, as Ishmael elaborates on the mode of agency that may have produced this spectacle of Ahab bursting into sight. "Crazy Ahab" the "steadfast hunter," this "Ahab that had gone to his hammock" was "not the agent that so caused him to burst from it in horror again." Ahab has split into two parts, an active "agent" and an acted-upon "him."

Ishmael explains that the "agent" is the "principle or soul." In sleep it is freed from the "characterizing mind," which otherwise "employed it for its outer vehicle or agent." This instrumental sense of "agent" opposes the motivating force that is being described, so that, it seems, the soul is now free to act as agent because it is not forced to serve as agent. Ishmael's metaphysical fantasia speculates further: "The tormented spirit that glared out of bodily eyes when what seemed Ahab rushed from his room, was for the time but a vacated thing." Ahab is not Ahab, for the "thing" if still frantic is now "vacated." The individual has been further divided. The self-created being is "formless," because if the soul has fled, the mind no longer has an "object" to shape through its "characterizing" power. Moreover, the being has no consciousness; it is "somnambulistic," because sleep is required for the psychic fissioning that in turn creates new elements. Ahab's pure will is a "blankness" like the horrifying "Whiteness of the Whale" that Ishmael had just analyzed and like the "blank" spaces on the chart that Ahab himself is painstakingly filling in at the beginning of this chapter.

To summarize Ishmael's analysis: when Ahab burst out "as though escaping from a bed that was on fire," he is not the agent. Instead, his soul is the agent, for its "escape from the scorching contiguity" of the mind has triggered the process by which pure will flares up, from which the body tries vainly to flee, thus projecting into visibility the simulacrum of Ahab. The "outer vehicle" of the body transports the "tormented spirit"; nonetheless, the body is not agent of the spirit, for in carrying the will out of the stateroom, it is not carrying out the will's will.

These involuted paradoxes of agency bring fully into literature a major theme from Romantic philosophy, particularly from Coleridge's *Biographia Literaria*. In "The Whiteness of the Whale," Coleridge is specifically mentioned, and the chapter is concerned with the need for "imagination," which is the major topic of the *Biographia*. In this chapter, whiteness is twice characterized as an "agent." Once whiteness is designated as "prime agent," the phrase Coleridge had reserved in the *Biographia* for his fundamental definition of the "primary imagination." In the second reference, whiteness is called an "intensifying agent." The word "intensifying" was a coinage of the *Biographia*, as Coleridge boasted in a footnote. It occurs in a sentence about the will, following a paragraph about the imagination, in a chapter that asserts the need for an active theory of mind against the passive mechanism that Coleridge found in eighteenth-century psychological theory. Coleridge criticizes this theory because it leaves no room for the soul as a "real separate being." Any effects that might be attributed to the soul are instead "produced by an agency independent and alien." Coleridge fears the alienation of agency, that is, the dispossession of a proper identity with the dispersal of soul, will, and self.

Melville does not share Coleridge's confidence in the relations between the soul and the will. Instead he works out a case—which "The Chart" lays out in its microscopic form—in which the real separability of the soul does not do as much good as Coleridge hoped and in which the independent, alien agency is constructed in considerable elaboration. To mock the mechanical theory, Coleridge proposed a hyperbolic reduction of the act of writing, in which "the whole universe co-operates to produce the minutest stroke of every letter, save only that I myself, and I alone, have nothing to do with it . . . for it is the mere motion of my muscles and nerves." Coleridge hoped his readers would reject such a conception, but Ahab cries out with full feeling, "Is Ahab, Ahab? Is it I, God, or who, that lifts this arm?"

Moby Dick, the whale itself, at every moment reminds readers that agency cannot be confined to human form or to human control. *Moby-Dick* explores the uncertain borders of agency. Things happen, but it remains a question how. Hawthorne argued in *The Marble Faun* that events might fall within ordinary human experience and yet not be explicable in relation to their origins or tendencies. The whale may be partially predictable as to time and place, but it is not known where it comes from or where it is going. To write a book that centered on the whale, rather than on its hunters, would go far beyond human powers of narrative, and yet even a narrative that merely includes Moby Dick shows that human individuality cannot account for the way the world works. In *Moby-Dick,* individuality is neither a goal nor a premise. At best, it is a puzzling possibility.

Issues of action, agent, and responsibility are first highlighted in "The Quarter-Deck." Behind the "pasteboard masks" of all "visible objects," Ahab seeks a subject, "some unknown but still reasoning thing" that may be surmised through its effects in "each event—in the living act, the undoubted deed." This "inscrutable thing," hidden behind the "wall" of the "whale," yet, to Ahab's sight, "sinewing it" with "malice," he seeks to reach, but his only access is through the whale. Therefore, "be the white whale agent, or be the white whale principal, I will wreak that hate upon him." Ahab denies the possibility of blasphemy, which Starbuck has warned against, because he denies hierarchy: "Who's over me?"

Ahab's stance points in two directions to the America in which Melville was writing. His pseudoutopian democratic promise—there is none above him, and he is not ruling the crew, but they are "one and all with" him in the enterprise—engages the political theory of John Calhoun. Calhoun argued that the southern states were made up not of "individuals," but of "communities": "Every plantation is a little community, with the master at its head, who concentrates in himself the united interests of capital and labor, of which he is the common representative." This organic model echoes the key term of Romantic aesthetics: all interests will be "harmonized." Yet "labor" here meant slaves, so Starbuck's critique of Ahab takes on even more force: "a democrat to all above; look, how he lords it over all below!"

Ahab's interpretation of agency as equality—his willingness to take the subordinate, the "agent," as responsible in place of the "principal," the master or owner—was not unique. It was shared by the American culture then reshaping itself to mobilize resources for the enormous industrial expansion that had followed the depression of 1837. In Ahab, coexisting with the residual political position of Calhoun, is an emergent legal position that began from railroad cases around 1840 and dominated the later nineteenth century. Ahab's multiple figurations are not all archaic: he is also cast in the language of modernity. In his "Sunset" soliloquy, Ahab identifies himself with the railroad: "the path to my fixed purpose is laid with iron rails." This figure of titanic will may seem to fit with Calhoun's "master," but there is another side to the railroad. Railroads were a notably impersonal system of employment. No American occupation had more employees who were less likely to have direct acquaintance, even by sight, with their employer. And the railroad image suits the whale as well as it does Ahab. The regularity of the whale's rate of travel resembles that of "the mighty iron Leviathan of the modern railway." This nonhuman force reduces humans to equality and shatters the system of representation that structured the relations of master to servant, principal to agent.

A whole new area of law, the law of torts, grew up to deal with railroad injuries, and, later, with factory injuries. For industrial expansion brought industrial accidents, and railroads were the scene and means of tremendous human damage. In common-law tradition, a "principal" was responsible for any damages done or caused by that principal's agent, slave, servant or other member of the household, or employee. In the new law, this "rule of agency" did not apply. Instead, a doctrine known as the "fellow-servant rule" held that an employee (servant, agent) could not sue the employer (master, principal) for injuries suffered through the negligence of another employee (a fellow servant), or "co-agent." The net effect of this was to protect corporations for decades from liability for much of the immense misery they caused. The judge who wrote the key decision (1842) in this area was Chief Justice Lemuel Shaw of Massachusetts, Melville's father-in-law.

The emergence of the American literature that readers still recognize today, the novel or the romance *(Roman)* as practiced by Hawthorne and Melville, is connected with the political crisis of the mid-nineteenth century, a situation of which Emerson could write, "Men live on the defensive, and go through life without an action, without one overt act, one initiated action." As argued earlier, the Compromise of 1850 defined political responsibility as regulation —preserving the Union—rather than as motion—extending freedom to the disadvantaged within the Union. Urgent questions of how best to share newly produced goods as well as new obligations were displaced from the electoral arena to the legal system, and the courts ultimately defined economic responsibility as motion—extending enterprise—rather than as regulation—preserving common-law protections.

Politics thus centered on the fiction of identity of the Union, but economics undid the "fiction of identity" (as Oliver Wendell Holmes, Jr. later called it) that had subordinated agents to principals. The new law multiplied the number of individuals who had no relations with each other other than those of contractual equality. These newly emergent individuals had little scope for action, however; they were "free agents" in a most restricted sense. The national consensus held that there was nothing to be done politically, and one's responsibility was to be silent; whatever was done economically was understood simply to have happened, and one's responsibility was to be patient, that is, to not take action, for injuries were not actionable. This consensus was not total. The movement against slavery stood emphatically outside it. *Uncle Tom's Cabin,* like *Moby-Dick,* drew on national, local, and personal narrative materials; and it emphasized not political change, but moral transformation. Nevertheless, it did not define itself as literary narrative, for it clearly engaged the shared world of its readers and did not make action a problem. *Uncle Tom's Cabin* was a polemically alternative national narrative.

Literary narrative offered a place to be heard separate from politics and only partially subordinated to the economy, but this privilege came at the cost of acknowledging literature as fiction, that is, as saying nothing that bore on the shared public world in the way that national, local, and personal narratives had done. To be thus outside partisan politics is to give ground in hope of finding a transcendent alternative. That is, the literary work acts as a one-way valve, drawing the materials of the world into its own world, from which they do not return. This is the effect of Ishmael's complex literary mediation. This literary compromise, a diminishment in the scope of the writer's action, may be seen also in the book itself, as Ahab's failure to achieve individual agency. In this particular American form of the generic problem of action in the novel, what marks and mars Ahab is also what places *Moby-Dick* in its moment.

In contrast to Hawthorne's romances, which hew closely to a conservative line of political quietism and thus shift attention from action to the "sensitive spectator," *Moby-Dick* more closely approaches the transformative energies of the economy and therefore places action as a problem in the foreground. Ahab most strongly asserts his individuality precisely at the moments that he is challenged by the impersonal structures of the economy. Rhetorically, he seizes that impersonality as freedom from hierarchy. When on "The Quarter-Deck" Starbuck challenges Ahab, "How many barrels will thy vengeance yield thee? . . . it will not fetch thee much in our Nantucket market," Ahab's response is to cut free from the question of "agent" or "principal," to proclaim that there is no power over himself, not even the invisible hand of the market: "But not my master, man, is even that fair play." In cutting off the "superior," the "principal," the "master," or the owner from responsibility for the injury caused one agent by another, courts transformed "servants," "agents," workers into individuals, even as they were also becoming "hands." Ahab offers a heroic fantasy—both nostalgic and critical—of such individuality. When Starbuck later challenges Ahab for the second time on economic grounds, he invokes the absent owners. Ahab rises to the challenge by applying an argument from John Locke that had once helped to make the American Revolution, "The only real owner of anything is its commander." This individuality has often impressed readers as the book's accomplishment.

Yet the complexity *of Moby-Dick* demonstrates, both in its overall shape and through the particular language of meditative moments, that such individuality cannot be sustained. As the nine-teenth century went on, however, an ever more intense rhetoric of individuality paralleled the unprecedented growth of corporations. Ahab dies asserting that "Ahab is for ever Ahab," but Ishmael has, for example in "The Chart," speculatively shown what Ahab does not know, the complex, alien causality that produces "what seemed Ahab." Or, as Ishmael also puts it, "That before living agent, now became the living instrument." Ahab's individual agency keeps col-lapsing into instrumentality or impotence because things happen on a scale—intrapsychic fission, cetacean power, an absent and irre-sponsible hierarchy of ownership—that is not commensurate with human individuality.

The writer's isolation as individual artist, cut off from the collec-tivity of local and national, and even personal, narratives, made possible the achievement of literary narrative in creating an alterna-tive world. However, the political and economic pressures that lim-ited the power of literary narrative to imagine action produced for-mal tensions that puzzled most readers, who were not fully content with the supplemental interpretive energy of the sensitive spectator. Amidst the political and economic crises from the mid-1850s into the Civil War and Reconstruction, readers and writers alike began to doubt the experiment of literary narrative, and national narra-tive returned to the fore.

5

Crisis of Literary Narrative and Consolidation of National Narrative

National Narrative in 1851

The Compromise of 1850 had displaced politics and opened a possibility for the literary narratives of Hawthorne and Melville, but in the years before the Civil War, American national narrative still flourished. Volumes 4 through 8 of Bancroft's *History of the United States* appeared from 1852 through 1860, and in 1851 *Moby-Dick* made far less of an impact than did two works that had adapted national narrative to establish careers for their authors which would outshine Melville's through the rest of the century: Harriet Beecher Stowe began serial publication of *Uncle Tom's Cabin* in the Washington abolitionist journal the *National Era,* and Francis Parkman published *The History of the Conspiracy of Pontiac.* Like *Moby-Dick,* both these works are on a large scale. They range broadly over the geography of North America, and they encompass a wide range of human experience, including shocking extremities of horror. Like *Moby-Dick,* too, they present problems that arise from the multiracial character of the United States, from its colonial past into the present. Their commitment to national narrative, as opposed to the subordination of national to literary narrative in *Moby-Dick,* may be gauged most readily through their narrative technique. They establish no fictional intermediary like Ishmael; rather, they encourage readers to identify the narrating presence with the author, who in each case holds a clear ideological position on issues of major national consequence.

In a letter to Hawthorne commenting on *The House of the Seven Gables,* which Hawthorne had just given him, Melville strikingly images the autonomy both he and Hawthorne associated with what I have been calling literary narrative. Hawthorne has caught a "certain tragic phase of humanity," which may be found in "human thought in its own unbiassed, native, and pro-founder workings." This "intense" exploration of the "mind" reveals what Melville calls "visible truth": "the apprehension of the absolute condition of present things as they strike the eye of the man who fears them not, though they do their worst to him." Such a man enjoys radical independence: "like Russia or the British Empire," he "declares himself a sovereign nature (in himself), amid the powers of heaven, hell, and earth." More solidly individual than anything Ahab achieved, this fearless, masculine vision makes possible the "grand truth about Nathaniel Hawthorne": "He says NO! in thunder; but the Devil himself cannot make him say *yes.*" The brave truth tellers who say no are "unincumbered," traveling through life with only their "Ego," but "all men who say *yes,* lie."

As American national narratives, *Uncle Tom's Cabin* and *The Conspiracy of Pontiac* would seem to Melville bound to a fundamental affirmation that compromises their power, even though each also exercises a powerful negation. Stowe redefined national narrative to oppose the compromised American consensus of 1850 that the Union required silence about slavery. Parkman challenged what he considered the idealization of Indians fostered by Cooper's national narrative. Even though the lives of Pontiac and Uncle Tom end terribly and might therefore be understood in Melville's terms as "tragic," neither work emphasizes the workings of "thought" or focuses intensely on the "mind." Parkman's elaborate renderings of settings, strategies, and events and Stowe's close attention to the details of regional speech and the fluxes of feeling might both seem external and conventional compared to the original, internalized profundity Melville found in Shakespeare and Hawthorne and sought to achieve for himself.

Different as they both are from *Moby-Dick, Uncle Tom's Cabin* and *The Conspiracy of Pontiac* also differ from each other. Their divergences demonstrate, in the same way as had William Hickling Prescott's approval of Bancroft, that national narrative covered a very broad ground, which made it hard for Hawthorne or Melville to maintain a place apart. Both Parkman and Stowe were children of New England ministers, but Lyman Beecher came from working-class, rural Connecticut, while Francis Parkman, Sr., was born to Boston wealth. Furthermore, Beecher was a fiercely orthodox Calvinist and Parkman one of the first for whom Unitarianism was already an established option. Each child turned away from the parent's direction—Stowe from fear of predestination to hope of universal love, and Parkman from bland optimism to severe struggle. The chosen sites for their narrations were the camp fire for Parkman and the home fire for Stowe. Parkman helped to form a national elite audience that prided itself on its tough, masculine strength. In his last years, he received the dedication of Theodore Roosevelt's *The Winning of the West* (1889–96). Stowe reached beyond the United States, and beyond the mass audience of women that were the base of her readership, so that in *What Is Art?* (1898) the great Russian novelist Leo Tolstoy could prefer *Uncle Tom's Cabin* to *King Lear*, opposing the century-long tendency to value the "literary."

The Conspiracy of Pontiac was the first fruit of the huge historical project that Parkman had formed in his youth and that had motivated his encounters with Indians narrated in *The Oregon Trail*. On his return from his trip west, Parkman suffered a physical collapse that all but totally incapacitated him for the next eighteen years. Nonetheless, after dictating *The Oregon Trail*, he began work on his history, employing the method perfected by Prescott, who was almost blind. Documents were read aloud to him, and by means of a mechanical device to guide his hands, Parkman wrote drafts in a darkened room without using his eyes. Parkman's theme of heroic struggle against natural obstacles strangely echoed his own situation of work, and his earlier periods of intense out-of-doors activity energized his representations of what others had done that he could do no longer.

Although Parkman was not yet thirty years old when *The Conspiracy of Pontiac* was published, the work, from its opening words, achieves the tone of authority, as it declares the meaning for North America of the British triumph over France in the Seven Years' War (French and Indian War, 1754–60):

> The conquest of Canada was an event of momentous consequence in American history. It changed the political aspect of the continent, prepared a way for the independence of the British colonies, rescued the vast tracts of the interior from the rule of military despotism, and gave them, eventually, to the keeping of an ordered democracy. Yet to the red natives of the soil its results were wholly disastrous.

Parkman details several resources for his authority—his research in archival materials, his first-hand knowledge of Indian life, and his personal investigation of "the sites of all the principal events recorded in the narrative." Moreover, his dedication of the volumes to President Jared Sparks of Harvard signals not only his authoritative institutional connections but also his command of the documentary and antiquarian basis for American historical research that Sparks had notably helped to establish.

Parkman's greatest authority is unacknowledged, however. The knowledge Parkman draws on in his opening, and which focuses his whole narrative through the seven further books that completed his history over the rest of the century, comes neither from the past nor from his personal experience: it is knowledge of the future. As part of the teleology of American "independence" and "democracy," he "aims to portray the American forest and the American Indian at the period when both received their final doom." In contrast to his knowledge, the Indians' "ignorance" leads them to their "desperate effort" to struggle against "the doom of the race," which "no human power could avert." Although Indians and forest survive, unacknowledged, at the time Parkman is writing, his prophetic frame of understanding is the American destiny to rule and civilize the continent. Parkman drew inspiration from Cooper and Bancroft, although he found each insufficiently severe within the outlines of the national narrative that all three shared.

Parkman takes on a pious responsibility toward the doomed peoples and landscape of the past. Pontiac (c. 1720–69) was chief of the Ottawa; his "conspiracy" was an attempt in 1760 to coordinate Indian resistance to British rule, uniting Indian groups across the whole western frontier. This "great and daring champion" led the Indians in their last possible moment of conceivably successful resistance, yet the story of this "heroism and endurance" lies "buried." Parkman seeks to "rescue it from oblivion." He must not only recover the story, however, but also improve it; his task is not only conservative but also progressive. Once encountered, the historical material takes on the shape of a savage landscape, "uncultured and unreclaimed." In order to "build" his book, Parkman must carry out "labour . . . like that of the border settler, who . . . must fell the forest-trees, burn the undergrowth, clear the ground, and hew the fallen trunks to due proportion." Parkman's labor of writing repeats the work of the settler, but this means that with every stroke of his pen he reenacts the doom of the forest at the same time that he is restoring it to knowledge. This paradox derives from Parkman's understanding of his social and cultural position. As a white American, he stands as the opposite to the Indian: "there is nothing progressive in the rigid, inflexible nature of an Indian. He will not open his mind to the idea of improvement." A white American is sufficiently flexible to respond to the Indian way of life, but the Indian is too pure to make use of what Cooper called white "gifts."

The Conspiracy of Pontiac draws strength and interest from the opportunity its subject presented: an event of world-historical significance, still recent enough to permit the gathering of oral traditions and radically different in character from the subjects of British and European historiography. The New World renewed its subject: "In America war assumed a new and striking aspect." Parkman was freed from the "old battle-ground of Europe," where "the same familiar features of violence and horror" were repeated from "former generations." Unlike the more pacific Bancroft, but much like Cooper, Parkman found in America not freedom from violence and horror, but a stirring freshness in horrors. The "western paradise" of America "is not free from the curse of Adam"; rather, its "wilderness" forms a "sublime arena," where "army met army under the shadows of primeval woods."

The setting, the "land thus prodigal of good and evil," figures more constantly in the narrative than any single character, for this warfare was widely dispersed over the frontier. Moreover, there was not really adequate documentation to allow Pontiac consistently to play the central role of "savage hero of this dark forest tragedy," the "Satan of this forest paradise," that Parkman at times rhetorically announces. This structural inconsistency points also to an inconsistency in the organization of the book's values. To imagine Pontiac as satanic corrupter is both to grant a purity to the wilderness and to enforce a distinction between the Indian and the wilderness that at other moments is denied. For the land is "not free from the curse of Adam," and the Indian is one with the land. At the climax of his first chapter, a long introduction to Indian life and character, Parkman defines the Indian as inseparable from the forest, the "irreclaimable son of the wilderness, the child who will not be weaned from the breast of his rugged mother."

Parkman never overcomes his triumphal, civilized contempt for Indians, and he never overcomes his fascination with the lost wildness they embody. His imagery is not stable; it shifts from one side to the other of the opposed forces. It is part of the Indians' doom, for example, that they are not flexible: "the Indian is hewn out of a rock"; yet they are doomed precisely because their futile ignorant revolt opposes "the rock-like strength of the Anglo-Saxon." At one point the massacre of a schoolmaster and nine pupils by Indians is proclaimed "an outrage . . . unmatched, in its fiend-like atrocity, through all the annals of the war." Yet it turns out that the savages are not unmatched. A white man named Owens, who has lived and married among the Indians, returns to civilization, after slaughtering his wife and children and several other Indian companions, to be rewarded with the bounty offered for each Indian scalp. Parkman finds this "one of many" cases in which "the worst acts of Indian ferocity have been thrown into shade by the enormities of white barbarians."

Both for such atrocities and for the large theme of the Indians' doom, Parkman's history is more "tragic" than Bancroft's, and Parkman disparages the "sentimental philanthropy" that might imagine a better or different outcome. Parkman relies fully as much as does Bancroft on the American narrative of destiny, but he is less happy with it, less able to soften past horrors by reference to present or future glories. Civilization, for Parkman, is the fate of American whites no less than it is of American Indians. At the end of Parkman's work, Pontiac, after the author has resurrected him, is again buried (on the site of present-day St. Louis, Missouri). The contrast between 1769 when Pontiac was murdered and 1851 rings with irony: "Neither mound nor tablet marked the burial-place of Pontiac. For a mausoleum, a city has risen above the forest hero; and the race whom he hated with such burning rancour trample with unceasing footsteps over his forgotten grave."

Against the ironic closure that ends *The Conspiracy of Pontiac,*

Uncle Tom's Cabin reaches out into an open future. Pontiac lies forgotten and dishonored, but the cabin in Kentucky from which Tom is sold early in the book stands at the very end as a memorial. The emancipationist son of the slaveowner who has sold Tom exhorts the freed blacks who had known and loved Tom: "Think of your freedom, every time you see UNCLE TOM'S CABIN." This last chapter of the fictional narration is entitled "The Liberator," echoing the title of William Lloyd Garrison's abolitionist journal, founded over twenty years earlier. The chapter title joins under a single description both the master who frees the slaves and Tom, the slave whose example of love and resistance frees that master from the system that supports slavery. Christ as the liberator of souls stands in turn as the model for Tom's actions.

As a theory of history, Christianity is often understood to be closed, because it anticipates the end of time in the apocalypse, and the social-scientific beliefs that support Parkman's version of national narrative are understood to be open, because the progress of civilization has no definite term. *The Conspiracy of Pontiac,* however, is more "closed" than *Uncle Tom's Cabin.* Parkman's national assurances about the relations of race and civilization place the Indians' doom beyond the reach of human alteration. In some senses the past is always beyond alteration, but for Parkman there was never a chance that Pontiac might have succeeded. Stowe, however, looks toward the future, and she understands that future as being formed through present human choice and action. She renews the radical potential within Christianity.

Stowe's "Concluding Remarks" turn from her completed fiction to the ongoing historical existence of the Union. Her last words warn of "the wrath of Almighty God," but her message is that it is not too late for "this Union to be saved" through "repentance, justice and mercy." The last chapter of *Uncle Tom's Cabin,* as already noted, ends by repeating the words of the title. In this respect Stowe comes close to Hawthorne, for the titular domicile of *The House of the Seven Gables* serves as the last words of Hawthorne's romance. Stowe, however, does not rest content with the aesthetic closure of literary narrative, by which, in thinking of the edifice, readers think too of the book that invented it and bears its name. The last chapter done, Stowe begins the supplementary "Concluding Remarks" with the issue that Hawthorne's preface was meant to disarm. She says many correspondents have written to inquire "whether this narrative is a true one." No less than Parkman's history, Stowe's novel claims the authority of truth, not of imagination. Different as they are, both speak to the nation of its destiny.

In order to achieve her national address, Stowe had an exceptionally difficult rhetorical task, for she began by writing in a partisan journal on the most explosively divisive issue of the day, one that had been barred from discussion within the national consensus. Once it had been published as a book, *Uncle Tom's Cabin* set a new standard for the sale of fiction, and it is especially notable that its popularity flourished also in the South, despite attempts to ban it there. The fascinating and powerful Civil War diary of Mary Boykin Chesnut from the South Carolina plantation aristocracy contains many references to *Uncle Tom's Cabin* as a provocation for thought about the realities of life with slaves. Stowe's act of cultural daring proved that there was more room in the national consensus than the established political parties allowed, and her example helped in the renewal of free-soil agitation and in the formation of the Republican party, which set the terms of national narrative for the rest of the century. Yet Stowe herself followed a resolutely antipolitical strategy. In reaching out as she did to address "Farmers of Massachusetts," "men of New York," "ye of the wide prairie states," "noble-minded men and women, of the South," Stowe built on the fundamental connection that she had established with her readership, not as legislators or even as voters, but as "mothers of

America." Women's exclusion from politics made it possible to address, through them, the politically forbidden issue in a nonpolitical way.

In the segregation of activities and values by gender in the nineteenth century, the male specializations of economic and political life were distinguished from the woman's "sphere" of the home, where the values of the "human" resided. Stowe's chapter that most focuses the technique of the book as a whole is entitled "In Which It Appears that a Senator Is but a Man." This title could appear in a satirical work, showing a high-talking political idealist taking a bribe ("man" connoting human weakness) or even taking sexual advantage ("man" connoting the simultaneous moral vulnerability and social power of the masculine gender). Stowe's reduction of "Senator" to "man," however, is not destructive but, it appears, improving. Face-to-face, caring responsibility replaces abstract legalism, as the Ohio state senator, who has participated in legislation forbidding assistance to fugitive slaves, nonetheless assists Eliza and her baby in their escape. As a politician, he had criticized the "sentimental weakness" of those who would threaten the Union for a few wretched fugitives, but "the magic of the real presence of distress" converts him—as, Stowe adds, it has also led many southerners themselves to assist runaways, "in Kentucky, as in Mississippi."

This transformation of political man to common humanity takes place through the power, called "influence," of women. The senator's wife, already disposed to sympathy, is fully won over when Eliza asks her, "Ma'am . . . have you ever lost a child?" Death here, unlike in Parkman's wilderness, opens connections, between present and past and between person and person. Across barriers of class, race, and gender, we "feel but one sorrow." This powerful theme and technique of "Union" distinguishes *Uncle Tom's Cabin* from Garrisonian abolitionism, which judged the Constitution an unholy compromise with slavery.

Stowe's revision of politics into humanity also affects the story of

George Harris, whose conventionally masculine escape and armed resistance are contrasted to Tom's conventionally feminine Christian quietism, even in resistance. The American revolutionary value of liberty energizes George. He begins by throwing in the face of southern whites their "Fourth-of-July speeches" that proclaim values belied by his condition as a slave, and he himself abandons America to seek liberty. Stowe meditates on his situation: "Liberty—electric word! . . . Is there anything more in it than a name—a rhetorical flourish? . . . To your fathers, freedom was the right of a nation to be a nation. To [George Harris] it is the right of a man to be a man." She rephrases the collective political rights as individual human rights.

As part of her national narrative strategy, Stowe takes special care not to give undue privilege to New England. Simon Legree, the villain who has Tom beaten to death on his plantation on the Red River frontier, comes from New England. Even more important for establishing Stowe's position, however, is Miss Ophelia from Vermont, who is cousin to St. Clare, Tom's good master in New Orleans. Miss Ophelia is ideologically an abolitionist, but at first she lacks human understanding and warmth. Neither being a Yankee nor being a woman makes her immediately able to do what for Stowe is the one thing needed for ending slavery: to *feel right.*

Miss Ophelia does not speak for Stowe in an early conversation with her cousin, when she declares, "This is perfectly horrible! you ought to be ashamed of yourselves." Her pharisaical righteousness is compromised by an earlier exchange in which she reveals that she could not imagine any white person, let alone herself, kissing a black person. As she undertakes the care of Topsy, she thinks that her "prejudice against Negroes" can remain hidden, even though she "could never bear to have that child touch" her. Only the death of little Eva breaks through to Miss Ophelia's feelings sufficiently to make it possible for her to love Topsy, and her commitment to that love takes a shocking form. In order to save Topsy from slavery,

Ophelia must first become her owner, so as then to take her north and free her. To learn what real abolitionism might be like, as opposed to the well-meaning complacencies of even liberal New England, Ophelia must experience not only personal, emotional relations to blacks, but also legal, institutional relations to slavery.

Miss Ophelia insists on having the papers for Topsy at once, "because now is the only time there ever is to do a thing in." As a result, after St. Clare's shocking, sudden accidental death, Topsy is the only slave to escape the breaking up of his household, in which Tom is sold to Legree. Despite his good intentions, St. Clare "hated the present tense of action." In St. Clare's ironic wit, anguished sensibility, and paralyzed self-contempt, Stowe severely yet sympathetically criticizes the sensitive spectator so fundamental to Hawthorne's literary narrative. "Instead of being actor and regenerator," St. Clare has deepened his interiority. In his inner self, he is a nay-sayer, but the cost of his autonomy is that he is a "natural spectator" in the life of his society. The course of events terribly bears out Miss Ophelia's conviction that "it is impossible for a person who does no good not to do harm."

Stowe's work stands in a long tradition of activist sentimentality. Commenting on a fictionalized version of Nat Turner in *Dred* (1856), Stowe observes that "under all systems of despotism," the Bible "always" has been "prolific of insurrectionary movements." From the first days of Christianity, the claim for valuable human feeling and spiritual dignity among the wretched of the earth had been felt as a challenge to the powers that ruled, even when as in Stowe, following Jesus' teachings, care was taken to indicate a political disengagement. In the generation after Stowe, Friedrich Nietzsche's analysis of "ascetic ideals" in his *Genealogy of Morals* (1887) traces the story, to him distasteful, of how "slave" morality from the time of St. Paul had achieved a reversal of hierarchy, so that first in the later days of the Roman Empire, and then again in the history of the modern West, "master" morality was marginalized, and in its place reigned democratic humanitarianism. Somehow the weak had triumphed over the strong. Feelings were not the only tactic, but they had played their part.

In the eighteenth century the rise of sentimental fiction and drama was understood by both sides as a challenge posed by newly emergent social groups against the values and position of the traditional elite. The greatest international success was Samuel Richardson's epistolary novel *Clarissa* (1748), in which Lovelace, a landed aristocrat, rapes Clarissa, a gentlewoman of a commercial family, whom he might have married. The outcome is disastrous for him, but a tragic, yet exemplary, moral triumph for her. In the *Key* (1853), published to document her portrayal of slavery in *Uncle Tom's Cabin*, Stowe refers to Laurence Sterne and Charles Dickens, significant English predecessors in the practice of sentimental writing that its readers understood to have social consequences. The effect she ascribes to Dickens is one that she sought to achieve with her own writing of "Life among the Lowly," as *Uncle Tom's Cabin* was subtitled: "the writings of Dickens awoke in noble and aristocratic bosoms the sense of a common humanity with the lowly." In contrast, the falsely sentimental Marie St. Clare demands that her own feelings as woman and mother be respected but cannot believe the same applies to her slave: "Mammy couldn't have the feelings that I should."

In the nineteenth century the groups that had earlier polemicized from feeling, having gained many of their goals, began to harden themselves. Malthusian demographics, laissez-faire economics, and what became known as Social Darwinism but which already appears in Parkman, all required resisting the appeals of what Parkman called "sentimental philanthropy." If *to feel* may seem weak, however, *not to feel* may seem brutal, and feeling was not utterly abandoned by the new ruling class. Feeling was segregated to the domestic sphere. Stowe's tactic was to bring this honored, but marginalized, value more powerfully into play, keeping alive a notion of "humanity" that included women as well as people of all classes and races.

In its original periodical publication, the subtitle for *Uncle Tom's Cabin* had been "The Man Who Was a Thing." Just as the "Lowly" in the final subtitle signals that the book is sentimental, this first version signals the systematic dimension of Stowe's analysis. Stowe's national rhetorical appeal emphasizes that southerners are as individuals no worse than northerners. As the problem with Miss Ophelia suggests, white southerners may even be more humane than northern whites in personal relations with blacks. The other side of this individual exculpation is national guilt: slavery exists as it does because it is part of a whole structure of commerce, law, and religion that defines the Union as it is. The religious subordination of slave to master, the legal denial of rights, and the commerce in bodies combine to make people "living property." By this process an institution that, if it were truly "patriarchal," might be tolerable is opened to the worst of abuses, which are held in check only by the decency of individuals. The existing system offers no protection against such a man as Legree; even public opinion cannot reach the owner of an isolated plantation. Although Legree is a spiritually haunted villain, it is essential to Stowe's design that he speak the language of market rationality: "I don't go for saving niggers. Use up, and buy more . . . makes you less trouble, and I'm quite sure it comes cheaper in the end."

When Tom is brutally beaten, he is thrown among economic refuse: "pieces of broken machinery, piles of damaged cotton." The closer the system approaches optimal market rationality in the economic understanding of the times, the more brutal it will become: "no tie, no duty, no relation, however sacred," can hold when "compared with money." This is the power of the "cash-nexus," which Thomas Carlyle had decried in *Past and Present* (1843) and which Karl Marx and Friedrich Engels analyzed in the *Communist*

Manifesto (1848). In the very opening pages of *Uncle Tom's Cabin,*
as Tom's master first discusses selling him, he explains to the slave
trader his reluctance in terms that powerfully evoke the tension between an organic and an economic sense of relation: "I don't like
parting with any of my hands." As a worker, a person is a hand, but
readers may also register the sense of hand as member of the body,
and the sentence then images a dreadful self-mutilation. Through
membership in the body of Christ, Stowe wishes to restore this sense.

Stowe's radical Christianity is also at issue in the twentieth-century African-American response to her novel. "Uncle Tom" has become the derogatory term for a submissively loyal or servile black.
The term is first recorded in 1922, used by the African American labor activist A. Philip Randolph, who is contrasting it to the "New
Negro," and there can be no doubt that the model of George's secular liberation may be more appealing. Yet current usages degrade
the "Uncle Tom" far more than Stowe ever did. Stowe's Uncle Tom
does not shuffle, clown, pull his forelock, or otherwise try to ingra-
tiate himself, as do those now called Uncle Toms. He repeatedly refuses to escape, but always in order to benefit other black people,
and his death culminates a protracted struggle to resist Legree. This
is how Stowe defines it in the *Key* and how the book shows it.
Stowe's hypothesis of nonviolent resistance stands with that of her
contemporary Henry David Thoreau and with the twentieth-century attempts to carry out such a strategy, from Gandhi to Martin
Luther King, Jr.

Uncle Tom's Echoes

Uncle Tom's Cabin helped to establish the audience and conventions for the best-selling sentimental fiction, and it also acted powerfully on the local, personal, and literary narratives that continued
to be produced in the decade after its publication. The path-break-

ing local narrative "Life in the Iron Mills" (1861) by Rebecca Harding Davis; the major woman's personal narrative of slavery, *Incidents in the Life of a Slave Girl, Written by Herself* (1861), by Harriet A. Jacobs; many of the revisions Frederick Douglass made in the 1855 edition of his narrative, *My Bondage and My Freedom;* and even Herman Melville's literary narrative *Pierre* (1852), all bear traces of their authors' engagement with Stowe's work.

"Life in the Iron Mills," the extraordinarily successful first publication of its thirty-year-old author, appeared in the *Atlantic Monthly* just as the Civil War was beginning in April 1861. The unnamed locale of the story is modeled on Davis's home, Wheeling, Virginia (now West Virginia), but Davis displaced attention from slavery, which existed there, to what was becoming widely understood as wage slavery, as, for example, in George Fitzhugh's prosouthern polemic *Cannibals All! or Slaves Without Masters* (1857). Davis renewed the local narrative sketch through the resources of the social-problem writing on "life among the lowly" that Stowe had pioneered but which had also been much practiced in England. In *Mary Barton* (1848), set among the textile mill workers of Manchester, the English writer Elizabeth Gaskell had preceded Stowe in developing the stance of earnest Christian sympathy that a concerned middle-class woman would feel for fellow human souls, whose miseries the existing political structure had no will to remedy. Not only in her attention to urban industrial workers but also in a crucial structural respect, Davis is closer to Gaskell than to Stowe: both *Mary Barton* and "Life in the Iron Mills" organize their plots around the legal process provoked by a worker's crime against an economic superior.

The work of an ambitious young writer often particularly illuminates the ethos of a literary institution. Founded in 1857 and edited from 1861 by Hawthorne's publisher James Fields, the *Atlantic Monthly* had serialized Stowe's New England historical fiction *The Minister's Wooing* (1859), while in these years the most consistent presence in its pages was Dr. Oliver Wendell Holmes, professor of medicine, essayist, and novelist. Davis's story appeals to a reader concerned with both art and social problems, at once urbane like Holmes, speculative like Hawthorne, and earnest like Stowe. It is a difficult feat, and it is hard to imagine Davis's accomplishing it without the model of "George Eliot" (Mary Ann Evans), whose works, themselves influenced by Stowe, had begun to appear in Britain in 1858. Eliot's novel *The Mill on the Floss* (1860) exemplified a narrative capaciousness that could range over high culture, reach out in human sympathy toward lives warped by "the emphasis of need," and sensuously render evocative details of remembered scenes. Like Eliot, but unlike Stowe and Gaskell, Davis mellows her narrative by setting the main action thirty years in the past, even though its interest was still urgent.

The *Atlantic Monthly* reader was more sophisticated than the reader of the *National Era*. Davis addresses her readers not collectively as "mothers" or "farmers," but individually as "amateur psychologist" (the Holmsian cultivated scientist) or as a more transcendentalist, "Egoist, or Pantheist, or Arminian." Although biblical references are as important for Davis as they are for Gaskell and Stowe, considerable further learning is assumed or imputed for her readers, as it is for Eliot's. Davis's story contains phrases in French and Latin and references to Dante, Goethe, and German philosophers. When the machinery is described at work, "the engines sob and shriek like 'gods in pain.'" This perfect line of iambic pentameter ironically alludes to John Keats's erotic medieval romance "The Eve of St. Agnes" (1819): "The music, yearning like a god in pain."

Echoing Richard Henry Dana from *Two Years before the Mast*, the narrator summons the reader: "I want you to hide your disgust, take no heed to your clean clothes, and come right down with me." Yet the narrator remains at a meditative distance, not actively involved like "personal" narrators or, in her different way, like Stowe. The narrator's attitude to the working characters fluctuates

between aesthetic and scientific and is never so fundamentally pas-
sional as in Stowe. They are a "figure," a "type," presenting a
"symptom" to be "read." Above all, Davis demands that readers
"judge" the worker-artist-criminal on whom the story centrally focuses: "Be just—not like man's law, which seizes on one isolated
fact, but like God's judging angel." Stowe would say, rather, "judge
not, lest ye be judged"; the divine mission is to love. Religion in
"Life in the Iron Mills" plays a much less active and potentially
transformative role than is claimed for it in *Mary Barton* or *Uncle
Tom's Cabin*. As in Stowe, there is an idealized Quaker woman, but
in Davis she appears only at the end, to help the working woman
expiate her crime, which has cost her the man she loved. The story
ends with God's "promise of the Dawn," but there seems no possibility of change in this world. Before James Fields, as editor, named
the story, Davis had suggested entitling it "Beyond," clearly differ-
entiating her from Stowe's or Gaskell's belief that religion operates
here and now.

Like religion, art also can offer a "beyond." Davis's alternative
story title was "The Korl-Woman," after the sculpture that the
worker Hugh Wolfe has made from korl, a "refuse" material.
When a group of privileged visitors comes through the mills, it encounters this "nude woman's form, muscular, grown coarse with labor, the powerful limbs instinct with some one poignant longing,"
what the narrator later calls "desperate need." Between the "gentleman" Mitchell and the "artist sense" of Hugh an inarticulate understanding arises, but neither can make anything of it. Mitchell insists that "reform is born of need, not pity," and that therefore it
must come from the oppressed themselves, not from above. Nothing in the story directly questions this circumscription of the notion
of need or suggests that Wolfe may offer something that Mitchell,
and the story's readers, need. Such an ironical reading is possible,
but only against the story's grain.

During the group's discussion around the sculpture, Deborah

("Deb"), a deformed worker who hopelessly loves Hugh, has stolen Mitchell's wallet, and later she gives it to Hugh, to allow him the freedom his poverty has denied him. This is "the crisis" of Hugh's life, and the story asserts that in choosing to keep the money, he "lost the victory." Hugh, we are told, "did not deceive himself"; he acknowledges, "Theft! That was it"; yet he hopes that good can come of it. Instead he is apprehended, sentenced to nineteen years in prison, and commits suicide. The story's power depends on the power of the ruling classes. Only the system of law enforcement allows this work its chosen tragedy. The speculative aesthete Mitchell had in conversation kept aloof from the mill owner's praise for the "American system," but Mitchell in practice adheres to that system by bringing legal charges against Hugh. Although the story is silent on the precise legal proceeding, the structure of the story requires the absolute inevitability of punishment after crime.

No less than Mitchell does, the worker-artist Hugh takes part in the system that has devastated his life. To Mitchell's disgust, the conversation on the "American system" had allowed "money" to appear as "the cure for all the world's diseases." Deb's hearing this has helped impel her to theft, and Hugh's "consciousness of power" from the money tempts him to dream of being "Free!" Art, it seems, can express the "need" for a beyond, and religion can fulfill that need for isolated individuals, but the "American system" is impervious to change. For Stowe, a decade earlier, there was no fictional need to punish people for breaking laws that supported an immoral system; for Horatio Alger, later in the 1860s, Deb's theft would have provided Hugh the chance to get a new start in life by returning the wallet and being rewarded by Mitchell's patronage. Unable to accept either popular agitation or popular fantasy as a solution, Davis, in her dense, complex, and powerful story, precociously sketches an impasse that would preoccupy many of the most serious, self-consciously elite, writers for the rest of the century.

The "crisis" that Harriet Jacobs recounted in her *Incidents in the*

Life of a Slave Girl differs greatly from that which Davis posed for Hugh. Jacobs's choice involved both morality and tactics, but not the law. For her, as for all her fellow fugitives, the absolute condition of freedom was to break the law, usually requiring also the implication of others in crime. The legal protections for slaveholders' property were "the regulations of robbers, who had no rights that I was bound to respect." The long-term happiness of herself and her children would depend on a struggle between two qualitatively different forces: "My master had power and law on his side; I had a determined will. There is might in each." Because she had lived without benefit of law, however, she greatly valued law when it was on her side. While visiting England as a nursemaid, she found even the "poorest poor" agricultural laborers to be better off than "the most favored slaves in America" because there was "no law forbidding them to learn to read and write" and their "very humble" homes were "protected by law." Therefore, sickening as it was to need to buy one's freedom, Jacobs acknowledges that she and her children will never be secure without "all due formalities of law." Her story ends "not in the usual way, with marriage," but instead "with freedom." In order for this to occur, however, Jacobs must first learn news that "struck [her] like a blow," even though it was good news: "So I was *sold* at last!"

Writing as a mother, Jacobs wishes to "arouse the women of the North" to realize the conditions of "two millions" of slave women in the South, still suffering as Jacobs had. Jacobs's personal narrative of testimony occupies the space opened by Stowe's sympathetic report on the vulnerability of parental love under the "patriarchal" institution. Jacobs's story does not end in marriage because she never married, and her shame over her social standing as an unmarried mother was one reason she chose to present her narrative displaced into the fictional identity of "Linda Brent." Despite her being what would conventionally, brutally, have been called a "loose" woman, her narrative shows that the ties of family love were the dominant feature in her life. The most astonishing feature of her story forms a real-life, yet grotesque, perfection of the woman's domestic role, within her own separate sphere. For seven years, while she was thought to have run away to freedom, Jacobs lay hidden in her hometown in the small attic of the house of her grandmother (known as "Aunt Martha"). This terrible confinement was the prerequisite of her liberty.

Jacobs's grandmother was a free black property owner who commanded respect in the small town of Edenton, North Carolina. (Symbolically as the name rings, it is not part of Jacobs's narrative and has only been discovered by modern research.) At a crucial stage in the escape, a white woman who had known the grandmother all her life came forward to hide Jacobs—just as Stowe had surmised that even in the South relations of sisterhood would prevail. Jacobs enjoyed a strong, positive sense of the Edenton community, while she also experienced the vulnerabilities and abuses of slavery. Even in the days of white vigilante terrorism after Nat Turner's rebellion of 1831, Jacobs's household was rightly confident that "we were in the midst of white families who would protect us." Stories were told that the grandmother had once "chased a white gentleman with a pistol, because he had insulted one of her daughters." The grandmother's expectations of sexual propriety offered protection when, from age twelve, Jacobs was subject to sexual harassment from the master of the household in which she lived. Despite her rejecting him and, further, his wife's jealousy, public opinion held him back from the whip: "how often did I rejoice that I lived in a town where all the inhabitants knew each other! If I had been on a remote plantation, or lost among the multitude of a crowded city, I should not be a living woman at this day."

The "crisis" was provoked when "Linda" was fifteen and the doctor set about building a "lonely cottage" where she would live isolated from the eyes and ears of the town and would therefore be helpless against him. The worst of it, according to Linda, was that the doctor was notorious for selling off his "victims," even with "his babies at the breast." At the same time, a sympathetic white gentleman, "educated and eloquent," was paying her attention. Although Linda recognized his interest in her as sexual, she also felt "something akin to freedom in having a lover who has no control over you, except that which he gains by kindness and attachment." This same attachment made it likely that she could "ask to have [their] children well supported." "With these thoughts revolving in [her] mind," Linda chose seduction over rape and "made a head-long plunge." Unlike the "drifting circumstance" by which Davis characterizes Hugh's step into crime, and unlike Hugh's crime itself, which is not so much a transgression as the failure to take restorative action, Linda here makes her choice and goes forward, although painfully. She appeals to the "virtuous reader" for pity and confesses that the "humiliating memory will haunt me to my dying day." Yet she has also achieved an independent standpoint: "Still, in looking back, calmly, on the events of my life, I feel that the slave woman ought not to be judged on the same standard as others."

In *My Bondage and My Freedom,* Frederick Douglass also argues that slave morality demands a different standard. Living under a master who fails to provide sufficient food, Douglass must steal to survive. This bare fact was recorded in the 1845 narrative, but in the 1855 revision, several pages of moral reasoning are added, which conclude, "The morality *of free* society can have no application to *slave* society." If a slave steals, he only "takes his own," and in killing his master, he would "imitate the heroes of the revolution." The reason for Douglass's claim is that "freedom of choice is the essence of all accountability," and therefore by enslaving a person, "you rob him of moral responsibility." This argument does not do justice to what any reader finds to be Douglass's own powers of choice, even in slavery, and to the moral admiration he wins, but as part of an ongoing struggle, it is an important polemical claim. In

Stowe's terms, this is more George Harris than Uncle Tom, and in her *Key* she cites Douglass's 1845 narrative to demonstrate that George's heroism has a basis in reality.

In several important respects Douglass's changes to the work in 1855 brought his narrative much closer to the world of Stowe than his 1845 version had been. In the decade between the versions, he had ceased to be a Garrisonian. He no longer understood the Constitution as a compromise with slavery, but rather as "in its letter and spirit, an anti-slavery instrument." Therefore, he no longer looked to a dissolution of the Union but committed himself to America. No longer prefaced by William Lloyd Garrison and Wendell Phillips, the 1855 narrative is introduced by James McCune Smith, a Scottish-educated black physician. Smith presents Douglass's life story as "an American book, for Americans, in the fullest sense of the idea." Douglass's 1855 work is more unequivocally national than the 1845, and it is also more strongly Christian. Although both versions severely criticize the complicity of American Christianity in slavery, only in 1855 does Douglass speak of his own conversion at age thirteen.

My Bondage and My Freedom resonates with *Uncle Tom's Cabin* in its increased concern with domestic and family issues. The whipping of Douglass's Aunt Esther concludes the first chapter of 1845, some five pages into the work; in 1855 the incident concludes the fifth chapter, over fifty pages on. The tremendous expansion of Douglass's experiences and reflections around his early childhood makes the single largest structural difference between the two versions. In 1845 he merely reports that at first he had "lived with his grandmother." In 1855 the expansion takes on a detail and emotional intensity that may owe as much literarily to Dickens's *David Copperfield* (1850) as it does ideologically to Stowe:

The old cabin, with its rail floor and rail bedsteads up stairs, and its clay floor down stairs . . . and the hole curiously dug in front of the fire-place, beneath which grandmammy placed the sweet potatoes to keep them from the frost, was MY HOME—the only home I ever had; and I loved it, and all connected with it.

In his early youth, before he becomes economically useful, the slave is free to be that emergent icon of America, "a genuine boy." In contrast to 1845, in which the whipping of Aunt Esther marks Douglass's "entrance to the hell of slavery," in 1855 it is his pain at separation from his grandmother, when she leaves him off at the house of "the old master," that becomes his "first introduction to the realities of slavery."

For Douglass in 1855, as for Stowe, the overwhelming reality of slavery was its destruction of the family, its failure in any way to fulfill its "patriarchal" self-presentation. Separating children from their mothers was part of the overall strategy of slavery "to reduce man to a level with the brute." Douglass asserts that slavery succeeds in "obliterating from the mind and heart of the slave, all just ideas of the sacredness *of the family*, as an institution." Only when he was first brought to the old master's house did he meet his brothers and sisters, but he does not understand or feel his relation to them: "I heard the words brother and sister and knew they must mean something, but slavery had robbed these terms of their true meaning." The system of slavery meant that Douglass's "poor mother . . . had *many children*, but NO FAMILY!" In his experience of slavery, there was no "domestic hearth, with its holy lessons and precious endearments."

Yet this cannot be exactly true, based on what he has just reported of life with his grandmother. A contradiction exists between the tremendous, real damage inflicted by systematic oppression and the astonishing resourcefulness that resisted by building relationship and love. This is a textual problem in Douglass and Stowe that is a living, historical problem in contemporary African-American life. By legally prohibiting marriage between slaves, the system,

Douglass argues, "does away with fathers as it does away with families." Then he complicates his statement: "When they *do* exist, they are not the outgrowths of slavery, but are antagonistic to that system." That creative antagonism against all odds remains an example to provoke readers' thought and action.

My Bondage and My Freedom shares Stowe's intense concern with the social bases of affective experience and the structural possibilities for moral education, but Douglass's experience does not support her hopes for the transformative power of face-to-face encounter between human suffering and human decency, at least when both parties are male. As if directly reflecting on Stowe's scene between the Ohio senator and the fugitive Eliza, Douglass revises a crucial episode in his own life. Before the decisive fight, after the slave breaker Covey had brutalized him for the first time, Douglass runs away to appeal to his master. In both versions, the master refuses to intervene despite Douglass's pitiable appearance: "From the crown of my head to my feet, I was covered with blood. My hair was all clotted with dust and blood; my shift was stiff with blood. My legs and feet were torn in sundry places with briers and thorns, and were also covered with blood." The 1855 version of the exchange begins with Stowe's premise: "It was impossible—as I stood before him at the first—for him to seem indifferent." The breakthrough by which a "master" would become a "man" seems imminent: "I distinctly saw his human nature asserting its conviction against the slave system, which made cases like mine *possible.*" What happens then, however, is that "humanity fell before the systematic tyranny of slavery." The master's initial "agitation" is calmed when he gets "*his* turn to talk," and by reiterating the commonplaces of the master class "he soon repressed his feelings and became cold as iron." Douglass implicitly takes issue with Stowe, even as he reshapes his work to make it at once, like *Uncle Tom's Cabin,* national, domestic, and sentimental. He follows with greater success a strategy also tried by Herman Melville.

Published less than a year after *Moby-Dick, Pierre: or, The Ambiguities* (1852) stands apart from Melville's earlier work in its mode of presentation and in the character and setting of its action. *Pierre* is not a personal narrative, even so much as *Mardi* or *Moby-Dick*. It is a third-person narrative primarily concerned with the moral and psychological development of the young man it is named after. It refers to and shapes itself in relation to *Hamlet*, in the literary-narrative mode opened by Goethe's *Wilhelm Meister*, the founding example of the *Bildungsroman*. Melville's first six books had largely exhausted his direct maritime experience, and unlike them, *Pierre* is set at home rather than abroad. It is doubly domestic, for within its American locales, its action springs from and remains within the network of family relations. Like *Uncle Tom's Cabin*, it begins with an apparently happy family that is then put to trials and brought to misery. In its domestic, familial focus, it seems aimed to engage the wider, "feminine" audience that had become defined since the middle forties, when Melville had begun writing, but it failed to satisfy this or any other audience.

Pierre lives in an idealized version of the Berkshire (Massachusetts) countryside, where Melville had moved during the writing of *Moby-Dick*. Pierre's situation draws on elements of the wealthy, civically outstanding families from which Melville was descended on both sides. A national framework is established by references to Indian land conveyances and revolutionary heroism, but these concerns are eclipsed by questions of Pierre's "interior development." Pierre's inheritance is "patriarchal": his grandfather, "grand old Pierre," was "loved" by his "stable slaves" just as "his shepherds loved old Abraham" in the Bible. As in *Hamlet*, but also in *Uncle Tom's Cabin*, the book's action springs from a crisis in patriarchy. Pierre's deceased, revered father, it appears, had fathered a daughter, Isabel, before he was married. The stern, heroic image of old Hamlet and the smiling, lecherous Claudius are suddenly combined. Isabel is now living, unacknowledged, in poverty nearby.

Pierre must decide whether to acknowledge his "dark" sister, whose hand is "hard" with "lonely labor." The color-coding evokes the narratives of slavery, and the social gap between siblings recalls *The Blithedale Romance,* also published this same year, in which Zenobia enjoys luxury while the hands of her sister Priscilla are hardened by labor as a seamstress. The question for Pierre is posed in the language of sentiment. Will he be "cold and selfish" and yield to the "dreary heart-vacancies of the conventional life," or will he choose "God's anointed," "the heart"? Despite her wild curls, Isabel is no "Gorgon." The Gorgon turned people to stone, but Isabel's face could "turn white marble into mother's milk," from conventionally masculine, cold hardness to conventionally feminine, flowing warmth. Pierre chooses the heart, and "thus, in the Enthusiast to Duty, the heaven-begotten Christ is born."

Roughly the first third of the book brings things to this point. Then a different approach to psychology begins to predominate, changing the book's focus, emphasis, and tone. For example, the narrator had earlier acknowledged that Pierre's decision to stand by Isabel was made easier because of her extraordinary, fascinating beauty, but the narrator disclaims any "censorious" intent. Later, however, a sharp distinction is emphasized between the thoughts presented "as Pierre's" and those of the narrator "concerning him." The narrative becomes more analytic and more ironically distanced, no longer claiming to be "magnanimous."

The further Pierre is subjected to individualizing scrutiny, the more ambiguous he becomes. As Pierre begins to glimpse his father's hidden life, he thinks of "two mutually absorbing shapes" that alternate from snake to human in Dante's *Inferno.* Later, at the culmination of an interview between Pierre and Isabel, he kisses her with a passion hardly fraternal: "Then they changed; they coiled together, and entangledly stood mute." Their transformation into joined serpentine coils identifies them with their morally compromised father. A strange speculative pamphlet no sooner read, near the book's middle, than lost, holds out a formula for the resolution of ambiguities, "by their very contradictions they are made to correspond," but its purport remains obscure.

Just like his father, Pierre hides a sexual secret. As he meditates his course of action, he is pained and frightened by the uncharitable rigor his mother reveals in discussing the illegitimate child of a neighboring farm girl. Both for this reason, and also to protect his mother's image of her husband, he determines not to confront her with what he understands to be the facts about Isabel. Moreover, the pointedly named clergyman Falsgrave shows a weak prudence, subservient to social authority, and so offers no alternative moral resource. Nor is the evidence of Isabel's birth sufficient to prove a legal case. In order to grant Isabel full familial honor and equality, Pierre therefore determines to present her to the world as his wife, but this has the effect not so much of raising her as of destroying his social position, as well as devastating his mother and his pale blond fiancée.

The first movement of *Pierre* criticizes the conventional social order, much in the mode of Stowe's radical sentimentality. In the second movement Pierre's "enthusiasm," the gush of spirit that shatters convention, is criticized by the narrator as "infatuated." Without the institutions of family, church, or state to guide and support action, the heart proves weak and dangerous. Pierre acts "without being consciously" aware of the upshot of what he is doing; his actions are oriented by feelings that spring from sources of which he is "unconscious." As in Freud's theory of the unconscious, Melville presents both a dynamic emphasis—the unconscious as an agency, a process of displacement by which things happen—and a topographic emphasis, in which the unconscious can be spatially figured as a place. Gothic figures, such as Poe's favorite topic of premature burial, turn into psychological theory: "as sometimes men are coffined in a trance, being thereby mistaken for dead; so it is possible to bury a tranced grief in the soul, erroneously supposing that it hath no more vitality of suffering"; but the feeling actually survives.

In the worldly psychological perspective associated with Machiavelli or La Rochefoucauld, a debunking analysis of idealism and self-sacrifice, like that enacted in this portion of *Pierre*, contributes to speculation on the dynamics of human life in social and political communities. This tradition accounts in part for Tocqueville's analysis of America. Although Melville also knew and valued such work, Pierre, in contrast, heads into isolation, and the novel offers a topographic play of figures rather than actions. In one of the most significant figures of the topographic unconscious, what a child ignorantly witnesses and overhears remains preserved in memory until certain adult experiences trigger understanding. Once the "key of the cipher" is provided, "how wonderfully, he reads all the obscurest and most obliterate inscriptions he finds in his memory; yea, and rummages himself all over, for still hidden writings to read."

This textualization of the unconscious points to literary narrative as the possible ground for bringing contradictions into correspondence. In the book's third and final movement, Pierre is revealed not only as a reader but also as a writer. He leaves his ancestral Saddle Meadows to start a new life with Isabel, as a writer in New York. Perhaps from Melville's bitterness at the reception of *Moby-Dick*, the New York literary world he had shared with the Duyckincks is severely satirized as "Young America in Literature." After the narrator's attitude toward Pierre has shifted in the second movement, the book's relation to the audience also changes, with a declaration of independence: "I write precisely as I please." In trying to follow the shifting "phases" of Pierre, readers must not hope for the guidance of any "canting showman" of a narrator: "Catch his phases as your insight may." The reader too is granted freedom. Declaring himself sovereign in his intense, tragic exploration of mind, Melville has broken the bonds of the institutions of reading and writing in his time just as Pierre breaks the institutional bonds of his home.

In trying to support himself as a writer, however, Pierre runs athwart of conventions that are just as firm as those at home had been, and even more crippling, because he is more vulnerable and needy. His publishers write, "Sir:—You are a swindler. Upon the pretense of writing a popular novel for us, you have been receiving cash advances from us, while passing through our press the sheets of a blasphemous rhapsody." Something like this was also the situation of Melville, who considered Ahab's diabolic baptism the "motto," but the "secret one," of *Moby-Dick*. "Dollars damn me," he wrote to Hawthorne while composing *Moby-Dick*: "What I feel most moved to write, that is banned,—it will not pay. Yet, altogether, write the *other* way I cannot. So the product is a final hash, and all my books are botches." As the brother and sister coiled together, entangled like lovers, so the satirical analyst and the object of his criticism, the author and character, threaten to merge in the last portion of *Pierre*. The deluded author Pierre, who has "directly plagiarized from his own experiences" in constructing his "apparent author-hero Vivia," becomes an object of pity to his author Melville, even as the plot leads to the final absurdities of murder and suicide.

During this last phase *of Pierre,* Pierre's "ever-present self," the individuality on which nineteenth-century psychology is based, proves unstable, for no thought or action "solely originates" in a single "defined identity." Such instability also challenges the "originality" on which literary narrative depends. The "creative mind" may promise a "latent infiniteness," but as surfaces are peeled away, influences foresworn, the final, central point may be "appallingly vacant." It seems improbable that critics will ever achieve a satisfactory definition of the central meaning of *Pierre* because to its own time, as to modern readers, the book stands as a failure, though now increasingly fascinating. Its central vacancy, it seems clear, was produced through the interaction of conflicting impulses and intentions that exercised their effects at different stages in the largely undocumented process of composition. Nonetheless, the power of literary narrative makes form even out of such absences.

The contradictions are brought into correspondence when Pierre sees a painting. This painting resembles a portrait of his father that had played a key role in making the case for Isabel's parentage, but there is no reason to think that this painting was drawn from his father. It may not even be a portrait at all, but a "pure fancy piece," that is, a work of pure imagination. If there is "no original" here, then Pierre has probably been wrong in trusting Isabel's story on which he has staked their lives, just as he has been wrong to trust in his literary originality. The combination of these two devastating errors prepares him for the final debacle. Ironically, however—and this irony is essential to the book's literary form—because "original" in this usage means "model," its absence would be the strongest testimony to the power of unaided artistic inspiration. Rather than a double loss, then, Pierre has been offered a chance to renew his confidence, but he proves incapable of taking the chance, and because he does not take it, it remains untried, unconsumed by the book's criticism. It betokens the alternative by which Melville as author of the work stands free of his character Pierre, building literary work from fictional disaster.

In reviews and sales, however, *Pierre* was a thorough disaster. Reviewers recognized that Melville was writing more like "Poe and Hawthorne" than he had in his earlier books, and they saw that *Pierre* was a "prose poem," based on a "new theory of art." But the result was judged a "perversion of talent." Like the "abuses" of the "German school," Melville's literary narrative ignored the "ordinary novel reader." The "supersensuousness" of *Pierre* provoked moral outrage, and it was a "dead failure."

Dead Ends for Literary Narrative

The severe setback posed by *Pierre* to Melville's career was especially disturbing because he needed income from his writing. Faced with this failure, after the election of Franklin Pierce, Melville's family and friends, including Hawthorne, worked, finally without success, to gain him a patronage position like that awarded Hawthorne. By the spring of 1853, Melville seems to have produced a new manuscript (never published and now lost), which Harper was not ready to take on so soon after *Pierre*. At the beginning of December, however, the publisher offered Melville an advance for a novel-in-progress on "tortoise-hunting." On December 10, 1853, a devastating fire destroyed Harper's stock of bound books and unbound sheets, including copies of Melville's earlier works that would have brought him about a thousand dollars when sold. For the same reason that Melville would have felt special need of money, Harper felt pinched; they were in no position to go ahead on the project, and Melville never completed it.

By late 1853, Melville was already launched on a new phase of his existence as a writer, as a magazinist. From late 1853 into 1856, when he traveled abroad for eight months, he published fourteen tales and sketches plus a serialized novel in the pages of *Harper's New Monthly Magazine* and *Putnam's Monthly Magazine of American Literature, Science, and Art*. *Harper's* had been founded in 1850 and immediately achieved great popularity by reprinting the most interesting current works of English writers. In contrast, *Putnam's,* founded in 1853, aimed to bring American writers to the fore, as in the previous decade Putnam's American Books series had. Evert Duyckinck was no longer involved in this Putnam American project, however. The editorial group of the new magazine included Charles Briggs, George William Curtis (a friend of Hawthorne's), Parke Godwin, and Frederick Law Olmsted.

Both magazines offered Melville a rate of five dollars per published page, the top rate they paid. Seven short pieces appeared in *Harper's*. *Putnam's* published the novel *Israel Potter*, in nine installments, and seven other pieces, three of which themselves appeared in more than one part: "Bartleby, The Scrivener," "The Encantadas," and "Benito Cereno." Melville thus appeared twenty-one times in the thirty-five monthly issues running from his first contribution to the magazine's termination in the financial crises of 1857. Immediately after its serialization, *Israel Potter* was published by Putnam as a book, and in 1856 Dix and Edwards, successors to Putnam as sponsors of the magazine, published *The Piazza Tales*, which collected the five pieces that had appeared in the magazine to that point. Both *Israel Potter* and *The Piazza Tales* were well reviewed, recouping for Melville the loss of esteem he had suffered after *Pierre*, even if not restoring the prominence he had held by the completion of *White-Jacket*.

After his initial success as a writer of personal narrative, and after his experiments with literary narrative in *Moby-Dick* and *Pierre*, Melville now worked in local narrative, and reviewers recognized his standing with Washington Irving, Edgar Allan Poe, and Nathaniel Hawthorne, who then as now marked the American norm for this kind of writing. Melville used established types: sketches of city characters ("Bartleby, "Jimmy Rose," "The Fiddler"), sketches of country characters ("Cock-A-Doodle-Doodle-Doo!," "The Lightning-Rod Man," "The Happy Failure"), travel sketches ("The Encantadas"), domestic sketches ("The Piazza," "I and My Chimney," "The Apple-Tree Table"), and tales ("The Bell-Tower," "Benito Cereno").

Melville also tried out a new way to achieve the effects of contrast so often essential in sketches. Three pieces are built from the doubled pairing of England and the United States, rich and poor. "Poor Man's Pudding and Rich Man's Crumbs" contrasts the mixed shame and dignity of a poor country family in the United States, neglected by the complacently well-off, with the terrifying

energy of a starving London crowd, maddened by the ostentatiously contemptuous charity of the rich. "The Two Temples" contrasts the stultifying hot air of a fancy society church in New York
with the hot breath of life at a popular theater in London. This
piece was rejected by *Putnam's* for fear of offending the New York
objects of its satire. "The Paradise of Bachelors and the Tartarus of
Maids" contrasts the blissful comfort of a London lawyers' club
with the dreadful misery of American factory "girls" in a moun-
tainside paper mill.

A similar technique of contrast gave a principle for constructing a
volume. The six pieces that make up *Piazza Tales* show off Melville's command of varied modes and locales. As Hawthorne had
introduced his *Mosses from an Old Manse* with a sketch of life in
the Concord Manse, so "The Piazza" (previously unpublished)
opens the volume in a setting like that of Melville's Pittsfield home.
This rustic domesticity is in contrast to the urban homelessness in
the sketch that follows, "Bartleby, The Scrivener," but "The Piazza" had already sounded notes of pathos that "Bartleby" deepens
and complicates. "Benito Cereno" comes next, a tale rather than a
sketch, emphasizing terror more than pity, and set at sea several
generations earlier. Between this long piece and the lengthy "Encantadas" (ten linked sketches of the Galapagos Islands) is placed "The
Lightning-Rod Man," the shortest and lightest piece in the volume,
which returns to the contemporary Berkshire countryside. "The
Encantadas" are meditative rather than touristic. These bleak vol-
canic islands, like "cinders" on the "vacant lot" of the sea, testify to
a "world" that is "fallen." The volume concludes with "The Bell-
Tower," a short tale of far away and long ago, vaguely set in Renaissance Italy, that speculates on technology and death with somewhat the feel of Hawthorne's "Ethan Brand."

"Bartleby, The Scrivener," as first published in *Putnam's,* had
been subtitled "A Story of Wall-Street." Part of the special force of
the story, its narrator thinks, conies from its setting in a "solitary
office," in a "building entirely unhallowed by humanizing domestic

associations." The office building—a structure devoted exclusively to commerce with no residential units—was a relatively new development in American urban life, and it added a third space to a world previously divided between "public street" and "private residence." This encounter of a narrator with the opacity of city misery plays a variation on Hawthorne's "Wakefield"—concerned especially with private residence—and Poe's "The Man of the Crowd" —concerned especially with the public street. Bartleby moves the narrator by his "solitude," the sense he conveys of being "absolutely alone," like Wakefield, who became the "outcast of the universe," and Poe's character, who "refuses to be alone" physically, presumably because of his terrifying inner state.

Each of these three characters fascinates the story's narrator, who struggles to penetrate the character's mystery. Melville, however, differs from Hawthorne and Poe by dramatizing the narrator, making him a character who speaks to the object of mystery rather than simply speculating, as in Hawthorne, or observing, as in Poe. The story thus becomes less metaphysical and more ethical. The narrator asks himself, "What shall I do?" The problem is to find a space for human action between the absurd, pseudopaternalistic claim of the next tenant in the office vacated by the narrator that "you are responsible for the man you left there" and the narrator's equally absurd legalistic response that he is "nothing to me—he is no relation or apprentice of mine." Despite the narrator's character as a "*safe*," prudent lawyer, he is moved by Bartleby. The problem is that Bartleby is immovable. Among all the other things he "would prefer not to," Bartleby is unresponsive to the narrator's attempts to assist him. His passive aggression puts Stowe's sentimental structure in a new light. What if not the rich and powerful but the objects of sympathy, the poor and needy themselves, are like stone? This may be the self-serving fantasy of those who find it easier to do nothing, or it may be a powerful claim that the poor too have the privilege of stoicism.

Putnam's was based in New York, and much that it published, like "Bartleby," had a New York flavor, but its ambitions were national. *Israel Potter: His Fifty Years of Exile* began serialization with the subtitle "A Fourth of July Story." Potter was a New England farm boy who became a revolutionary soldier, fought at Bunker Hill, served as a secret courier for Benjamin Franklin, and was stranded in London after the Revolution, only returning to the United States in advanced old age. In adapting Potter's story, Melville made different use of a technique he had developed for his first-person narratives. From *Typee* through *Moby-Dick,* he had freely supplemented his own experience with materials drawn from travel books and others' personal narratives. For *Israel Potter,* Melville made a third-person account out of an existing personal narrative, which had evidently preoccupied him. As early as 1849, he had bought an old map of London "in case I serve up the Revolutionary narrative of the beggar."

In the early decades of the nineteenth century, some two hundred personal narratives of the Revolution were in print. *The Life and Remarkable Adventures of Israel R. Potter* (1824) was published in an inexpensive pamphlet, the year of Potter's return to America, by a Providence, Rhode Island, printer whose publications included such other popular personal narratives as a version of Daniel Boone's and *Life and Adventures of Robert, the Hermit of Massachusetts,* an escaped slave. Despite Melville's claim to offer "almost a reprint" of the Potter narrative, save for "change in the grammatical person," he made very substantial changes. Perhaps because he and Potter shared the birthdate of August 1 and had both served on whalers, Melville shifted Potter's birthplace from Rhode Island to the Berkshire region, where Melville was then living. The first six chapters of *Israel Potter* otherwise correspond fairly closely to the first half of the 1824 narrative, and Melville's last four chapters follow, although drastically abridging, the last half.

In between these opening and closing chapters, Melville has sixteen chapters that extensively add to and elaborate the 1824 work.

They nationalize the personal narrative by devoting several chapters to Benjamin Franklin and some fifty pages to John Paul Jones, the great naval hero of the Revolution, who did not at all figure in the original. Israel's adventures culminate in Jones's naval battle between the British *Serapis* and the revolutionary *Bonhomme Richard*. As the two ships grapple, the bloody horrors of this great victory become a figure of civil war: "It was a partnership and joint-stock combustion company of both ships; yet divided, even in participation. The two vessels were as two houses, through whose party-walls doors have been cut." Appalled witticism turns the language of commercial enterprise to destruction and cooperation to "combustion"; the door joining two houses opens only to let death enter. Jones himself had been earlier revealed as tattooed, like Queequeg in *Moby-Dick,* in a way "only seen on thorough-bred savages—deep blue, elaborate, labyrinthine, cabalistic."

After the battle, the narrator asks whether civilization is indeed "a thing distinct," or "is it an advanced stage of barbarism?" Through this reflection on a founding deed of the nation, the categories that grounded American national narrative in Parkman, Bancroft, and Cooper come under severe questioning. This narrative of the wanderings and exile of "Israel" resonates suggestively because, ever since the seventeenth century, America had been understood as what in *White-Jacket* is called the "Israel of our time." Melville, therefore, is licensed to find in the story of Israel Potter "a type, a parallel, and a prophecy" for America. America may prove to be "the Paul Jones of nations" because like him it is "intrepid, unprincipled, reckless, predatory, with boundless ambitions, civilized in externals but a savage at heart." One review found notable political virtue in this passage, contrasting its directness to the "fine phrases" of current American expansionist political discourse.

After the election of Pierce, the problems of slavery, supposedly settled by the Compromise of 1850, reemerged over the organization of the Kansas and Nebraska territories, which soon escalated into guerrilla civil warfare, and with the "filibuster" activity of Americans determined to bring the Caribbean into American hands as slave territory. In October 1854, Pierce's ambassadors to Spain, France, and Great Britain (James Buchanan, who would succeed Pierce as president) signed a memorandum known as the Ostend Manifesto, which proclaimed that Cuba was "necessary to the North American republic," and that if the United States determined to possess it and Spain refused to sell it, then "by every law, human and divine, we shall be justified in wresting it from Spain." Appalled that this "scheme of spoliation" made high-flown appeals to "conscious rectitude" and to the "approbation of nations," the reviewer found that Melville's speculation, in contrast, "comes to the point." By drawing on popular traditions of personal narrative to gain a purchase on national narrative, *Israel Potter* succeeded in pleasing readers and provoking thought on important contemporary issues.

A similar strategy directs "Benito Cereno," which Melville had originally intended to be the title and lead piece in the volume of *Putnam's* pieces that became *Piazza Tales*. Without acknowledging his source, Melville takes his action from *A Narrative of Voyages and Travels* by Captain Amasa Delano (1817). Going on board a Spanish ship in trouble off the coast of South America, Delano is unaware that the ship is actually controlled not by its captain, Don Benito Cereno, but by the blacks on board, whom Delano believes to be slaves and who act the part, but who have previously mutinied and taken charge; nonetheless, he finally learns the truth, and his ship recaptures the blacks. Even the technical peculiarities in Melville's piece, what he calls the "nature of this narrative," the "intricacies" of materials "retrospectively" or "irregularly" ordered, have precedent in Delano's account, which begins with a summary of the events from the ship's log and ends with a dossier of court records, placing Delano's own first-person version in the middle. By removing the preliminary logbook record and shifting from Delano's retrospective first-person to a third-person narration closely tied to Delano's flawed perception and fluctuating thoughts, Melville gains the potential for both the suspense of a good magazine tale and the ironies of literary reflection.

In transforming the personal narrative into a tale, Melville uses the rhetoric of gothic fiction, which combines the glamor of ruinous dilapidation with the danger arising from moral weakness. The ship is like a "strange house," perhaps "haunted." The "influence" of its atmosphere produces "heightened" impressions, "enchantments" such as might be felt by the "prisoner in some deserted chateau." The courtly reserve, the sudden coldnesses, and the agitated gnawing of his fingers by Benito Cereno recall Poe's Roderick Usher. The climax of Poe's tale figures here as a simile; the final revelation is like a "vault whose door has been flung back." Gothicism is not just decor. In "Benito Cereno," no less than in William Faulkner's *Absalom, Absalom!* (1936), gothicism is a technique for historical tragedy, representing the continuing power of the past in the present as the consequence of ancestral crime.

By changing the name of Cereno's ship from the *Tryal* to the *San Dominick,* Melville serves his gothic motif while directly engaging a history living on into the present. The saint's name enhances the gothic aura of Spanish Catholicism, fearsomely strange to antebellum America. More crucially, however, it names a place. This place, first called Hispaniola, was the Caribbean island where Columbus had landed, and Melville invents a figurehead for the ship, "the image of Christopher Colon, the discoverer of the New World." After the extermination of its native Indian population, this island received the first African slaves brought to the New World. In a historical irony already noted by Bancroft, this was also where the largest and most important uprising in the history of African-American slavery occurred, in the days of the French Revolution, establishing the independent, black-governed state of Haiti as the second free nation in the western hemisphere.

The Haitian revolution immediately affected the United States because many thousands of the island's slaveholding class emigrated to the United States. It further affected the United States, as Henry Adams first recognized and W. E. B. Du Bois emphasized, because once France no longer held the "pearl of the Antilles," its Louisiana holdings lost their point. Napoleon's sale of the Louisiana territory and the chance for the United States to expand westward followed from the revolution. Most importantly, Haiti's revolution stood as archetype of the terror that some imagined inevitably would follow any slackening of white control over slaves. As late as the 1860 election, Chief Justice Roger Taney of the U.S. Supreme Court wrote in fear of race war if Lincoln were elected, "I am old enough to remember the horrors of St. Domingo." Taney's fearful memory played some role in his judgment in the Dred Scott case of 1857. In determining that black people had no rights that the United States was constitutionally obligated to honor, Taney, while hoping to assuage southern concerns, further exacerbated sectional antagonism.

Delano, too, has fearful memories, of things heard "as stories" of pirates, and he worried lest "the San Dominick, like a slumbering volcano, suddenly let loose energies now hid." No figure was more used by the nineteenth century for revolutionary violence than that of the volcano, yet it is fundamental to the ironic form of "Benito Cereno" that Delano be capable of every fear about his circumstances except the right one. His racist underestimation of the powers of blacks is so entrenched that even the ship's name does not bring to his mind the "horrors of St. Domingo." After Nat Turner's rebellion, a series of shipboard uprisings, such as on the *Amistad* (1839) and on the *Creole* (1841), were the most notable instances of mass black resistance. Frederick Douglass devoted his one attempt at fiction to "The Heroic Slave," a version of the life of Madison Washington, who led the *Creole* slaves. Delano's incapacity to imagine black revolutionary agency is ironically repeated by Melville's scrupulous refusal to enter the mind of Babo, the leader of the uprising. Even Douglass, after having established the character of Madison Washington, leaves the narrative of the uprising to be recounted externally and retrospectively by a white survivor. Only in Stowe's *Dred* (1856) and in *Blake; or The Huts of America* (1859), by the black activist Martin R. Delany, is there any attempt to represent large-scale slave rebellion from the inside.

Delano's misdirected fears might recall the polite squeamishness of *Putnam's*, which had rejected "The Two Temples" in 1854 for fear of "offending the religious sensibilities of the public," as was explained to Melville in separate letters from the editor Charles Briggs and the publisher George Palmer Putnam. But as times changed, the journal proved not at all timid. In May 1856 the most outspoken congressional voice against slavery, Senator Charles Sumner of Massachusetts, was assaulted, while seated in the Senate, by a South Carolina congressman, and beaten unconscious; that June the Republican party nominated its first presidential candidate. An 1856 advertisement by *Putnam's* new publisher, Dix and Edwards, stated that the journal's work "cannot always be done without offense." While establishing a standard of quality that led the great English novelist William Makepeace Thackeray to call it "much the best Mag. in the world," the editors of *Putnam's* were responding to the challenges of American politics. Frederick Law Olmsted was publishing controversial travel books with Dix and Edwards, beginning with *A Journey in the Seaboard Slave States* (1856). George William Curtis, the journal's literary editor and author of five volumes of minor sketches, underwent a political conversion. Soon after his 1856 Wesleyan University oration on "The Duty of the American Scholar to Politics and the Times," published by Dix and Edwards as a pamphlet, he became primarily a political publicist, imitating the "sublime scholarship of John Milton," which "began in literature and ended in life."

Parke Godwin collected his pieces from *Putnam's* as *Political Es-*

says (1856), also from Dix and Edwards, and dedicated the volume to Sumner. In "The Vestiges of Despotism" (1854), Godwin attacked the stifling of fundamental debate by the combined efforts of the churches, the party system, and the slave interest. He also defended the legitimacy of his own kind of writing appearing in a magazine of "American literature, science, and art": "Literature is the full and free expression of the nation's mind, not in *belles-lettres* alone, nor in art alone, nor in science alone, but in all of these, combined with politics and religion." Writers, as the "cultivated men," the "literary men of the nation," must be "free to utter their wisest thoughts" wherever they saw the need, on "every subject which concerns the interests, the sensibilities, and the hopes of our humanity." In such a magazine, which preserved an older sense of "literature" and resisted the specialization to belles lettres characteristic of Poe and Hawthorne, and at times Melville, "Benito Cereno" might seem part of a new moment in the formation of national consciousness.

In *The Confidence-Man: His Masquerade* (1857) Melville draws on more recent popular narrative materials than he used in *Israel Potter* or "Benito Cereno." The term "confidence man" was coined in 1849, to describe a particular New York shyster named William Thompson. The key to his criminal technique was a direct appeal to a stranger to trust him. The term was immediately recognized as suggestive for thinking about many aspects of American life. The Duyckincks' *Literary World,* in reprinting some paragraphs that characterize "the young confidence man of politics" and the middle-aged "confidence man of merchandise," reflected that "it is not the worst thing that can be said of a country that it gives birth to a confidence man." Melville nationalizes his scene by removing the confidence man from the urban East to the American heartland, setting the action on a Mississippi steamer going south from Saint Louis, like Thomas Bangs Thorpe in "The Big Bear of Arkansas." Thorpe had localized his tale by focusing on the hunter's narrative, but Melville stays with the diversely representative characters gathered on board.

The tall talkers of southwestern local narratives, as well as the specific tricks of a rogue like Simon Suggs, stand behind Melville's procedure. *The Confidence-Man* focuses on a series of appeals to trust, made both to groups and in one-on-one conversations, by a variety of figures—among them a crippled black man, a mourning widower, an agent for Indian charities, an official of the "Black Rapids Coal company," an herb doctor, and a "Cosmopolitan"—all of whom may be a "masquerade" by the single titular figure. The "Wall Street spirit" pervading contemporary America is tested through the various traditional perspectives that the characters offer, such as "this ship of fools" and "All the world's a stage." Most notably, on this steamer named *Fidèle*, the first scene shows a deaf and mute man writing out St. Paul's words on "charity," including that "charity believeth all things," and the last chapter includes discussion of what belief should be granted the Apocrypha, the "uncanonical" part of the Bible.

The work's diverting incidents seem intended to provoke thought on ultimate matters, but how seriously? St. Paul spoke earnestly of charity, but *The Confidence-Man* presents a "game of charity." In a time and place very different from Melville's America, the street theater of medieval mystery plays provided a ritually institutionalized space that integrated play and devotion into communal life. The *Fidèle*, however, can only contain such disparities as a problem. One character complains to another, "You pun with ideas as another man may with words." The book dwells on paradoxes, such as the "genial misanthrope," and in the midst of this complexly satiric work, a character exclaims, "God defend me from Irony, and Satire." This book's repeated staging of its incommensurability with itself is a virtuoso performance of literary narrative that reveals how marginal and improvisatory that literary narrative remained.

As the various speakers make their appeals, they tell stories to and elicit stories from their interlocutors. The variety of voices is notable. At moments the narrator and some characters use a disingenuous gentility: "the merchant, though not used to be very indiscreet, yet, being not entirely inhumane, remained not entirely unmoved." Other characters burst out in vernacular freedom, "Look you, nature! I don't deny but your clover is sweet, and your dandelions don't roar, but whose hailstones smashed my windows?" Structurally the work is a frame narrative, confined within the hours from sunrise to midnight on the thematically apt April Fools' Day. In mentioning "Chaucer's Canterbury pilgrims," Melville signals a traditional affiliation that, however, had not easily been available for earlier American use. Hawthorne in "The Storyteller" and Poe in "The Folio Club" both had wished to make books out of their local narratives by establishing a social context to frame, motivate, and complicate the narratives as Chaucer had done, but they had found no support from publishers.

In the speculative intellectual perspectives and complex techniques of construction through which Melville raises his contemporary American life into exemplary shapes of human possibility, he returns again to literary narrative. He comments on his own procedures in three chapters that reflect on the art of fiction. These chapters address the topic of character, with regard to consistency, realism, and originality. In the 1850s claims had begun to be made that certain "psychological novelists," such as Thackeray, gave positive knowledge of the motives for their characters' otherwise incomprehensible actions. Deprecating any claims to scientifically "fixed principles," Melville still allies himself with the search to reveal "the heart of man." The "nature" that readers seek in fiction must be "exhilarated" and "transformed." Fiction may provide even "more reality, than real life itself can show." Fiction serves the same function as religion: "it should present another world, and yet one to which we feel the tie." The power required to produce a character "original in the sense that Hamlet is, or Don Quixote, or Milton's Satan" is as great and rare as that of a "new law-giver" or "the founder of a new religion."

One sentence extraordinarily exemplifies the interplay between the world and the writer's power that Melville is concerned to elucidate. The truly original character is "like a revolving Drummond light, raying away from itself all round it—everything is lit by it, everything starts up to it." Named after the British engineer who invented it in the 1820s, the Drummond light, now most familiar as the limelight, provided by far the most brilliant artificial illumination known in its time. It had aroused a tremendous sensation when first introduced to New York in the 1840s by P. T. Barnum to advertise his American Museum (as recounted in his personal narrative, *The Life of P. T. Barnum, Written by Himself,* 1855). This technical device, then, was associated with the man who epitomized fame and fortune through hoax and humbug. Melville lifts the Drummond light from the world of technology and shady commerce, and he makes it a figure for the highest moments in the psychology of creation. The light's brilliance is like the "effect" produced when "certain minds" receive "the adequate conception" of a truly original character. In turn, the psychology of artistic creation is joined to the first and highest creation. It is "akin to that which in Genesis attends upon the beginning of things." The divine "Let there be light" is echoed in the flash of literary genius but also in the glare of advertising practices. In these chapters of reflection, Melville went beyond Poe in developing the theory of literary narrative, a form that Melville was about to abandon.

For Hawthorne and Poe, the failure to publish their frame narratives defined the beginnings of their careers as professional writers; for Melville the failure of his frame narrative's publisher marked the end of his career. *The Confidence-Man* was published by Dix and Edwards on April 1, 1857, and before the end of the month the publisher was bankrupt. By September, so were its successor firms, and the stereotype plates of their books were auctioned off. No one was willing to bid on Melville's works; he could not raise funds to purchase them himself; and he authorized their sale for scrap. He had realized no income from either *The Piazza Tales* or *The Confidence-Man*. *Putnam's*, too, was sold off and merged into another magazine. Melville had another chance, however; in August 1857 he was invited to contribute to the projected *Atlantic Monthly*. He agreed to be listed as a contributor, but he had nothing ready nor any date at which he expected to. In fact, he did not publish prose again in his lifetime. From 1857 into 1860, he earned money lecturing; after the Civil War he finally received a position in the New York customhouse. Although he produced a good deal after 1857, he chose to write only poetry until the last years of his life, when he began work on "Billy Budd," which remained incomplete at his death.

During the years that Melville's career came to its end, Hawthorne was American consul in Liverpool. Anticipating their use for fiction at a later point, Hawthorne kept voluminous notebooks while he was in England, bulking larger in four years there than those he had kept for decades in the United States, and he continued his notes after leaving the consulship and taking up residence in Italy from 1858 into 1860. Yet before his death in 1864, Hawthorne published only two more books, *The Marble Faun* (1860) and *Our Old Home* (1863), sketches of England that had appeared in the *Atlantic Monthly* from 1860. Beginning in 1858, he also worked on some six different drafts of romances, which his modern editors have grouped as the "American Claimant" manuscripts (including "The Ancestral Footstep," "Etherege," and "Grimshawe") and the "Elixir of Life" manuscripts (including "Septimius Felton," "Septimius Norton," and "The Dolliver Romance"). After *The Marble Faun*, with Melville not writing and Hawthorne not publishing, it would be some twenty years before American literary narrative was resumed, by Henry James, under new circumstances. Meanwhile, Hawthorne's heirs gradually released the materials he had left in manuscript at his death: *Passages from the American Note-Books* (1868), *Passages from the English Note-Books* (1870), *Passages from the French and Italian Note-Books* (1871), *Septimius Felton; or the Elixir of Life* (1872), *The Dolliver Romance and Other Pieces* (1876); *Dr. Grimshawe's Secret* (1883), and *The Ancestral Footstep* (1883). These seven posthumous volumes helped preserve the idea of literary narrative in America.

Although Melville did not directly participate in the political engagements of his editors at *Putnam's,* he successfully wrote in consonance with them, until the economic crisis of 1857 destroyed the institutional basis that had allowed him to earn a living. Hawthorne was more directly affected by the political crises of secession and civil war. He was not converted to a militant antislavery position, nor even to hearty unionism, and he felt himself wholly out of touch with the enthusiastic feelings around him. The best he could imagine was an independent New England. Hawthorne registered his extreme discomfort in "Chiefly about War Matters" (*Atlantic,* 1862), which ironically supplements its text with footnotes written by a straightforward unionist "Editor." Ostentatiously placing friendship over politics, Hawthorne dedicated *Our Old Home* to Franklin Pierce, who was in extremely bad repute because of his concessions to the South while he was president, but whose patronage had made the book possible by allowing Hawthorne to live in England. The Compromise of 1850 had defined a moment of political suspension, in which Hawthorne's speculative uncertainties about action could be meditatively elaborated, but during the decisive action of the war, Hawthorne pushed his distrust of action so far that he could no longer imagine a plot for romance. The plot of *The Marble Faun* had scarcely animated the massive descriptive passages that distract the reader and, it seems, comfort the writer by burying the action. The new work showed a further erosion in Hawthorne's commitment to reaching any audience.

The "American Claimant" project stemmed from a paragraph in

the notebooks of 1855, sketching an English emigrant to America who bears a family secret that could ruin the family. He passes on the secret until, "at last, the hero of the romance comes to England, and finds that . . . he still has it in his power to procure the downfall of the family." Originally named "Middleton," the protagonist is a man in the middle, isolated between America and England and hoping to mediate between them. He seeks "links" or a "connection," but anything that will join him to England will sever him from America, and the project gets stuck in this dilemma. Although Middleton is "sensitive," he has led an active political life, which, however, he has recently abandoned in "disgust." It is a significant innovation for Hawthorne to make his central figure someone who is in between actions. This figure is only temporarily a spectator; unlike major characters in Hawthorne's earlier romances, he is not a photographer, poet, or sculptor. Hawthorne cannot carry this plan through. The protagonist's possible action is swallowed up by his antagonists (representing the current possessors of his English inheritance) and his helpers (figures from his American childhood). Yet even with these characters, Hawthorne struggles at an impasse.

In fascinating notes to himself that interrupt the incomplete manuscripts, Hawthorne wrote, "Still there is something wanting to make an action for the story." Frustrated, he notes, "The story must not be founded at all on remorse or secret guilt—all that I've worn out." Struggling to devise a motivation for the Italianate villain, he tries and discards many possibilities: is his peculiarity "a leprosy?—a eunuch?—a cork leg?—a golden touch?—a dead hand? —a false nose?—a glass eye?" Turning to the tutor of the protagonist, he decides to make this old man the "real hero," but as a "martyr," in contrast to the "young American politican" and all other "self-seekers." The legendary "bloody footstep" shall be the track "not of guilt, but of persecution," because the old man and all his family have always exemplified "the weakness of too much conscience," its "indecision" and "incapacity for action." In his "inability for anything but suffering," the old man raises Hamletism to the pitch of Uncle Tom. Against the grain of his own narrative intention, Hawthorne notes that conscience is incomparably "disorganizing": it is "certain to overthrow everything earthly." Where he wants a motive, he can find none, and where he expects weakness he finds strength. This was no way to organize a romance, but it does suggest Hawthorne's struggle to grasp the dynamics of southern secession and the northern response.

In the "Elixir of Life" project, the first two versions focus on Septimius, a theology student in Concord at the outbreak of the revolutionary war, whose identity is defined by his killing of a British soldier and by his quest for physical immortality. Hawthorne acknowledges the excitement of the revolutionary moment as something "we" know "now," as the Civil War carries off young men, yet despite killing the soldier, Septimius stands aloof. Hawthorne intends "dealing as little as possible with outward events," because "our story is an internal one." Like everything else "outside of Septimius's brains," the "great historic incident" figures in the narrative only to help "develop and illustrate what went on within" him. Yet Septimius is criticized because his "characteristic egotism" makes him think that "the war would hardly have a more important result than the vivifying of his thought" by the secret learned from the dying Englishman. Hawthorne's own narrative technique, however, has prescribed that self-centeredness, and it is hard for this criticism of Septimius to work without also working against the romance.

Hawthorne directly relates the character's psychology to his own experience as a "Romance writer." Septimius's disappointment with his elixir is a disillusion with which a romancer can "sympathize." For a romancer suffers equal pain when the world of fiction is confronted by the ordinary world. Outside the "magic influence" of romance, "destruction, disturbance, incongruity" ruin the "nicely adjusted relations" that had established a "truer world" than everyday, with a "fitness of events" otherwise unavailable. Hawthorne could no longer extend faith to his literary narrative. By comparing his character to himself, he attempts to buttress the fiction with fact, seeking to draw stability from the world of chaotic confusion. Hawthorne failed to separate himself from his hero even to the extent that Melville had achieved in *Pierre,* and he could not complete the work.

In "The Dolliver Romance," Hawthorne no longer tries to command such challenging materials as the revolutionary war or a politician in temporary exile. The romance springs from a simple, sketchlike domestic setting, yet even in his notes for this extremely truncated manuscript, Hawthorne struggles to structure and motivate action. Given a magical potion that makes an old person gradually younger, Hawthorne tries to determine why someone would want to "live back" in this way. Perhaps he wants to "confer a material benefit on the world," to "get rid of poverty, or slavery, or war." The point of the story would be that his "toil," which threatens to "disturb . . . the order of nature" and "destroy . . . the whole economy of the world," had no effect. On the contrary, "without any agency of his," the goal would be accomplished by "the real tendency and progress of mankind." Faced with the "convulsive action" of the Civil War, however, Hawthorne could no longer effectively commit himself to this faith in romance as progress without agency, which had made possible the independent worlds of his literary narratives.

Epilogue: Postwar National Narrative

The Civil War debilitated Hawthorne and inhibited literary narrative, but it did not prevent all new narratives. The greatest talent to emerge during the war was Mark Twain. His first books clearly link him to the traditions of local and personal narratives: *The Celebrated Jumping Frog of Calaveras County and Other Sketches*

(1867), *The Innocents Abroad* (1869), and *Roughing It* (1872), which the preface characterizes as "merely a personal narrative." During the war, Francis Parkman recovered from his nearly two decades of debility and renewed his national narrative. Dedicated to three of his relatives who had fallen in the Civil War, Parkman's *Pioneers of France in the New World* appeared in 1865; after twenty-three reprintings it was revised in 1885 to take account of research in Florida that Parkman had been unable to accomplish during the war. Over the last decades of the century, until his death in 1893, he completed his series on "France and England in North America," to which *The Conspiracy of Pontiac* had formed a proleptic coda: *The Jesuits in North America* (1867); *The Discovery of the Great West* (1869; revised and enlarged as *La Salle and the Discovery of the Great West,* 1879); *The Old Regime in Canada* (1874; revised and enlarged, 1893); *Count Frontenac and New France under Louis XIV* (1877); *Montcalm and Wolfe* (1884); and *A Half-Century of Conflict* (1892).

In the "Introduction" which from the first edition stood at the front of *Pioneers of France,* Parkman set out the conceptual terms and antithetical oppositions that govern the whole history as he wrote it over the next thirty years. His work lays bare the "springs of American civilization," for "France in America" is subsumed within American national narrative. It was France that "conquered for Civilization" the land of America, but the United States is fulfilling the course of civilization. In Parkman's allegory of historical principles, his series recovers "the attempt of Feudalism, Monarchy, and Rome to master a continent where, at this hour," as Parkman writes during the Civil War, "half a million of bayonets are vindicating the ascendancy of a regulated freedom." France in America was "all head." Pope and king stood for the principle of "Centralization," which infantilized the French by denying them their independence, just as savagery had made Indians remain children. The principle of "steadfast growth" was to be found in New

England's "body without a head." (Parkman shows no awareness of the grotesquery.) New England was "fruitful" and offered "hope" because it was based on "Liberty"; New France was "barren" and doomed to "despair" because it was the "representative" of "Absolutism."

British "blood and muscle" made New England "pre-eminently the land of material progress." In contrast, however, the aristocratic, archaic, and savage qualities of the French and Indians made New France rich in "striking and salient forms of character." The greatest effort of Parkman's thousands of pages goes to recovering the "contrast"—grave priests and naked Indians, sober merchants and bushrangers "tricked out with savage finery"—that made the "whole course of French Canadian history" so "picturesque." Because the further course of events has "dwarfed" the French period and reduced it "to an episode," it now must be evoked as a "memory of the past" that rises in "strange, romantic" shape: "A boundless vision grows upon us; an untamed continent; vast wastes of forest verdure," in which "plumed helmets gleamed." All this Parkman undertakes to represent with "photographic clearness and truth," employing the best documentary methods of scientific historical technique in the service of recovering glamor.

The heroic figures of Champlain and La Salle among the explorers, Marquette and Jogues among the Jesuits, Frontenac and Montcalm among the governing aristocrats, organize the narrative for large stretches, but as in *The Conspiracy of Pontiac*, the land itself provides the largest continuity. Parkman notes at times his own recent visits to the scenes about which he writes. Sometimes they had remained wilderness; sometimes they were more casually accessible, and the "tourist," the "sportsman," the "wandering artist" might take leisure where Indians once had lived in deadly earnest. Some wilderness had been painfully lost. A great rock, once covered with Indian religious images visible from afar, now advertises "Plantation Bitters." The "great natural beauty" at the Falls of St.

Anthony has been "utterly spoiled" by the new city of Minneapolis. Other wilderness has been gained for progress. The "yellow . . . ripened wheat" of a "hardy and valiant yeomanry" has "strangely transformed" the "rolling sea of dull green prairie," once "boundless pasture of the buffalo."

The interplay of science and glamor, the use of photographic precision to allegoric effect, may be seen in a notable passage from Parkman's last years. To introduce "Queen Anne's War," Parkman begins with the "unbroken forest" of Maine, a "waste of savage vegetation," which, he notes, "survives, in some part, to this day." Its "prodigality of vital force" in "the struggle for existence," however, does not distinguish it, but only makes visible the "same" process at work in "all organized beings, from men to mushrooms." The forest scene carries implications beyond itself:

> Young seedlings in millions spring every summer from the black mould, rich with the decay of those that had preceded them, crowding, choking, and killing each other, perishing by their very abundance; all but a scattered few, stronger than the rest, or more fortunate in position, which survive by blighting those about them. They in turn, as they grow, interlock their boughs, and repeat in a season or two the same process of mutual suffocation. The forest is full of lean saplings dead or dying with vainly stretching towards the light. Not one infant tree in a thousand lives to maturity; yet these survivors form an innumerable host, pressed together in struggling confusion, squeezed out of symmetry and robbed of normal development, as men are said to be in the level sameness of democratic society.

In such a passage Parkman's intense feeling for the "universal tragedy of nature" is in contrast to his progressive national narrative framework. Checked only by the irony of "said to be," it threatens to reduce the course of history to the mere "revolution" (in the astronomical sense) that marked Indian life: "mutable as the wind" in power relations, but "hopelessly unchanging" in cultural "development." It was a "gloomy and meaningless history . . . of extermination, absorption, or expatriation."

For the United States, however, the experience of the Civil War gave a powerful new shape to national narrative. By virtue of the war and of Lincoln's death, understood as martyrdom, the state itself (in the sense of the sovereign power, not in the sense of the united "states") became sanctified, taking on the prestige that had previously been reserved for the "Union" and the "People." This new American reverence for earthly power made possible Melville's final work of prose fiction, "Billy Budd," on which he worked for the last several years of his life and left near completion at his death in 1891.

"Billy Budd" is the most wholly fictional of Melville's works. It is not drawn at all directly from his experience, nor does it rework specific documents. It is set in 1797 on a British warship, and Billy is not even an American. America is no longer so unique that major work by an American writer must treat an American subject (or one with obvious bearing on the United States, such as Prescott's *Conquest of Mexico*). Parkman's history even praises the continuing spread of British colonialism in the nineteenth century, rather than treating empire as superseded by democracy. A Britain threatened by revolutionary France might begin to seem a congenial figure for the United States. After the Civil War, slavery was ended, but other forms of social inequality increased until farmers' populism and industrial workers' agitation to unionize threatened the existing order.

Although "Billy Budd" is fiction, Melville's rhetoric is antifictional. Subtitled "An Inside Narrative," "Billy Budd" repeatedly appeals to the documentary expectations of narrative. Readers should understand that this is "no romance," and it must, therefore, lack "the symmetry of form attainable in pure fiction." Using a term not yet in the language when he began his career, Melville defends his procedures as "realism." As an "inside" narrative, the work corrects the news account (itself part of the fiction) of the events it recounts. In 1851, Melville had been happy to encounter a newspaper report that confirmed *Moby-Dick* by reporting a whale's sinking a ship, but now he reenacts a fundamental gesture of self-consciously innovative high culture, from William Wordsworth in the preface to *Lyrical Ballads* (1800) to Joseph Conrad in *The Secret Agent* (1907): defining the truth of one's writing by the falsity of newspapers. As "romance" had been in the 1850s, "realism" in the 1880s was the password for literary narrative.

"Billy Budd" performs an extraordinary historical reconstruction. It defines a limited fictional action within the "juncture" of important public events. These events are not just the revolutionary wars, but, specifically, the mutinies of 1797 within the British navy, and, yet more precisely, the constraints of commanding a ship detached from the fleet. Its "inside narrative" does not function like the "internal story" of *Septimius Felton* to displace attention from history to psychology. Two paragraphs from the manuscript that served as the work's preface from its first publication in 1924 until the scholarly edition of 1962 greatly enrich the complexity of historical thought by arguing that "not the wisest could have foreseen" at the time that the revolutionary excesses, or the sailors' mutiny, would eventually lead to "political advance" and "important reforms." It seems that only because they were opposed by the wisest have these movements succeeded; progress requires resistance.

Combined with the complex realism of its historical narrative, "Billy Budd" equally gains power through allegorical simplification. Billy Budd, the natural child of an unknown lord, an illiterate "upright barbarian," is like "Adam." Claggart, the master-at-arms, serves the ship as its corrupt "chief of police"; his eyes exercise "serpent fascination," and he satanically lies in accusing Billy of treason. Tongue-tied by a natural speech defect, Billy tries to speak in self-defense, but he "could only say it with a blow," and he strikes Claggart dead. Captain Vere, a hero in action yet a meditative reader of "unconventional" books, is the "troubled patriarch" who must resolve the situation, which he summarizes, "Struck dead by an angel of God! Yet the angel must hang!" The "jugglery of circumstances" means that Billy's righteousness counts as mutiny. In explaining the case to the drumhead court-martial he has summoned, Vere emphasizes the need to "strive against scruples that may tend to enervate decision." At whatever pain, he avoids Hamletism. Hawthorne's "American Claimant" had similarly argued on behalf of "efficient actors," those "who mould the world." But the claimant's life in "politics" had taught him that such efficiency required an ugly "something else" to be "developed more strongly than conscience," and upon reflection, his argument pains him with its "ugliness and indefensibleness." Vere shows that power may have conscience, and even moral beauty. Feeling still the "primeval" in "our formalized humanity," he takes Billy Budd to his bosom like Abraham when he is about to sacrifice Isaac.

When Melville in *Typee* first challenged his readers as "state-room sailors," it was on behalf of the crew. "Billy Budd," however, invokes "snug card players in the cabin" to set them against the lonely, agonized responsibility of "the sleepless man on the bridge" who guides the craft. Billy himself, condemned by Vere for his deed, cries out before being hanged, "God bless Captain Vere!" The narrator concludes that "the condemned one suffered less" than his judge did, for Billy's consciousness is like that of "children," but Vere is a mature adult.

The Civil War, fought for the Union and against slavery, had brought the state an imaginative moral legitimacy unavailable in the 1850s. Nothing admirable stood behind Legree as Vere stands behind Claggart. After the Civil War, the "conservative" position no longer had to be also progressive—as was Judge Temple in Cooper's *Pioneers*—in order to be right. Billy Budd and Uncle Tom are both innocent martyrs, but the feelings Tom provokes reach out to the reader; those of Billy are contained by Vere. In Melville's pre-war "Benito Cereno," the revolutionary slave Babo remains opaque to Cereno, to Delano, and to the reader. This is far different from the moral and intellectual comprehensiveness that allows Vere to sympathize with Billy and still judge him. Vere has incorporated Stowe's lesson of feeling, and his power to give himself pain by his own judgment enhances his authority.

To the extent that readers accept Vere, "Billy Budd" reconciles force with principle. Parkman had emphasized the dominance of principle. Only at moments in Parkman did the predominance of force over principle produce a complicating undercurrent, but this imbalance becomes the primary irony in Henry Adams's *History of the United States During the Administrations of Thomas Jefferson and James Madison* (9 volumes, 1889–91). Adams aims for thoughtful, "scientific," rather than spectacular, "dramatic," history. For Adams human agents may no longer be "heroes" but only "types" that are illustrative rather than in themselves "sources of power." He transforms the narrative of America from prophetic to analytic. Parkman's concluding paragraph looks forward from the end of the Seven Years' War to anticipate the present nation: "the disunited colonies became the United States. The string of discordant colonies along the Atlantic coast has grown to a mighty people, joined in a union which the earthquake of civil war served only to compact and consolidate." Adams looks back within the history of the United States and places the consolidation much earlier than the Civil War; his unstated premise is that the nation must have been consolidated already for the North to have had the will and capacity to defeat the South's secession.

Parkman took his analytic topic of "centralization" from Tocqueville, who had broached in *Democracy in America* and developed in *The Old Regime and the French Revolution* (1856) the thesis that it was not the French Revolution that had introduced centralization to French government (even though the term itself was a revolutionary neologism). Rather, Tocqueville argued, the process had begun in the Middle Ages and developed with unparalleled rapidity and complexity from the Age of Louis XIV. This argument concerning centralization helped Parkman explain what was wrong with New France: "the government, and not the individual, acted always the foremost part." Adams, who during the Civil War had made Tocqueville's life and work "the Gospel of my private religion," does not simply appropriate Tocqueville's argument. He reverses Parkman's evaluation by treating centralization as strength, and he transposes Tocqueville's analysis from old France to new America. Centralization of the government of the United States had not occurred during the Civil War, as usually understood, but had begun much earlier, in fact, during the administration of Thomas Jefferson, the president most associated with the anticentralist principles of strict construction and states' rights.

Implicitly rebuking the theoretical grounds offered for southern secession, Adams proposes an ironic thesis: "The Constitution was violated more frequently by its friends than by its enemies, and often the extent of such violations measured the increasing strength of the Union." From the moment of his first presidential message to Congress in 1801, Jefferson did not try to block up "loopholes for the admission of European sovereignty into the citadel of American liberty." Instead, he "stretched out his hand to seize the powers he had denounced" before becoming president. The debate over Jefferson's purchase of Louisiana from Napoleon came down to the particulars of whether it should be a state, colony, or territory, rather than the basic question of whether the Constitution permitted such an acquisition. Adams draws the moral: "for the first time in the national history all parties agreed in admitting that the government could govern." Reduced to a tautological triviality, the fundamental debate of the first decades after the Declaration of Independence no longer counted and should have had no force when resuscitated in midcentury.

Centralization occurred not only in mute practice but also in public opinion. Adams notes that the Constitution never mentions the "nation" but only the "Union" in order to characterize the American collectivity, and he argues that only through the War of 1812 did the Union become a nation (which in turn could be mobilized to preserve the "Union" in the Civil War). Adams identifies June 1807 as the moment when "for the first time in their history the people of the United States learned . . . the feeling of a true national emotion." The British had humiliated the U.S. frigate *Chesapeake,* and the outrage "seethed and hissed like the glowing olive-stake of Ulysses in the Cyclops' eye, until the whole American people, like Cyclops, roared with pain, and stood frantic on the shore, hurling abuse at their enemy, who taunted them from his safe ships." This crucial phase in American consciousness becomes mock-epic. The new-found national unity is figured in the single, centralized, but blinded eye of the Cyclops: great force but little understanding or control.

Adams fixes the moment when "the rhetorical marks" of antebellum political discourse were established. In February 1810, the young Henry Clay spoke for a new generation that "for fifty years" would prevail through its "devotion to ideas of nationality and union." The key figures of this discourse were the Union itself and the Founding Fathers. This national rhetoric was powerful because it belonged "to no party." It was available "with equal advantage" to "orators of every section." This new political language was formed to serve a counsel of war. Idealizing as the Fathers and the Union may seem, they were part of the "War Hawk" movement. Led by Clay and John Calhoun, the War Hawks sought to end in practice America's exceptional status among nations, even while sanctifying it figuratively. Adams sees their goal as granting the government "the attributes of old-world sovereignty under pretext of the war power." Moving into the war, "America began slowly to struggle, under the consciousness of pain, toward a conviction that she must bear the common burdens of humanity, and fight with the weapons of other races in the same bloody arena."

Adams sets at the beginning of the national period a loss of America's uniqueness, a transition from innocence to force. "Billy Budd" shows a comparable transition at about the same time. A major difference between 1800 and 1815, Adams explains, was that "the Rights of Man occupied public thoughts less, and the price of cotton more." This shift was not just from idealism to worldliness, but from an age of liberation to an age in which slavery would seem more and more indispensable. Melville seems to allegorize this change. The action of his story begins with the "handsome sailor," the Adamic Billy Budd, forced to leave the merchant ship *Rights of Man* in order to serve the king on the battleship *Bellipotent*.

Many of Adams's generation, however, preferred to date this shift from the Civil War. In his study of Hawthorne (1879), Henry James claims that Hawthorne's contemporaries, "that generation which grew up with the century," held a "superstitious faith in the grandeur of the country." Because they thought a "special Providence" protected America (as we have seen in Bancroft's *History*), they were free to enjoy "simple and uncritical" faith and "genial optimism." But since the Civil War, the "good American," Hawthorne's equivalent in sensibility and seriousness, "has eaten of the tree of knowledge." James claims experience against Hawthorne's innocence, but Adams finds even such knowingness still caught in American innocence of history, as James's residual biblical myth might suggest. James claims to know better than the national narrative of Hawthorne's time, with its optimistic providentialism, but Adams shows how little James knows of the cyclopean fires of war and pain that forged the supposedly innocent tools of American national narrative. James claims that "good" Americans are now beyond the seductive powers of national narrative. Adams's ironic genealogy must discount James's claim as a wish, yet by showing a beginning, Adams's account may make possible an end.

In the first chapter, I suggested that American national narrative is now much more recognizable in movies, television, and political rhetoric than in the culturally honored realm of "literature." Adams's *History* may stand for the point at which national narrative became an object of study for American high culture rather than, as in Bancroft or Webster, being the very substance of that culture. In the fifty years after Adams's *History*, modernism brought literary narrative a far higher authority and prestige than it had ever won in its first decades, the time of this study. In its own time, however, literary narrative could not maintain its separate realm against the crises that from *Uncle Tom's Cabin* through the end of Reconstruction again brought to the fore national narrative. Hawthorne and Melville incorporated in their literary narratives the emphasis on experience of personal narratives and the keen observation and complex tonal modulations of local narratives; in *The Scarlet Letter* and *Moby-Dick* they also subdued national narrative to their purposes. They produced a kind of narrative that was new to the United States and that is now known through much of the world and valued as a living heritage.

Bibliographic Essay

The bibliography that follows this essay lists alphabetically the works of scholarship, criticism, and history mentioned here, all of which have contributed to my work. It excludes primary sources, except a few collections that present lesser-known or scattered materials. It focuses on major, synthetic works—even then, not all that might be included—and does not detail dissertations, articles, or studies of individual authors, from which I have also greatly benefited. I have not updated it since the submission of my text for publication in 1993; many of the authors listed have continued to produce important writing. Readers who wish more extensive references should consult *American Literary Scholarship,* an annual volume published by Duke University Press.

For primary texts, reliable editions of major works by most writers treated in this book are published by the invaluable Library of America, including (in the order they are discussed) Cooper, Tocqueville, Irving, Hawthorne, Poe, Douglass, Parkman, Melville, Thoreau, Stowe, and Adams. For Bancroft, one must consult nineteenth-century sets, readily available in research libraries; my citations have been drawn from the ten-volume edition, not from either of the revised six-volume editions. For Southwestern humor, see the collections listed below by Blair, Cohen and Dillingham, Lynn, and Meine. *Two Years before the Mast* is widely available; I used the Penguin edition. For Harriet Jacobs's *Incidents in the Life of a Slave Girl,* see the edition by Jean Fagan Yellin (Harvard University Press).

This book is unusual for choosing to focus on several, interrelated forms of narrative, not a single form or a pair such as the novel or romance, nor authors, nor a thematically related body of works. This choice allows specific attention to individual exemplary works and also a broadly sociologi-

243

cal consideration of what it means to choose one mode of writing over another in a particular historical situation. Certain emphases arise from my work's being originally part of a multiauthor collaboration in the *Cambridge History of American Literature,* edited by Sacvan Bercovitch, the volumes of which began appearing in 1994, and all eight of which should have appeared by the time this edition does. I address Irving, Cooper, and Thoreau only briefly because Irving and Cooper are treated at length by Michael T. Gilmore in volume 1 and Thoreau by Barbara Packer in volume 2. Likewise, slave narrative and other writing on race questions are treated more fully by Eric Sundquist in volume 2, as are Harriet Beecher Stowe and a larger body of sentimental fiction by Michael Davitt Bell in volume 2.

This book began to be planned in 1983–84, was written from 1987 to 1989, and was finally revised by 1993. In this decade the study of American literature was transformed by "New Americanists," and my work has been placed in this category. The term arose in debate provoked by collections of new essays by many hands, particularly those edited by Pease and Michaels, Bercovitch, and Bercovitch and Jehlen. Exemplary books of this moment include those by Philip Fisher, Gilmore, Pease, Thomas, and Tompkins, all of which, quite diversely, understand literature as socially valued "cultural work."

This revisionary movement arose independently in projects by a number of scholars born in the 1940s, who were therefore originally formed by the great works that defined the first academic flourishing of American Literature, from about 1940 to 1970. These earlier works have by no means been superseded; one respect in which the humanities differ from sciences is the continuing obligation to read major works of scholarship or interpretation from earlier times. For the study of antebellum narrative, by far the single most important earlier work is Matthiessen, who measured Melville and Hawthorne by the scale of Shakespeare and Milton and affirmed their merit. Matthiessen built from earlier studies by Parrington and Rourke and expressed special debt both to the boldly speculative creative exploration by Lawrence and also to the new understanding of New England colonial intellectual history accomplished by Perry Miller, who later published important work on the nineteenth century.

In the wake of Matthiessen and Miller, there followed major interpretive studies later known as the "myth and symbol school," including landmarks by Smith, Lewis, Feidelson, Marx, Fussell, and Quentin Anderson, all of which analyze important works, genres, or authors in a broader cultural context, organized around a compelling theme. Slotkin continues this line and also sharply departs from it in taking a much less happy view of the cultural symbolism analyzed. Ziff offers a mature reconsideration of Matthiessen's key concern, "the possibilities of democracy" in antebellum American literature. From the years before Matthiessen, Winters remains critically challenging, a reminder that major American writing from the nineteenth century has not always awakened assent from gifted readers.

The Cold War years emphasized the unique distinctiveness, the exceptionalism, of American literature, culture, and history, and accordingly a rich body of studies focused on the American romance as distinct from the English and European novel. Founding works of this approach appeared in the late 1950s by Bewley, Chase, Harry Levin, and Fiedler, whose work has proved the most influential. Poirier's distinctive attention to style especially affected my thinking about literary narrative. Later important studies in this tradition include Bell, Hoffman, and Porte. Newer ways of thinking about the institution of American fiction may be found in Arac, Baym (1984), Brodhead, and Howard Horwitz.

In contrast to exceptionalist attention to romance, Auerbach's great study of Western realism, even while not discussing any American works, shows that in literature writers reveal the human seriousness of everyday life. They do so through subtle choices in the vocabulary, syntax, and rhythm of their prose. Auerbach's example helps to explain why my book quotes far more than is usual in a work of literary history. Harding's modest but valuable study adapts Auerbach's procedure, and Bridgman aids in the specific analysis of prose style, as does Simpson by different means. Scholarly counter-emphases to the isolationist tendency of American exceptionalism may be found in international and comparative studies by Arac, Chai, Larry Reynolds, Weisbuch, and Wellek.

As scholars of my generation began their studies, the Vietnam War affected how one felt the place of the United States in the world and thus put national narrative into question. My conception of national narrative arises from the study of American history and historiography but also from geographically wider-ranging, comparative, and global work by Benedict Anderson and Jameson, who understand nationalism as produced or reinforced by various forms of writing. On the specifically American side, crucial studies include those by Wilson, Merk, Tuveson, and above all Bercovitch. The presence of Native Americans was particularly important and troubling for national narrative, as is shown by Pearce, Rogin, and Drinnon.

The classic study of American historians as literary writers is David

Levin's, while the innovative work of White analyzes the formal articulations of historical narrative together with its political implication. Colacurcio's study of Hawthorne offers much that is relevant to national narrative. Diehl and Herbst provide important scholarly background for Bancroft's relation to German historiography. The emergence of a national literature in the United States involves crucial economic issues addressed in studies of publication, the book trade, and authorship by Charvat, Mott, Hart, Tebbel, and Ferguson (in a comparison of law and letters as careers), while Spencer summarizes literary debates and exhortations.

As war abroad changed America in the 1960s, the Civil Rights movement and the women's movement made it necessary within the United States to think anew about who would count as important writers. The study of writing by nineteenth-century American women emerged as a vital field of inquiry in the 1970s in pathbreaking studies by Baym (1978), Douglas, Gilbert and Gubar, and Moers (the latter two include more British than American writers). In their modes of social and literary analysis, these works differed greatly from the still-useful earlier surveys by Pattee and Herbert Brown. Important later works in this new mode include those by Kelley, Tompkins, and Gillian Brown.

Rich WPA interview material on slavery was gathered in the 1930s. Some of it was published by Botkin; other material lay fallow for decades. Reconceiving African American cultural history was first achieved in the 1970s by historians such as Blassingame, Rawick, Genovese, and Levine. Blassingame established the validity of slave narratives as historical sources; literary analyses tended to build from this newly certified authenticity to develop further modes of interpretation and description in books edited by Davis and Gates, Fisher and Stepto, and Pryse and Spillers and written by Andrews, Baker, Foster, and Stepto. Key later works by Gates, Fox-Genovese, and McDowell and Rampersad already point in some quite different directions. Studies of African American literature and culture are complemented by studies that focus on race from multiple perspectives. These include Fredrickson, Horsman, and Takaki on modes of racism, Toll on minstrelsy, Sollors on negotiations of race and ethnicity, and Sundquist's massive reframing of black and white writing together.

In addition to the expanded horizons for Americanists produced by these social movements, new intellectual perspectives also opened in the 1970s. Literary studies at large were influenced by recent European thinking in the fields of philosophy, linguistics, and anthropology as well as in literature more simply. This encounter was known as the "theory boom" and some of its components included structuralism and poststructuralism. Foucault's books analyze both the emergence of individual psychology in the nineteenth century (1975) and also the newly specialized conception of literature (1966). Among the American critics active in this area, Jameson is especially important for thinking about the operations and significance of narrative.

More broadly, the journal *New Literary History,* which began publication in 1969, created an international conversation that helped to make possible work such as mine and the dramatically innovative new histories of French and German literature (published by Harvard University Press and edited by Denis Hollier [1989] and David Wellbery [2004]). My work aspires to some kinship with these two texts.

Moreover, in Britain the development of cultural studies helped to inspire new approaches to the interrelations between literature and the culture at large, such as may be seen in Wicke. Williams offers particular resources for understanding the new conception of literature in the nineteenth century (1976) and also for the social analysis of narrative forms (1959). Older models of cultural history also remain valuable when pursued with the intelligence of Bender or the assiduity of David Reynolds. Other useful studies in cultural history include Green on Boston, Grimsted on popular theater, and Harris on popular exhibition and entertainment more broadly. For local narrative, important studies of regional culture include Brooks and Buell on the Northeast and Hubbell and Taylor on the South. On Southwestern humor, Yates studies the most important national venue for this writing, *The Spirit of the Times,* and Lynn shows the impact of this writing on Mark Twain.

This confluence of field renovation, national and world politics, and intellectual ferment all helped to produce the distinctive emphases of New Americanists. In preparing this study, I read widely in American historiography, but I restrict my citations to a few major syntheses, including Pessen on the Jacksonian era and Potter on the coming of the Civil War. Welter's intellectual history, Morton Horwitz's legal history, and especially Forgie's psychohistory all provide valuable materials for what Raymond Williams would call the structure of feeling around the Compromise of 1850, which is crucial to my argument for the emergence of literary narrative.

Bibliography

Anderson, Benedict. *Imagined Communities: Reflections on the Origin and Spread of Nationalism*. London: Verso, 1983.

Anderson, Quentin. *The Imperial Self: An Essay in American Literary and Cultural History*. New York: Knopf, 1971.

Andrews, William L. *To Tell a Free Story: The First Century of Afro-American Autobiography, 1760–1865*. Urbana: University of Illinois Press, 1988.

Arac, Jonathan. *Commissioned Spirits: The Shaping of Social Motion in Dickens, Carlyle, Melville, and Hawthorne*. 1979. New York: Columbia University Press, 1989.

Auerbach, Erich. *Mimesis: The Representation of Reality in Western Literature*. 1946. Trans. Willard Trask. Princeton, N.J.: Princeton University Press, 1953.

Baker, Houston A., Jr. *Blues, Ideology, and Afro-American Literature: A Vernacular Theory*. Chicago: University of Chicago Press, 1984.

———. *The Journey Back: Issues in Black Literature and Criticism*. Chicago: University of Chicago Press, 1980.

Baym, Nina. *Novels, Readers, and Reviewers: Responses to Fiction in Antebellum America*. Ithaca, N.Y.: Cornell University Press, 1984.

———. *Women's Fiction: A Guide to Novels by and About Women*. Ithaca, N.Y.: Cornell University Press, 1978.

Bell, Michael Davitt. *The Development of American Romance: The Sacrifice of Relation*. Chicago: University of Chicago Press, 1980.

Bender, Thomas. *New York Intellect: A History of Intellectual Life in New York City, from 1750 to the Beginnings of Our Own Time*. New York: Knopf-Random House, 1987.

Bercovitch, Sacvan. *The American Jeremiad*. Madison: University of Wisconsin Press, 1978.

———. *The Puritan Origins of the American Self*. New Haven, Conn.: Yale University Press, 1975.

———. *The Rites of Assent: Transformations in the Symbolic Construction of America*. New York: Routledge, 1993.

———, ed. *Reconstructing American Literary History*. Harvard English Studies 13. Cambridge, Mass.: Harvard University Press, 1986.

Bercovitch, Sacvan, and Myra Jehlen, eds. *Ideology and Classic American Literature*. New York: Cambridge University Press, 1986.

Bewley, Marius. *The Eccentric Design: Form in the Classic American Novel*. New York: Columbia University Press, 1959.

Blair, Walter, ed. *Native American Humor (1800–1900)*. New York: American Book Company, 1937.

Blassingame, John. *The Slave Community: Plantation Life in the Antebellum South*. Rev. ed. New York: Oxford University Press, 1979.

Botkin, B. A., ed. *Lay My Burden Down: A Folk History of Slavery*. Chicago: University of Chicago Press, 1945.

Bridgman, Richard. *The Colloquial Style in America*. New York: Oxford University Press, 1966.

Brodhead, Richard. *The School of Hawthorne*. New York: Oxford University Press, 1986.

Brooks, Van Wyck. *The Flowering of New England, 1815–1865*. New York: E. P. Dutton, 1936.

———. *The Times of Melville and Whitman*. New York: Dutton, 1947.

———. *The World of Washington Irving*. New York: Dutton, 1944.

Brown, Gillian. *Domestic Individualism: Imagining Self in Nineteenth-Century America*. Berkeley and Los Angeles: University of California Press, 1990.

Brown, Herbert Ross. *The Sentimental Novel in America, 1789–1860*. Durham, N.C.: Duke University Press, 1940.

Buell, Lawrence. *New England Literary Culture: From Revolution Through Renaissance*. New York: Cambridge University Press, 1986.

Chai, Leon. *Romantic Foundations of the American Renaissance*. Ithaca, N.Y.: Cornell University Press, 1985.

Charvat, William. *Literary Publishing in America, 1790–1850*. Philadelphia: University of Pennsylvania Press, 1959.

———. *The Profession of Authorship in America, 1790–1850.* New York: Columbia University Press, 1992.

Chase, Richard. *The American Novel and Its Tradition.* 1957. Baltimore: Johns Hopkins University Press, 1979.

Cohen, Hennig, and William B. Dillingham, eds. *Humor of the Old Southwest.* 3d ed. Athens: University of Georgia Press, 1994.

Colacurcio, Michael. *The Province of Piety: Moral History in Hawthorne's Early Tales.* Cambridge, Mass.: Harvard University Press, 1984.

Davis, Charles T., and Henry Louis Gates, Jr., eds. *The Slave's Narrative.* New York: Oxford University Press, 1985.

Diehl, Carl. *Americans and German Scholarship, 1770–1870.* New Haven, Conn.: Yale University Press, 1978.

Douglas, Ann. *The Feminization of American Culture.* New York: Knopf, 1977.

Drinnon, Richard. *Facing West: The Metaphysics of Indian-Hating and Empire Building.* Minneapolis: University of Minnesota Press, 1980.

Feidelson, Charles, Jr. *Symbolism and American Literature.* Chicago: University of Chicago Press, 1953.

Ferguson, Robert. *Law and Letters in American Culture.* Cambridge, Mass.: Harvard University Press, 1984.

Fiedler, Leslie A. *Love and Death in the American Novel.* 1960. Rev. ed. New York: Stein & Day, 1982.

Fisher, Dexter, and Robert B. Stepto, eds. *Afro-American Literature: The Reconstruction of Instruction.* New York: Modern Language Association, 1979.

Fisher, Philip. *Hard Facts: Form and Setting in the American Novel.* New York: Oxford University Press, 1985.

Forgie, George. *Patricide in the House Divided: A Psychological Interpretation of Lincoln and His Age.* New York: Norton, 1979.

Foster, Frances Smith. *Witnessing Slavery: The Development of Antebellum Slave Narratives.* Westport, Conn.: Greenwood, 1979.

Foucault, Michel. *Discipline and Punish: Birth of the Prison.* 1975. Trans. Alan Sheridan. New York: Random House, 1977

———. *The Order of Things: An Archeology of the Human Sciences.* 1966. Trans. New York: Random House, 1970.

Fox-Genovese, Elizabeth. *Within the Plantation Household: Black and*

White Women of the Old South. Chapel Hill: University of North Carolina Press, 1988.

Frederickson, George M. *The Black Image in the White Mind: The Debate on Afro-American Character and Destiny, 1817–1914.* New York: Harper & Row, 1971.

Fussell, Edwin. *Frontier: American Literature and the American West.* Princeton, N.J.: Princeton University Press, 1965.

Gates, Henry Louis, Jr. *Figures in Black: Words, Signs, and the "Racial Self."* New York: Oxford University Press, 1987.

———. *The Signifying Monkey.* New York: Oxford University Press, 1988.

Genovese, Eugene D. *Roll, Jordan, Roll: The World the Slaves Made.* New York: Pantheon, 1974.

Gilbert, Sandra, and Susan Gubar. *The Madwoman in the Attic: The Woman Writer and the Nineteenth-Century Literary Imagination.* New Haven, Conn.: Yale University Press, 1979.

Gilmore, Michael T. *American Romanticism and the Marketplace.* Chicago: University of Chicago Press. 1985.

Green, Martin. *The Problem of Boston: Some Readings in Cultural History.* New York: Norton, 1966.

Grimsted, David. *Melodrama Unveiled: American Theater and Culture, 1800–1850.* Chicago: University of Chicago Press, 1968.

Harding, Brian. *American Literature in Context (1830–1865).* London: Methuen, 1982.

Harris, Neil. *Humbug: The Art of P. T. Barnum.* Boston: Little, Brown, 1973.

Hart, James D. *The Popular Book: A History of America's Literary Taste.* Berkeley and Los Angeles: University of California Press, 1961.

Herbst, Jurgen. *The German Historical School in American Scholarship: A Study in the Transfer of Culture.* Ithaca, N.Y.: Cornell University Press, 1965.

Hoffman, Daniel. *Form and Fable in American Fiction.* New York: Oxford University Press, 1965.

Horsman, Reginald. *Race and Manifest Destiny: The Origins of American Racial Anglo-Saxonism.* Cambridge, Mass.: Harvard University Press, 1981.

Horwitz, Howard. *By the Law of Nature: Form and Value in Nineteenth-Century America.* New York: Oxford University Press, 1991.

Horwitz, Morton J. *The Transformation of American Law, 1780–1860.* Cambridge, Mass.: Harvard University Press, 1977.

Hubbell, Jay B. *The South in American Literature, 1607–1900.* Durham, N.C.: Duke University Press, 1954.

Jameson, Fredric. *The Political Unconscious: Narrative as a Socially Symbolic Act.* Ithaca, N.Y.: Cornell University Press, 1981.

Kelley, Mary. *Private Woman, Public Stage: Literary Domesticity in Nineteenth-Century America.* New York: Oxford University Press, 1984.

Lawrence, D. H. *Studies in Classic American Literature.* 1923. Garden City, N.Y.: Doubleday, 1951.

Levin, David. *History as Romantic Art: Bancroft, Prescott, Motley and Parkman.* New York: Harcourt, Brace, & World, 1963.

Levin, Harry. *The Power of Blackness: Hawthorne, Poe, Melville.* New York: Knopf, 1958.

Levine, Lawrence W. *Black Culture and Black Consciousness: Afro-American Folk Thought from Slavery to Freedom.* New York: Oxford University Press, 1977.

Lewis, R. W. B. *The American Adam: Innocence, Tragedy, and Tradition in the Nineteenth Century.* Chicago: University of Chicago Press, 1955.

Lynn, Kenneth. *Mark Twain and Southwestern Humor.* 1959. Westport, Conn.: Greenwood, 1972.

———, ed. *The Comic Tradition in America.* Garden City, N.Y.: Doubleday, 1958.

Marx, Leo. *The Machine in the Garden: Technology and the Pastoral Ideal in America.* New York: Oxford University Press, 1964.

Matthiessen, F. O. *American Renaissance: Art and Expression in the Age of Emerson and Whitman.* New York: Oxford University Press, 1941.

McDowell, Deborah, and Arnold Rampersad, eds. *Slavery and the Literary Imagination.* Baltimore: Johns Hopkins University Press, 1989.

Meine, Franklin J., ed. *Tall Tales of the Southwest: An Anthology of Southern and Southwestern Humor, 1830–1860.* New York: Knopf, 1930.

Merk, Frederick. *Manifest Destiny and Mission in American History.* New York: Knopf, 1963.

Michaels, Walter Benn, and Donald Pease, eds. *The American Renaissance Reconsidered.* Baltimore: Johns Hopkins University Press, 1985.

Miller, Perry. *The Life of the Mind in America: From the Revolution to the Civil War*. New York: Harcourt, Brace, 1965.

———. *Nature's Nation*. Cambridge, Mass.: Harvard University Press, 1967.

———. *The Raven and the Whale: The War of Words and Wits in the Era of Poe and Melville*. New York: Harcourt, Brace, 1956.

Moers, Ellen. *Literary Women*. 1977. New York: Oxford University Press, 1985.

Mott, Frank Luther. *Golden Multitudes: The Story of Best Sellers in the United States*. New York: Macmillan, 1947.

———. *A History of American Magazines, 1741–1850*. New York: Appleton, 1930. Republished as Vol. I of *A History of American Magazines*, 5 Vols., Cambridge, Mass.: Harvard University Press, 1938–68.

Parrington, Vernon L. *Main Currents in American Thought*. Vol. 2, 1800–1860, *The Romantic Revolution in America*. New York: Harcourt, Brace, 1927.

Pattee, Fred. *The Feminine Fifties*. New York: Appleton-Century, 1940.

Pearce, Roy Harvey. *Savagism and Civilization*. Baltimore: Johns Hopkins University Press, 1965.

Pease, Donald E. *Visionary Compacts: American Renaissance Writings in Cultural Context*. Madison: University of Wisconsin Press, 1987.

Pessen, Edward. *Jacksonian America: Society, Personality, and Politics*. 1978. Urbana: University of Illinois Press, 1985.

Poirier, Richard. *A World Elsewhere: The Place of Style in American Literature*. New York: Oxford University Press, 1966.

Porte, Joel. *The Romance in America: Studies in Cooper, Poe, Hawthorne, Melville, and James*. Middletown, Conn.: Wesleyan University Press, 1969.

Potter, David. *The Impending Crisis, 1848–1861*. Edited by Don E. Fehrenbacher. New York: Harper & Row, 1976.

Pryse, Marjorie, and Hortense J. Spillers, eds. *Conjuring: Black Women, Fiction, and Literary Tradition*. Bloomington: Indiana University Press, 1985.

Rawick, George. *From Sundown to Sunup: The Making of the Black Community*. Westport, Conn.: Greenwood, 1972.

Reynolds, David S. *Beneath the American Renaissance: The Subversive Imagination in the Age of Emerson and Melville*. New York: Knopf, 1988.

Reynolds, Larry J. *European Revolutions and the American Literary Renaissance.* New Haven, Conn.: Yale University Press, 1988.

Rogin, Michael Paul. *Fathers and Children: Andrew Jackson and the Subjugation of the American Indian.* New York: Knopf, 1975.

Rourke, Constance. *American Humor: A Study of the National Character.*
New York: Harcourt, Brace, 1931.

Simpson, David. *The Politics of American English, 1776–1850.* New
York: Oxford University Press, 1986.

Slotkin, Richard. *The Fatal Environment: The Myth of the Frontier in the
Age of Industrialization, 1800–1890.* New York: Atheneum, 1985.

———. *Regeneration through Violence: The Mythology of the American
Frontier, 1600–1860.* Middletown, Conn.: Wesleyan University Press,
1974.

Smith, Henry Nash. *Democracy and the Novel: Popular Resistance to
Classic American Writers.* Oxford: Oxford University Press, 1978.

———. *Virgin Land: The American West as Symbol and Myth.* 1950. Reissued with a new preface, Cambridge, Mass.: Harvard University
Press, 1970.

Sollors, Werner. *Beyond Ethnicity: Consent and Descent in American Culture.* New York: Oxford University Press, 1986.

Spencer, Benjamin T. *The Quest for Nationality: An American Literary
Campaign.* Syracuse, N.Y.: Syracuse University Press, 1957.

Stepto, Robert B. *From Behind the Veil: A Study of Afro-American Narrative.* Urbana: University of Illinois Press, 1979.

Sundquist, Eric J. *To Wake the Nations: Race in the Making of American
Literature.* Cambridge, Mass.: Harvard University Press, 1993.

Takaki, Ronald T. *Iron Cages: Race and Culture in Nineteenth-Century
America.* New York: Oxford University Press, 1979.

Taylor, William R. *Cavalier and Yankee: The Old South and the American
National Character.* New York: Doubleday, 1963.

Tebbel, John. *Between Covers: The Rise and Transformation of Book
Publishing in America.* New York: Oxford University Press, 1987.

Thomas, Brook. *Cross-Examinations of Law and Literature: Cooper,
Hawthorne, Stowe, and Melville.* New York: Oxford University
Press, 1987.

Toll, Robert. *Blacking Up: The Minstrel Show in Nineteenth-Century
America.* New York: Oxford University Press, 1974.

Tompkins, Jane. *Sensational Designs: The Cultural Work of American
Fiction, 1790–1860.* New York: Oxford University Press, 1985.

Tuveson, Ernest. *Redeemer Nation: The Idea of America's Millennial Role.* Chicago: University of Chicago Press, 1971.

Weisbuch, Robert. *Atlantic Double-Cross: American Literature and British Influence in the Age of Emerson.* Chicago: University of Chicago Press, 1986.

Wellek, René. *Confrontations: Studies in the Intellectual and Literary Relations between Germany, England, and the United States during the Nineteenth Century.* Princeton, N.J.: Princeton University Press, 1965.

Welter, Rush. *The Mind of America, 1820–1860.* New York: Columbia University Press, 1975.

White, Hayden V. *Metahistory: The Historical Imagination in Nineteenth-Century Europe.* Baltimore: Johns Hopkins University Press, 1973.

Wicke, Jennifer. *Advertising Fictions: Literature, Advertisement, and Social Reading.* New York: Columbia University Press, 1988.

Williams, Raymond. *Culture and Society.* New York: Columbia University Press, 1959.

———. *Keywords: A Vocabulary of Culture and Society.* 1976. Rev. ed. New York: Oxford University Press, 1983.

Wilson, Edmund. *Patriotic Gore: Studies in the Literature of the Civil War.* New York: Oxford University Press, 1962.

Winters, Yvor. *Maule's Curse: Seven Studies in the History of American Obscurantism: Hawthorne, Cooper, Melville, Poe, Emerson, Jones Very, Emily Dickinson, Henry James.* Norfolk, Conn.: New Directions, 1938.

Yates, Norris Wilson. *William S. Porter and the "Spirit of the Times."* Baton Rouge: Louisiana State University Press, 1957.

Ziff, Larzer. *Literary Democracy: The Declaration of Cultural Independence in America.* New York: Viking, 1981.

Index

257